Katherine really is a Me Ada

by Rose Gordy

Praise for
"The Green That Never Died"

"I loved the book. I was so happy to see my name in it. Many memories revisited. You came off as very sincere. I very much liked the way you used prose and poetry. I cannot put the book down."

- Joe Batya, former priest

"Congratulations on this rich and wonderful read. You must be very proud. I've checked out all the pictures and just loved them. It's going to take some time to digest and enjoy every page as thoroughly as I want."

- Pat Downey, former nun

"The Masterpiece arrived! I started to read it last night and of course went straight to the Notre Dame days. Brings back lots of warm memories."

- Joellen, former nun

The Green That Never Died

A Convent Memoir
of the 50's and 60's

by Rose Gordy

Every Day We Really Live and Love is a
Mysterious Adventure into the Green Unknown.

ISBN-13: 978-1478356301
ISBN-10: 1478356308

Cover design courtesy of Stephen Charles and SuperClusterMedia.com

Rosewords Books
Rosewords.com

To my Mom and Dad

INTRODUCTION

As I relive my convent days of long ago,
I will share my experiences
in a "Word Collage"
of relevant letters,
journal entries,
commentaries,
dialogues,
essays,
prayers,
short stories,
dreams and poetry.

Other women in and out of the convent
as Pittsburgh Sisters of Mercy
in the 50's and 60's
may have different recollections,
all of them real and valuable.

But this is my story.

I don't regret the years
in that Hallowed World.

I never lost my Life Force,
My Green of Spring
with new buds and blossoms.

My Past as a nun
was prologue
to the rest of my life.

The Green Never Died.

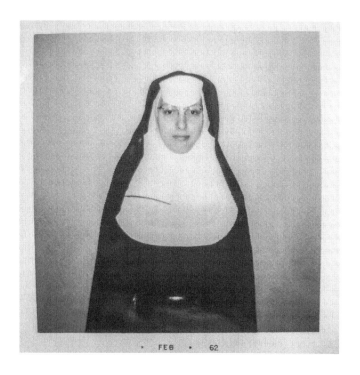

PROLOGUE

The Significance of GREEN in My Life

"Into every created thing God has breathed a certain power of
germination, i.e. the greenness."
Mylius, an alchemist, quoted by Carl Jung

Often I have wondered about the series of
mysterious twists of fate and fortune that
have guided me through life. By virtue of
the heights and depths of the years I spent in the convent, my
dreams and the Green symbolizing them have never died.
Though sometimes trampled on, sometimes smothered,
sometimes uprooted and let lie fallow, they have survived.

     Green - such a hopeful word to me. Trees and grass
and especially my houseplants, my treasured Greens. As each
of them shows signs of growth with a bud, a flower or a new
leaf, I glory because I grow as well somehow tasting that
Green. My link to life at its most profound level.

     A plant's existence mirrors my own. A rooting in
water. An enveloping in soil. A reaching out to water and dirt

to grow and leaf and bud and be strong and sure and smile out to the universe despite everything.

Despite the open affection denied me as a child. Despite the self-consciousness of an awkward elementary student. Despite the frustration of trying to make it but not make it in high school. Despite the loneliness and the negativity of my twenties in confinement living under the vows of Poverty, Chastity and Obedience. As the writer David Bates has said, "To be alone and lonely, to be without nurturance or a consistent source of erotic gratification are among the worst and most commonplace emotional pains humans must endure."

Despite the railings against who I was and wasn't and could never be as well. The wrenching feelings of nausea no medicine could cure. Alone in a land of indecision, upset and hate turned in, upon and against myself.

What had I been searching for all those years behind closed doors? What am I always searching to find? The Green.

Nevertheless, always the questions. What do I want to make of my existence? How do I retrieve my Green when Blackness surrounds and envelops? How to get the Green back when I have denied its wondrous worth? Why have I bound my being in a circle of discord and upset without color?

Still the Greens have sustained me. The glory-filled moments. The days I never wanted to end. All the life changing events long past, far down the lanes of my experiences. They rest inside me - the Green, the Gold, the Glorious. I replay their fun and their joy to bring me release in trying times.

I would never have arrived where I am in the present moment or will ever reach that wondrous tomorrow, my future, if my unique past had never happened. Such a fundamental thought yet so crucial. Through all I experienced in the past, the Green and my dreams have never died. My Winters have always foreshadowed wondrous Springs. The dark, colorless days of snow and cold and death quietly yet eventually have given way to the glorious Green of Spring.

How long ago did I write the line: "Every day we really live and love is a mysterious adventure into the Green Unknown?" Why Green? Why did it have to be the "Green Unknown?" everyone has always asked. The Green is for growth and life and rebirth and vitality and freshness. The Green is for Spring and New Life.

Spring my season. A time of nature's celebration. Once my eighth grade students created a "Celebrate Spring Day" with collages, mobiles, songs and dances. Celebrating Spring is to celebrate Life - to glory in new birth and rebirth growing and glowing. The challenge to keep the Green inside when the "earth" there is dank and dark and hard or cold and frozen and white like Wordsworth's "emotion recollected in tranquility." Soothing Green thoughts when tension squirms and screams inside trying to smother my Spring. My Green.

When my dream world opened up and I started to record and honor them, a common dream involved "*pacing the Motherhouse corridors back and forth, back and forth. Finally changing directions when I realized I was wrong.*" I am duly fascinated by how prophetic and symbolic the subconscious is.

Inevitably, the Winters returned but always as harbingers of Springs and afterwards more Winters followed by more Springs. Endless cycles of days and minutes and seconds not just months or years. In the midst of it all, Keats' question continued to reassure me. "If Winter comes, can Spring be far behind?" The Winters of my life - my days and nights of frustration, sorrow and depression - somehow were always harbingers of the Springs of new hope in their stead.

Spring with its Glorious Green and its sun warm and soothing. My sign - Leo - A Sun Sign. I glory in the sun. I blossom and grow and am nourished by it and in it and through it. All of the Up times of my life have come in sun - in Spring and Summer. Maybe someday I'd be able to love, to embrace and cherish the Winters too - to come to realize that only through them in life's cycle could the Springs be born. That only through dying does one live. The line of the New Testament I had frequently meditated upon in the convent, paraphrased as "Unless the seed falls to the ground and dies, it cannot live." Unless the seeds of rage, discontent, discouragement, resentment, hate and all the other destructive emotions within me die, go to dust and blow away, I, my true self, can never live fully in the Glory of the Green.

Above me now the sun at its peak of afternoon brilliance has been blackened out by clouds forecasting rain. How nature speaks to my own inner state. The questions in the night. The haunting questions of when and if or how. As F. Scott Fitzgerald wrote at the end of The Great Gatsby, "So we beat on, boats against the current, borne back ceaselessly into the past."

Yet as surely as the Winter is a harbinger of Spring, the clouds will give way to the sun in time too. After all isn't everything resolved in the end to a question of time? A few minutes perhaps or later after rain. The vital thing is to be ready for the whatever - the inevitable or the unforeseen - the surprise or the revelation.

Now the sun begins to shine again light and delicious. I'm closing my eyes, my mind tense and tired yet at peace for these few moments. The sun speaks to me in mellow tones of solace, in soothing sounds a Mother would coo to her child, about to go to sleep and dream.

Ah, Spring!

Change.	Flux.
Ebb.	Flow.

New birth.
Nascent blooms.
Tiny shoots.
Crocuses peeping up.
Buds bursting into being.
Breezes warm and caressing.
Skies blue or cloudy white.
Sunshine or showers.
Luscious landscapes
of Green. Growth. Change.
Sprouting. Flowering. Glorying.

As a nun I chanted the Office of the Blessed Mother three times a day. This was a devotional series of psalms, hymns and scripture which changed daily. The following verses are part of this "Office."

Psalm 51

"Have mercy on me, O God,
according to your great mercy.
And according to the multitude
of your tender mercies blot out my iniquity.

Wash me yet more from my iniquity,
and cleanse me from my sin.

For I know my iniquity,
and my sin is always before me.

To you only have I sinned,
and have done evil before you:

that you may be justified in your words,
and may overcome when you are judged.

For behold I was conceived in iniquities;
and in sins did my mother conceive me."

My sins were of denying the Good - the God within me. Sins of depression and despair. Of jealousy of those who seemed to me so secure and vibrant and alive while I was always wondering, searching, and slowly dying. Of upset with my uncertainties, frustrations and negative feelings.

Yet I never stopped fighting and wanting to be born again every day during the years I lived "in the world but not of it." During that time keeping the Green, the Spring alive in my heart and soul. And so my life has flourished because the Green has never died inside me.

MY CONVENT YEARS

For reference, the following is the breakdown of the years I lived as a Sister of Mercy. **Note**: If you want to be surprised by events, then skip these two pages.

'57 -'58   A new nun called a Postulant and a Freshman at Mount Mercy College (now Carlow College) in Oakland, PA.

'58-'59   A White Novice having received the habit of the Community and a white veil on August 26, 1958 now in my Canonical or Contemplative Year taking mostly theology classes but no regular college classes.

'59-'60   A Senior White Novice and a Sophomore at Mount Mercy College.

'60-'61   A Junior Professed (before taking Final Vows) and a Junior at Mount Mercy College.

'61-'62   A Junior Professed and a Senior at Mount Mercy College.

'62   BA English Major and Secondary Education and French Minor at Mount Mercy College.

'62-'63   Two Summers at Kansas State Teacher's College on government grants for French study.

'62-'63   My First year teaching. Seventh grade at Epiphany Elementary School in Pittsburgh, PA. Still living at the Motherhouse as a Junior Professed.

'63 August   Final Profession.

'63-'64   My second year teaching. Seventh grade at Cathedral Elementary School in Oakland, PA. Living not at the Motherhouse but at my first "local house" (local convent.)

'64-'68   Four years teaching English, French and Religion and coaching Speech and Debate at Saint Xavier's Academy in Latrobe, PA.

'65-'69   Four Summers at Notre Dame University in South Bend, Indiana working on my MA.

'68-'69   Teacher at Saint Elizabeth's High School in Pleasant Hills, PA. Seventh year teaching English and coaching Speech and Debate.

'69-'70   Teacher at Greensburg Central High in Greensburg, PA. Eighth year teaching English and coaching Speech and Debate. During the summer my MA thesis is accepted. Receive an MA for English Major and French Minor from Notre Dame University.

Part One

"I will go to the Altar of God"

Becoming a Sister of Mercy

**I knew in my heart during those early years
I would become the finest nun I could be.**

PROCESSION INTO CHAPEL ON
FIRST PROFESSION DAY

The World, The Flesh and The Devil

My high school boyfriend begged. He insisted that he needed me and that I "could save my soul in the world." But I couldn't listen to his impassioned pleas; I wouldn't let myself even hear them.

Three weeks after my eighteenth birthday, on September 7 of 1957, I left home. On that momentous day I put my past life behind me or so I believed then in the heady idealism of my youth. I became a lamb to the slaughter. A seed dying to be born again. A willing victim to a holy guillotine to be cut off from "the World, the Flesh and the Devil" by becoming a Sister of Mercy in Oakland, Pennsylvania.

I died to the world as a daughter and a sister and a girlfriend and a silly teenage girl. But was reborn into a new life ultimately as a nun under my three vows of Poverty, Chastity and Obedience. Everything done on a schedule by bell or chime or clock - from waking, to praying, to eating and finishing eating, to recreating, to sleeping. Always with the underlying belief as the old nuns put it, "Your reward will be great in Heaven."

With the slightest effort I can still smell the Novitiate on the third floor of the Motherhouse where we young nuns lived. On certain Saturday mornings we Postulants and Novices waxed and polished the old fashioned furniture in the Community Room. I remember being crouched down on my hands and knees scrubbing the white lines in the hallway floor with old toothbrushes. Or on a Lenten noon smelling the inviting aroma of homemade bread wafting up from the kitchen to the Novitiate Chapel too temptingly, especially since we had been dutifully fasting even though mere teenagers.

I also recall the dank and pungent odor that came from pressing a habit that should have been washed instead. Or the bland odor of the dry house on a Saturday morning as I pushed the long heavy carriers in and out. Or the sweet smell of lilies in Chapel on Easter Sundays.

I can also feel my heart pounding erratically the day I entered and walked upstairs in high heels and a stylish jumper and blouse. Shortly afterwards coming down in the "Possie" outfit: a full length pleated black skirt, long sleeved black cotton blouse, black old lady shoes over black opaque stockings and, to top it off, a funny looking black veil on my head ruffled around the crown. How my Mom must have had tears in her eyes when she saw me dressed like this.

A year later on August 26, 1958 the girls I entered the convent with and I received our "Holy Habit of Religion," consisting of:

- A white heavily starched headpiece, called a coif, that covered all except the edges of the back of my head. The swooping forehead part dug into my skin sometimes and chaffed.

- The also white circular bodice piece called a guimp, also heavily starched.

- A floor-length white veil with the small waist length opaque veil underneath.

- The black serge habit, unpleated to the top of my breast and from there following the form of my body to my waist and flowing to the floor in multiple one inch pleats.

- A cincture: a two inch black leather belt hanging from it oversized Rosary beads reaching to the floor.

All of these parts of our Holy Habit covered, protected(?) and enshrined us. I can also feel my silver ring on the second finger of my right hand. Engraved inside it was the word I had chosen, "Maranatha," Aramaic for "Come, Lord Jesus." This modest ring came to symbolize the reasons why I had entered to "Strive for Perfection." Yes, I tried to accomplish the impossible and be perfect, thinking that once I was Professed, I'd be nearer the day when I would actually be perfect - our main "raison d'etre."

As Sisters of Mercy we followed "The Rule" of our community which encompassed numerous and arcane directives. The 9 p.m. Grand Silence, when at the toll of the large bell everyone ceased talking even midway through a word and didn't speak again until after breakfast the next day.

Keeping "Custody of the Eyes" which meant we didn't look directly at anyone. Also, we were not allowed to talk to lay people unless there were extenuating circumstances. We couldn't visit our fellow nuns in their cells, as our bedrooms were called, because there was a fear of "Particular Friendships," a euphemism for a word never spoken, lesbianism. We could not use any object in any way except for its intended purpose. We didn't have any regular clothes including anything with color. We were not allowed to possess or wear anything feminine. No scented soaps. No silk undergarments. We were not permitted to seal our letters to our parents so that they could be read by our Superiors. No radio. No TV. No newspapers. We also had to perform a daily Particular Examen to acknowledge our sins and go to Confession every week.

We were forced to endure the monthly "Chapter of Faults" where each of us announced to the rest of the community some violation of The Rule like talking at the wrong time of day. It was actually an entire process of events. First, I had to go see the Mistress of Novices and kneel down by her wooden desk. Then I would ask her to tell me one of my faults. Later I would "confess" this "fault" in front of the Community assembled in the Main Chapel. All the young nuns sat in the front pews, with senior nuns behind us. In turn each of us young nuns walked up to the front of the Chapel, faced all the other nuns and then announced, "I accuse myself before God and the Community...." and then admitted a fault such as being uncharitable to one of our fellow Sisters or talking after the Grand Silence.

Until we made our Final Profession, we had to leave the Chapel in a group as soon as all of us unprofessed nuns were finished. This was because we weren't permitted to be privy to the faults of "the Old Girls," the name we gave to those over forty. When years later I could stay, it was no surprise that I heard certain nuns accuse themselves of the same superficial and meaningless faults month after month.

During those first few years I was so serious about following The Rule that I felt guilty for the ones who didn't. I embraced my new life fully without question.

(Revised from an essay "The World, the Flesh and the Devil" published in a 2014 anthology entitled Nothing But the Truth So Help Me God: 73 Women on Life's Transitions by the organization "A Band of Women" in California)

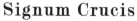
WITH MY PARENTS ROSE & CHARLIE

The Sign of the Cross

"In the Name of the Father and of the Son and of the Holy Ghost. Amen."

Signum Crucis
The Latin Version of The Sign of the Cross

"In nomine Patris et Filii et Spiritus Sancti. Amen."

My Pilgrimage to Mercy Internationale

Several years ago I went on a spiritual pilgrimage to Ireland led by my New Camaldoli monk friend, Father Michael Fish. There I visited the Mercy Internationale Center on Baggot Street in Dublin. Built by Mother McAuley, the Foundress of the Sisters of Mercy in 1831 in response to the needs of the poor in that area, it is now a "Center of Hospitality, Heritage, Pilgrimage and Renewal" and in particular, Mother's burial site.

In a letter home to my parents, two sisters and brother shortly after Easter '58, I wrote,

> For our Mother McAuley Class Project I made a poster giving a sketch of Mother Francis Xavier Warde's life. Next to Mother McAuley, our holy Foundress, Mother Warde is the most important person to us. It was she who in December of 1843 arrived in Pittsburgh as Superior of the first group of Sisters of Mercy in the United States. She went on to found 43 houses all over the country, to name a few, Chicago, Rhode Island, New York. Mother Warde was the first Sister received and professed by Mother McAuley and the first Sister of Mercy to celebrate her Golden Jubilee. (Mother McAuley only lived about ten years after becoming a Sister. Today her community ranks the second largest in the world.)

As I toured the building, I heard Mother McAuley speaking to me from a July 1841 letter to Mary Ann Doyle, one of the first members of her new community. "Do not fear offending anyone. Speak as your mind directs and always act with more courage when the 'mammon of unrighteousness' is in question." These wise words from across the years gave me the needed resolve to face the challenges before me.

**THE CHAPEL AT
MERCY INTERNATIONALE IN DUBLIN**

Next in a February 1838 letter to Mother Frances Warde, Mother wrote, "The comfort comes soon after a well-received trial." Then in May of the last year of her life, she wrote to her, "This is your life, joys and sorrow mingled, one succeeding the other." Finally, mere weeks before going to Heaven, she wrote, "God bless and preserve you and send you every blessing."

These words resonated in my mind as I walked through the building and the grounds of the Mercy Internationale in Dublin. Making my way to Mother's Chapel, I sat in contemplation pondering my service to God.

My Final Profession

Now I'm in another chapel. The Main Chapel on the first floor of the Motherhouse of the Sisters of Mercy in Oakland, Pennsylvania. It's August 26, 1963. I'm walking in procession down the main aisle with the eight women who entered with me. While the tall ceremonial candles on the altar flicker and the sunlight flitters in through the stained glass windows, all the eyes of the people in the pews are on us nuns. We are dressed in our best black Holy Habits of Religion and our long black veils. Our families and friends and the other nuns of the Community watch quietly as each of us then lie down prostrate on the floor in front of the imposing altar.

A two feet wide by thirty feet long opaque black cotton cloth, called a pall, is then carried over to us. Palls are traditionally used to cover a casket at a funeral or to wrap a corpse. Per the Catholic Encyclopedia (1913), "Symbols of death, such as skulls and cross-bones are forbidden on the altar and ministers' vestments," but are allowed on palls. If there was any ornamentation on the cloth then I was not aware of it because I was lying face down on the floor. So this black cloth was then stretched out over our nine backs signifying our deaths to "the World, the Flesh and the Devil."

Across time and space I can still hear my voice as I in turn recite the words of my Final Profession:

> In the name of our Lord and Savior
> Jesus Christ, and under the protection of
> His Immaculate Mother Mary, ever Virgin,
> I, Rose Marie Engle, called in
> religion Sister Mary Raymond
> do vow and promise to God poverty,
> chastity, and obedience, and the service
> of the poor, the sick, and the ignorant, and
> to persevere until my death according to
> the Constitutions of the Congregation of
> the Sisters of Mercy, in your presence
> Mother Margaret Mary,
> Mother General of this Congregation.
>
> This 26th day of August in the year of
> Our Lord 1963.

Many holy thoughts streamed through my mind as I lay there on the floor in front of the altar. As the chanting of the nuns echoed through the Main Chapel, I prayed.

"I'm yours, My Jesus. I'm doing what I've been meant to do from all eternity. Help me. Help me."

I sincerely believed that morning that I was on the Right Path of My Life.

Our Father
The Lord's Prayer

"Our Father, Who art in heaven,
Hallowed be Thy Name.
Thy Kingdom come.
Thy Will be done,
on earth as it is in Heaven.
Give us this day our daily bread.
And forgive us our trespasses,
as we forgive those who trespass against us.
And lead us not into temptation,
but deliver us from evil.
Amen."

Pater Noster (Oratio Dominica)
The Latin Version of Our Father

"Pater noster, qui es in caelis,
sanctificetur Nomen tuum.
Adveniat regnum tuum.
Fiat voluntas tua,
sicut in caelo et in terra.
Panem nostrum quotidianum da nobis hodie,
et dimitte nobis debita nostra sicut et nos dimittimus
debitoribus nostris.
Et ne nos inducas in tentationem,
sed libera nos a malo."

The Sacred Vow of Chastity

Yet what did I or any of us on that marble floor that August morning know about foreplay, intercourse or orgasms as we took our Vow of Chastity? Some would argue it didn't matter whether or not we had experienced or even understood what sex or love was before we took that vow.

"We belong to God. All in us is His. The chastity to which a religious binds herself by vow is a virtue which makes her, in some manner, equal to the angels."
    Mother McAuley

There was no "sex education" in school then. Women would frequently "learn" about sex on their wedding night. My sense is that ideally we should have been told more about what we were giving up. And yes, although it would have been an unrealistic expectation, I wish we had a deeper understanding of our femininity, our sexuality and our basic human selves before we ever made our three vows, especially the Vow of Chastity.

We could have been better prepared by our Community to make this vow. In the Spring before our Final Profession, the women who entered with me called my "Crowd" were in a vow class in the long room across from the

Novitiate Chapel. That morning Sister Eleanor, the outspoken one of our group, asked a frank and pointed question about sex like "What should we do if we feel stirrings inside us after seeing a handsome man? Or what if it was the priest on the altar at Mass?"

Without adequate words to respond, the Mistress of Novices could only sidestep the issue. By reverting to a passage from Scripture, she, in effect, slammed the lid down on the Pandora's Box in the room. She probably had less knowledge about the sexual world than some of us young women. Had she been able to answer the question up front, it may have led to even more uncomfortable questions. So the woman closed the box and That Was That. No one had a voice to question or legs to stand on to challenge her decision or to ask any other relevant questions that morning. None of us ever even tried again in those months prior to our Final Profession or in our continuing formative years to lift the lid on that Pandora's Box to try to get some answers. And so we all took the Vow of Chastity, without comprehending what we were actually giving up and away.

Did I know that momentous day that it was not so easy to leave "the World, the Flesh and the Devil?" Even if I could live as a hermit in a secret underground cave for the rest of my life, wouldn't I still be flesh? Even there I couldn't leave all of life and the temptations of the devil. Nevertheless, with a serious resolve and devotion, I accepted this belief about leaving the world.

Yes, on that morning of my Final Profession two weeks after my twenty-fourth birthday, I believed I gave myself to God forever. I would be His and His only. Through and by Him to serve and love all those who crossed my path over the years as fellow Sisters, students, colleagues or whoever else. As close to having an orgasm as I vaguely knew then, I felt I was truly "with" Jesus on that altar floor as tears of joy flowed from my eyes.

Afterwards the Community threw a fine celebration breakfast of waffles and eggs and all the accompaniments. Then we enjoyed an exceptional visit with our families and friends with remarks from my Mom and other relatives like "You all looked like Angels walking into Chapel" or "I cried when I saw you lie down on the floor in front of the altar" or "May God be with you on your journey, Sister."

How could I know what God had planned for me? No matter, I believed I was meant to do what I was doing. This was the path I was meant to take.

Those days and events are now like a clouded vision of Another World as I talk to myself.

"Who was that girl, that woman in black? Who was that person no longer of 'This World?' Who was the good nun, that holy young woman prostrate on the floor in front of the altar at Mount Mercy?"

"It wasn't me," one part of my being replies.

"You're wrong," the other part corrects.

"Yes. It was me. I did live it all. I did believe in it and want it...."

"Where did all those years get you? Happiness? Fulfillment?"

Given a New Name

As I continue to relive the morning of my Final Profession, I'm thinking about how they gave me my name in religion. In writing I had submitted a number of other possibilities for the consideration of my Superiors. Among the thirty names were: Rosarita, Charlita, Mary Ralph, Rosita and Mary Abraham. Other names on my list had already been given to older nuns in the Community: Sylvia, Robert, Anthony and Rene. But it all was a foregone conclusion.

Local Student Gets Mercy Sister Habit

Rose Marie Engle, daughter of Mr. and Mrs. Charles Engle of 205 James avenue, East McKeesport, was clothed in the habit of the Sisters of Mercy at a ceremony held last Tuesday, Aug. 26 at Mt. Mercy Motherhouse, Pittsburgh.

A graduate of St. Peter's High School, McKeesport, she took the religious name of Sister Mary Raymond upon completion of the first year of religious life last week.

I had written numerous letters to my family over the years about what was happening in particular the following one telling them how I came to be given my Name in Religion.

Feast of Our Lady of Mount Carmel
July 16, 1958

I think I've more or less 'known' that this would be my new name for about a month. When Mother Patrick came home from her retreat at St. Xavier's, she said to me, "I was down to see Sister Raymond's grave and I told Mother Superior I thought that name would be fine for you." Then not to get my hopes up too high, she added, "But I don't know if she'll give it to you or not." After that

conversation something seemed to make me feel
that no matter what, I was meant to be called Sister
Mary Raymond. I looked up the lives. To my
approval I found two Saint Raymonds. Raymond of
Pennsfort and Raymond Nonnatus both of whom
were members of the first order of Our Lady of
Mercy for the ransom of the captives of the
Crusades. The one for whom I am especially named
is Raymond Nonnatus. I was so happy to receive
him as my patron saint because of his singular
devotion to Our Lady. He never knew his Mother
because she died at his birth. He thus prayed to
Mary to take her place as his special Protectress.
Incidentally, I'll be the first in my crowd to have my
feast day after Reception next month on the 26th.
It's the day after my other patron Saint Rose of
Lima's feast - August 31st.

Mom, I finished my charge or work habit.
Now I just have my Reception one to go. Don't
forget each one of you keep praying as hard as you
can for me especially August 6-15 Solemn Retreat.
Remember you all are always in all my prayers.
Mary loves you. God bless you!

Your loving daughter,
Sister Rose Marie
(Sister Mary Raymond, R.S.M.)

The Sisters of Mercy
respectfully invite you to be present at the

Religious Clothing

of

Sister Rose Marie Eng

which will take place in the Convent Chapel, Mount Mercy
Fifth Avenue, Pittsburgh, Pennsylvania

August 26 19_5?_, at _??_ a.m.

Doors In and Out

"Actual doors haunt me.
They are the heavy wings of metaphor."
        Robert Kelley

Fall '57

Recently I watched a video made
of the film my Dad took years ago.
Time traveling back
to the teenager I used to be,
I watched my Before and After Self
the day I entered the convent.

Before:
I'm a ponytailed teenaged girl
wearing a fashionable green jumper,

a white long sleeved blouse,
sheer silk stockings
with seams up the middle
of the backs
and black high heels.

After:
I'm a black veiled young woman,
with my bangs barely visible.
My head encircled by a black
ruffle-edged headpiece.
My young body swathed in black:
a black long sleeved cotton blouse,
a floor-length pleated black serge skirt,
a black serge short-to-the-waist cape,
black opaque stockings under black-stringed
two inch high Cuban heeled shoes.

As the fourth in my Crowd to enter that day,
Sister Barbara being the first and
ultimately also the first to die years later,
I walked up the wide marble stairs
in the front hall of the Motherhouse
an attractive young teenage girl
and walked back down
less than a half hour later
a new young nun called a Postulant
essentially "Dead to the World" already.

Years later my next younger sister
would tell the story about how
the image of the closing
of the wooden front door
of the Motherhouse continued
to haunt her for a long time.
How when it closed on me,
it locked me away from her
and the rest of our family.

That same tall wooden door
my high school classmate
Mary Louise and I
had stood in front of
waiting for our knocks
to be answered one afternoon
in the spring of our senior year
when we were to meet the Mother Superior
for the first time to announce our desire
to enter the Community that fall.

How I announced to my friend that day
when it seemed we had been
waiting an eternity
for someone to open the door,
"Well, if no one's going to answer,
I guess that means we don't belong here.
They don't want us. So let's leave!"

No sooner had those words
tumbled out of my mouth,
the door finally squeaked open.
Behind it stood the strict nun who
taught us social studies in high school.

(How well I recall being in her class
at the beginning of my Freshman year.
I know this because I was wearing a dress,
not yet the white blouse and blue jumper uniform.
Since the building was only yards away
from a railroad track, all the other nuns
stopped trying to teach when the train chugged by.
But not Sister Rosalia.
She would raise her voice
above the loud noise outside.
On this certain day I was wearing a dress
with a bow at the back of it.
As the train barreled by,

a guy nicknamed "Hooda" sitting behind me
kept undoing that bow over and over.
Then I would laugh out loud
each time I retied it.
After the train passed by,
I realized to my embarrassment,
that Sister had been yelling
at me the whole time,
not continuing the lesson as usual.)

Now to return to my story with Mary Louise.
All we could hear as we clip clopped
in our high heels across the marble floor
of the front hall of the Motherhouse,
that significant threshold of our young lives,
were the "Hail Mary's" of the Rosary
repeated over and over again.

We found out later that this was the Rosary Ritual
to "welcome" the body of a recently deceased nun
about to be brought back to the Motherhouse
and laid out in the front parlor.
This particular day it was the body
of the "Old Sister Raymond"
as she was always referred to,
whose name I would be given
several years later as my name in religion
because in a college speech class that fall,
I would share this story with my peers
and later be directed by my Superior
to share it also with the nuns in the Novitiate
as part of an "entertainment" at recreation one night.

When I was told my name would be
what I presumed it would be,
I insisted that "Mary" be added
before "Raymond"
so it would sound feminine.

I will never forget what
Mother Margaret Mary,
who lived past 104,
told Mary Louise and me that afternoon
when the recitation of the Rosary ended,
"God takes one and brings two in her place."

Doors:
Shutting in and
Opening out.

Doors:
Hiding people and
Leading them forward.

Doors:
Two sides of the Coin of Life.
At Once In and Also Out.

Doors:
Undercover and Uncovered.
Closed Away and Moving Outward.

Doors:
Enclosing and Liberating.
Closing and Opening.

The Holy Rosary
(The Order of Prayers)

The Sign of the Cross
Apostle's Creed
Our Father
Hail Mary
Glory Be
Five Mysteries
Hail Holy Queen
The Sign of the Cross

Hail Mary

A prayer for the intercession of the Blessed Virgin Mary,
Mother of Jesus Christ.

"Hail Mary, full of grace.
Our Lord is with thee.
Blessed art thou among women,
and blessed is the fruit of thy womb,
Jesus.
Holy Mary, Mother of God,
pray for us sinners,
now and at the hour of our death.
Amen."

Ave Maria (or Salutatio Angelica)

The Latin version of Hail Mary

"Ave Maria, gratia plena,
Dominus tecum.
Benedicta tu in mulieribus,
et benedictus fructus ventris tui,
Jesus.
Sancta Maria, Mater Dei,
ora pro nobis peccatoribus,
nunc, et in hora mortis nostrae.
Amen"

The Winter of My Final Depression

During the dark days of '63, prior to the monumental day of my Final Profession, I endured an inner winter. Despite the friendship and support of the closest women in my Crowd in the Novitiate, I was languishing in a deep depression, my being quicksanded in doubt. Angry at myself for being angry. Upset for being upset. Caught up in a circle of anguish, every day I sank deeper and deeper into this darkness of my spirit. It seemed to me that the only way to go was down further and further into the abyss.

I was no good. I hated myself. Well, not really hated, that was too strong a word. But I was disgusted with myself. There was no escape. No light even faintly in the distance at the end of this tunnel of exile. I allowed myself no hope, no respite, no possibility of coming up, of breaking the circle, of unpainting myself out of the corner. Nothing was right with me in the world.

Two friends from my Crowd, Sisters Matilda and Imogine, provided comfort to my soul. By them being themselves, they kept the traces of Green inside me alive as I went about doing my assigned duties. Among these responsibilities: working in the laundry and the kitchen, serving meals to the afflicted nuns and volunteering at places like the Pennsylvania School for the Blind.

How many hours, days and years I spent under the conditioning of harsh self-judgment and negativism. Every noon during the first three years as a Postulant, Canonical White Novice and Senior Novice, I spent kneeling in Chapel doing a Particular Examen searching for my supposed "faults," such as washing my hair or pressing my habit without permission. As a result I became a nitpicking, scrupulous, self-pitying reject of a person to myself.

Thankfully, Sister Regis, my dear Mistress of the Juniorate, realized I was in need of significant help. The following poem is to honor her and especially thank her for her inveterate awareness of me.

Some Person Else
For Sister Regis Grace, R.S.M.

Her philosophy of life:
"Live it to the hilt and like it!"
She who understood me
long before I began
to understand myself.

Making me the ongoing companion
for other nuns to dentist, doctor,
hospital or funeral home.
Giving me permission
to walk to the flower shows
in spring and fall on Sunday afternoons.
Sometimes even without a companion.

Or giving me permission
to walk just to walk
with no destination
determined in advance.

She knew I needed to get out.
But her insight was deeper.
Significantly Deeper.
I think she knew I needed
to get out all the way.
And what's more she knew
before I knew.

But she never violated my personhood
by trying to push me out
before I was ready.

During those challenging months
before my Final Profession,
Sister Matilda was assigned
to be my companion
for my once a week conference
with Father Bonaventure,
a Capuchin priest.

I routinely stared down at the floor.
Never up at him or into his eyes.
As I tried to empty my soul of pain.
As I pleaded with him for Answers.
Answers that ran for cover at every turn.
Leaving in their stead Questions.
Only Questions.

One stellar day I realized
that in the end Life itself is a Question.
Still, to paraphrase Sister Regis' words,
How live it to the hilt,
yet like it at the same time?

That lovely Spring
after my Depression started to lift
like a curtain on a breezy morning,
I began to know me as me
and could look directly into Father's eyes.
And I knew I would make my Final Profession
in the Community the following August.

୬ଡ଼ୖ ଗ୶

Dear Sister Regis,
I've felt your understanding of me
as I was then and am now.
Once I stood on the banks
of the Hudson River in spirit
feeling your hand in mine
as a tall weed leaned into my left side.
I sensed your spirit with me
as my eyes are lifted upward
to the top of a skeleton tree
to a lovely bright yellow bird,
a kind I had never seen before,
perched there on the topmost branch.

Seconds later it flew gloriously
across my line of vision
to the left and away.
I wrote a mantra
of my life that morning,
"Out on a limb
and waiting passionately."

How we rolled our eyes
as young adult nuns
under your care
every time you said,
"some person else."
An expression
we had never heard before.

And yet how well those words
described you, Sister Regis.
For you surely were
"some person else" yourself.
If there ever was one.
A wise mentor.
An inspiring role model.
A Woman's Woman.

Insightfulness. Sensitivity.
Understanding. Caring.
You were blessed
with these traits.
You were One Remarkable Woman.

Throughout the 60's I wondered
where that your expression
"some person else" came from.
While later reading Act III
of Julius Caesar with my students,
Brutus' words to Publius jumped out at me,

"There is no harm intended to your person,
or to no Roman else."

The answer from the Bard himself!
I know you'd smile,
dear Sister Regis,
at my belated awareness.
You who were
"Some Person Else!"
A woman who has made
All the Difference in My Life.

Living in Honor of Sister Regis

My ideal as a nun was to emulate Sister Regis and follow her example to become the perceptive, understanding, honorable and intuitive woman that she was. A nun who was a good listener with enduring qualities of deep friendship and honest concern for others. Her family's last name "Grace" sums up what a model Sister of Mercy would be. Even today she inspires me to further develop these traits as I continue to emulate her in my Other Life.

In those early years one of our priest teachers asked us to decide, "Which one of your senses would you give up to God if asked?"

Because I treasured it the most, I answered, "My sight."

How would Sister Regis have reacted to my choice? I imagine she would have shaken her head, pushed her glasses up and smiled her inimitable smile as she told me, "We each decide what we decide."

The Decision of My Life

How did I decide at seventeen to enter the convent? One major event was in '56 when I was a junior at Saint Peter's High School in McKeesport, PA, a school that no longer exists. After classes that afternoon, Sisters Clement and Eugenia, two of the most outspoken nuns at Saint Peter's, became caught up in a heated altercation in front of us students. The issue was about whose group was to meet at a certain time, the Class Officers or the members of the National Honor Society. The conflict centered on the fact that eight of us students were members of both groups.

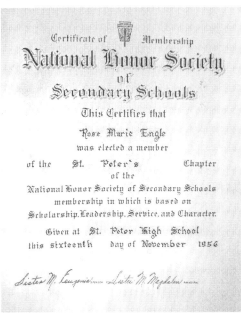

Certificate of Membership

National Honor Society of Secondary Schools

This Certifies that

Rose Marie Engle
was elected a member

of the   St.   Peter's   Chapter
of the
National Honor Society of Secondary Schools
membership in which is based on
Scholarship, Leadership, Service, and Character.

Given at St. Peter High School
this sixteenth day of November 1956

Sister M. Eugenia   Sister M. Magdalen

It didn't matter which nun won the debate that day. But as I walked down the street afterwards with my best friend Alberta, we discussed what happened. (We hardly ever ventured into the after school hangout called Lorelei's where all the cool kids drank pop and had a good time after school.)

I vowed to her that "If I ever enter, it won't be *that* Community!"

Within the next year, I realized that if those two nuns could show human emotions like real women "in the world," then I could join them and remain a real person too. So I "knew" the Christmas of '56 would to be my last one at home as a lay person. Even so, I didn't tell anyone yet.

LAST CHRISTMAS AT HOME

As a senior at Saint Peter's in '57, my English and Religion teacher, Sister Eugenia, would have someone open the window even if snow was coming in (there were no screens on the windows in the building) to get everyone to wake up and become re-involved in class. One day she volunteered my best friend Alberta and me to play the witches of Macbeth with her. "Double. Double. Toil and Trouble!" we cried out as we danced in place around an imaginary cauldron.

Without a doubt in my mind, Sister Eugenia was the nun who essentially convinced me to enter the convent with the following logic, "If you have good health and a good mind, a desire to serve God and the Community accepts you, you have a Vocation." Carl Jung had put it another way, "Anyone with a vocation hears the inner voice...the voice of a fuller life, of a wider, more comprehensive consciousness."

When I announced my decision, my always supportive Mom insisted, "Whatever will make you happy."

The Physical Examen

O n Ash Wednesday February 19, 1957, Sister Patrick, the Mistress of Novices, wrote the following letter to me.

Dear Miss Engle,

As you asked I have arranged for your physical examination at Mercy Hospital prior to completing your plans for September. You could go to the hospital, Medical Social Service Office, first floor near the front entrance and ask for Sister Richard. Sister will have arranged for the various examinations which you will need. Your appointment is for Thursday, March 14 as close to one o'clock as possible. If for any reason you cannot keep the appointment, please let me know.

Just as soon as I have the results, I shall inform you and I shall then send you your application for entrance to the Mercy postulancy.

I have been praying for you and asking God to give you the generosity and courage needful to do His Holy Will.

Make a good Lent, I shall write soon. In the mean time write to me if you wish or better still come up to see me.

P.S. God love you, Rose Marie, dear, I'll be anticipating seeing you again.

Sister M. Patrick

With a few coins in my pocket for the ride, I took a bus to the appointment. The doctor methodically checked out my eyes, ears and all the other parts of my body. Sister Patrick sent me another letter regarding the results of the physical.

Feast of Saint Benedict
March 21,1957

Dear Rose Marie,

The results of the physical examination came today. They are all favorable. The way is now clear to answer Our Lord's call to give Him the gift of yourself.

It will be impossible to describe the peace, love and rewards He has for you in return. He will not be outdone in generosity. Just now I'm sure you are inclined to look on what you plan to do as a great sacrifice - and it is - It is all you have. Still, it won't be long - just as soon as you have acquired a certain spiritual insight - before you will realize that what you give Our Lord is nothing in comparison to the honor He does you - in extending you the invitation to be His - and His alone. Remember when you are inclined to doubt the reality that you don't choose Him - He has chosen you and the only reason why you are able to take even these preliminary steps is because He is giving the grace. "This isn't your idea." It is entirely too big for a little body like yourself.

I expect the devil to be very busy insinuating a thousand doubts and objections. It is his last chance to spoil God's plan for you. Multiply your acts of confidence and love of the Sacred Heart - Heart of Jesus, in Thee I trust - Have the firm will to go ahead with what you believe in God's Will and trust Our Lady to watch over the outcome. We are praying for you.

Affectionately in Christ,
Sister M. Patrick

Then the same nun, now with the title "Mother," wrote another letter months later inviting me to the Profession ceremonies at the Mount. I wasn't able to attend because my family and I were on a special "Goodbye" trip for me in New York City. A cherished moment of that visit was walking up into the arm of the Statue of Liberty with my Dad, something no longer possible.

August 3, 1957
Dear Rose Marie,

We would love to have you at either one or other or both ceremonies on August 26. As the times come closer to September 7, I suppose that you are becoming as anxious as we are to have you with us to begin your new life.

I can imagine that around this time you are experiencing the common affliction of "being scared" yourselves and of hearing many of your friends lament your choice. They don't understand. But you should - and you do appreciate too the wonderful fact that You mean much to God and that following His plan means happiness for yourself.

You have a special vocation that no one else can answer. Out Lord needs "live wires" like yourself who will carry light and love; a young lady who is willing to give Him everything -simply because He wants it.

I am sure that the good God has called many other young women besides the nine of you to St. Mary's Novitiate this September. Selfishness, inability to make a decision, larger opportunities for careers and the whole worldly spirit of our times are causing them to turn down Christ. Thank God He has given you the special grace to be true to His call. If your sacrifice looms especially large at this time, (and it is a worthy sacrifice) it won't be long before you will realize that though you have been generous - God knows how to be infinitely more so.

Let me know if I can help you at any time in anything. The new Novices and newly professed will be happy to see you on the 26th, if you can come.

Sincerely in Christ,
Mother M. Patrick

The Tour of the Novitiate

During those precious last months of living "in the world," several of us who were to enter in the Fall were invited to tour the Novitiate on the third floor of the Motherhouse. This was where we were to live in dorms for our first few years as new nuns. The first floor had a Community Room for the Professed nuns, several living rooms and especially the Main Chapel. The second floor contained the cells of the Professed nuns.

While on the tour, there was a nun standing on top of a table having the bottom edge of her habit trimmed. Towering above me in her black outfit, she seemed stately and reserved. In time she would become my friend Sister Monica.

If ever there was a time to be scared off from joining the Community, it was during this tour in this huge old building with no radios or TV's and full of older strange women.

The Required Interview

To make sure I was of sound mind regarding my Vocation to become a nun, that summer Father Bailey interviewed me. He was my Mom's good friend, the dark-haired middle-aged Pastor of our parish church Saint Robert Bellarmine in East McKeesport, PA. Wearing a light blue dress, I took the short walk to the Rectory from my home. Father asked me relevant questions like "Why do you want to do this?" "How do you know this is your vocation?" "Are you prepared for the sacrifice of leaving your parents and your siblings?" Apparently, I responded appropriately to his queries.

Next my Mom and I met with a woman selling the clothing required for entering the convent. My Mom answered the door.

(Note: My nickname from childhood was "Ree" because it was easier to pronounce than "Rose Marie" for my youngest sister and baby brother.)

Hello, Mrs. Weaver, do come in. Did you have a hard time finding the house?

Not at all, Mrs. Engle. Shall we get started?

Hold on, she's upstairs. Ree! Mrs. Weaver is here!

I'm coming, Mom... Hi, Mrs. Weaver.

Good afternoon, dear.

Oh gosh, are those the stockings? They look so heavy.

Well, we do have one that's more of a sheer type.

No, they're the right ones. I'll get used to them.

I'm sure you will, dear. What about night gowns? One of these long plain white cotton ones?

Yes. Nothing fancy.

How about some black cotton slips for her, Mrs. Weaver?

Yes. Stand up, my dear, and let me see the length.

They're fine I guess.

What about some aprons? A checkered one?

No, Mom's friend is making me some.

Did you know her daughter entered the same Community last September?

Are you talking about Faithy?

Yes, Ree used to double date with her.

So she's becoming a nun as well?

God's ways are not ours.

MY DAD AND HIS FIREPLACE

Burning the Remnants of My Past

That summer, my last before entering the convent, I made another momentous decision. Picking up a box of personal items and a matchbox, I walked out of the house to the backyard brick fireplace my Dad built. It was to be a Grand Production of burning all my diaries and other writings.

As the flames roared and the smoke flew up into the afternoon sky, my next younger sister was not pleased about this decision because she naturally would have liked to have read them. She was one of several who were bewildered by the finality of my decisions.

The Final Masquerade?

I thought I would never dance again once entering the convent. So the week before leaving home I went to Bert's Glenn, my favorite dance place a half hour from our house. To drink up every last moment of dancing opportunity, I got my dance partner to dance all the way out of the building during the last song. It felt like a sentimental scene of a movie as the music got softer and the night air cooled us off.

The Dancing Changes of My Life

"I could only believe in a God who could dance."
        Nietzsche

I danced out of Bert's Glenn Ballroom
with my date
four days before
I entered the convent.

It was a Statement. A Symbolic Action.
A coming Full Circle to my decided reality
because I believed without question
I would never dance again
once I became a nun.

I can't forget the song that was playing,
"Good Night, Sweetheart, it's time to go.

I hate to leave you,
but I really must say,
Good Night, Sweetheart,
Good night."

How could I have known
that the night after I entered,
convinced I would never dance again,
that I would read a sign on the bulletin board
which announced the directive,
"Sisters, report to St. Joseph's Hall
at 8:00 for a Square Dance."

At first I was repulsed dancing only with women,
but over the next decade it was that or keep still,
which wasn't an option for me.
I square danced & round danced & modern danced
to whatever music we could find on old records.
One song stays on the edge of my mind,
Al Hurt's "Cherry Pink and Apple Blossom White."

One afternoon twenty of us
danced B.I.N.G.O. out in the back circle
on a break from study and work.
When she saw us dancing,
Sister Patrick appeared at the third floor window
extremely angry at us
because neighborhood people
across from our property
could watch us enjoying ourselves.
We had to stop immediately.

In my first "local house,"
one of the small convents
away from the Motherhouse,
the second year I taught,
three of us young Professed
collapsed the nuns into tearful laughter
with our performance of the Beatles' hit,

"I Want to Hold Your Hand."
Wearing mops on our heads,
we danced our way into the room,
lip-syncing what was to become a rock classic.

I also thought I'd never eat seafood again after becoming a nun. So the night before leaving home, my whole family dressed up and we piled into the Chrysler. My Dad drove us a half hour away to celebrate at a restaurant called Poli's, which has since been torn down. I enjoyed the famous shrimp platter, the same dish my Dad would always order. At this last-blow-of-the-horn special family meal, the evening was filled with laughing, talking and farewells. Since I truly believed this was the last time we'd be together like this, it was a particularly bittersweet celebration.

MY DAD AND HIS CHRYSLER

Losing My Hair

One thing I didn't mind giving up after entering the convent was my hair. To wear the coif, a special "tight against the skull" headpiece, we needed to have what looked like a boy's haircut. It was cut short in Room 101, where we could also get away with a little talking and a quiet laugh.

A Senior Novice, only a year older than I, would do the job. She would scissor off all the excess and use a razor to do the sides up to the ear and edge of the neck. Losing mine didn't matter much because my hair was not so beautiful. Nevertheless, it must have been traumatic for Jean, who entered two years before me, to have her lovely long blond hair cut off like a part of her femininity.

Repression of Our Female Selves

Femininity... now that was one thing hardly ever mentioned. In those days in the Novitiate we weren't allowed to use any kind of scented soap, only "Ivory." No colored nightgowns or silk lingerie either. They were feminine, the implication being they violated our Vow of Chastity. It was wrong to want to show concern for one's body beyond ordinary hygiene. One could not wear or have in one's possession anything colored, not even writing paper or anything scented. Johnson's Baby Powder was all we could use for talc. Any kind of cosmetics were out of the question, as was any item with lace. Our handkerchiefs had to be the large white square men's cotton ones. No flowers or trim or design of any kind on our nightgowns.

All of these "no no's" were outright attempts to deny our femininity. But one Christmas when I was a Novice, my Mom tried "beating the game" by giving me a white flannel nightgown with tiny lilac flowers on it. It also had a lilac ribbon belt. If I hadn't told my Mistress of Novices about how much I needed a new one, they would have taken it away.

Our night cap hassle still makes me smile. We were required to wear these small white caps in the hall after hours and in bed when our regular headpieces were off. Our heads had to always be covered to honor the Blessed Sacrament in the Chapel - in the same way we had to wear hats to Mass on Sundays as lay women and girls. As Novices we had started trimming the edges of these head coverings with strips of colored material we found. However, after an "Old Girl" complained about these trimmings, we had to hand them all in. After that, we could only wear the time-honored all white caps.

When we were still Junior Professed three years after entering, we were told to move into the building across from the Motherhouse called McAuley Hall. There each of us had our own cell that still had throw rugs on the floor from the days when college girls lived there. When one of the "Old Girls" heard about these rugs, apparently jealous since she didn't have one in her cell in the Motherhouse, she complained to the Mistress of Novices. As a result we had to hand them all in to her only days after we moved into the building. We accepted this decision without question thanks to our Vow of Obedience.

At recreation each evening from 8 to 9, we were permitted to eat one piece of chocolate as a treat (except during Advent and Lent.) During this hour we were required to be busy instead of just sitting and talking. We learned multitasking by fine stitching our habits or pressing them or, in my case in the earliest years, redoing my sewing as we talked. I was teased mercilessly for sewing patches on patches on the male style undershirts we wore.

We also had to wear large underarm dress shields to protect our habits since we only had three - an every day one, a special occasion one and a "charge" or work one. We had to also wear girdles because the nun who taught biology at the college thought they were healthy for us. In retrospect, maybe she thought that our wearing these restrictive garments would help us control our sexual yearnings as well.

Femininity was an albatross we had to guard against in every way.

The Secret Escape
Under Cover of Night

We were not allowed to look out windows as part of the Rule, but in that first year I absentmindedly did once....

It started like all the other Saturday mornings of the past six months ever since I and the other eight teenage girls in my group entered the Sisters of Mercy. Roused at 5:30 a.m. by the ringing of the ever so loud chapel bell, we would hurriedly dress. After less than twenty minutes, having taken care of our personal needs in the nearest communal mirror-less bathroom, we would be sleepily kneeling in our assigned places in Chapel. First, we'd meditate using the Exercises or Meditations of Saint Ignatius, then chant the Office of the Blessed Virgin Mary, our special daily prayers, and finally attend Mass. Afterwards we young nuns ate breakfast served family style in oversized white earthen crocks. We were not permitted to talk at this meal.

Following breakfast cleanup, we walked next door to the rooms of the laundry to do our weekly chores. Then after lunch and our cleanup duties, we Postulants had some time to shower and get our good clothes cleaned and pressed for Sunday before we chanted the afternoon Office of the Blessed Virgin Mary, ate dinner and did our other mandatory chores.

After that we'd have a class or study hall for an hour followed by recreation from 8 to 9.

On one particular Saturday evening I was re-sewing my name tag on one of my long white nightgowns. Before the welcome distraction of the nightly box of chocolates was passed around, our sugar fix for the day, my attention was drawn to a noise by the back door of the kitchen three floors down. Although we were not supposed to look out the windows, I gave into the temptation and glanced out the one beside me. As I did, a car door slammed shut and then the vehicle squealed out into the darkness. I didn't see anyone get into it with my cursory look, but I knew whatever happened was out of the ordinary.

Mystified, I continued sewing as I remarked to one of my Sister friends who entered the Community two years before me, "Sister, I just saw something odd down by the kitchen door."

"You know we're not allowed to look windows."

"I didn't mean to really. It's just that I heard a noise and automatically glanced down."

"It's part of the Rule, Sister. If you don't follow it, you could be sent home."

"Just for glancing out a window without thinking? "

"Yes, if you want to be professed."

"Well, let me tell you what I saw. There was a car down near the exit. The car door closed and it sped away. I can't stop wondering about it."

"It won't do you any good to keep thinking about it. Why don't you help me measure the hem on my habit instead."

It wasn't until after the bell rang at 9pm for the beginning of the Grand Silence when I returned to my alcove in the large dorm that "The Mystery of the Disappearing Car" was solved. Sister Betty Ann's dresser was empty; there wasn't one telltale sign that she'd ever even been here! She had disappeared without a word of goodbye to anyone. All I had was the haunting remembrance of the sound of the car door slamming in the night.

I tried hard to put her leaving out of my mind. I didn't feel confident enough to bring up the subject with the Mistress of Postulants afraid she'd just give me a penance for being too inquisitive if I did. Determined to be a good nun and obey all the rules, I kept quiet.

Within the next decade more than half of the women at recreation that strange night many years ago when Sister Betty Ann left, would themselves also disappear into the outside world under cover of night or day. They'd hand in their specially engraved rings and Holy Habits of Religion and virtually climb over the walls of their convents to live other lives in other places with other people on the Other Side.

Going into the Outside World

T he first time we got to leave the Motherhouse was to walk the mile, two by two, to the Cathedral Church on Holy Soul's Day in November of '58. Rachel, one of the teens who entered the convent a year after me, had been a parishioner in that parish. When we left the church, she saw her high school boyfriend standing by his car watching us walk out of the Cathedral. Taking a considerable risk, Rachel walked over to talk to him. Speaking to people in the "outside world" was not permitted, especially boys from our past lives. As a result she could have been sent home, "a Fate worse than Death." However, her transgression was overlooked because her aunt, who was a nun, was coming to visit her. Instead of being told to leave she became Sister Naomi.

When I was seventeen, I was aware my parents didn't have the money to send me to college, but I knew I could get a good education in the convent. Interestingly, by chance years later I found a receipt my Mom had kept. It indicated my parents paid the convent $100 a month in my first year there for my room and board and education. This was a significant amount of money for them since my Dad was a factory worker at the Westinghouse in Homestead, PA and my Mom didn't have a job at the time. The bigger issue that bothered me is that none of us were ever told about these quiet payments.

Spiritual Reading to the Novitiate

F requently I was given the assignment to sit in the middle of the refectory at dinner where I would read aloud for twenty minutes. The assembled group of about forty Postulants, Novices and Junior Professed would hear me read from a spiritual book selected by the Mistress of Novices. She would be sitting at the Head Table with the Mistress of Postulants as well as the nun in charge of our sewing our habits. From that vantage point these three could see whether we listened to the reading and what we ate or didn't eat. My next poem is a tribute to them.

To Mother Patrick, Sister Regina & Sister Anna Rose

The Trio in Command of the Ship of the Novitiate '57-'60

By your names
and personalities,
Patrick, you were our firm aunt.
Regina, our sophisticated lady cousin.
Anna Rose, our home town great aunt.

As teenage nuns so long ago
we lived and learned from you.
Through trying times,
you each stood beside us
to support us in our new lives.
Lives so diametrically different
from anything we as girls
had experienced beforehand.

The three of you sat up "in state"
at the Head table in the Novice's Refectory.
Did you share "holy" thoughts
regarding scripture and rituals
or discuss the problems
like homesickness and violations of the Rule
we nuns under your care
were suffering and guilty of?

Sister Regina, you were the first
we conferred with
during our earliest days.
As Mistress of Postulants,
a rather young woman yourself,
you were our role model
on how we should act
as gracious Women of God.

Sister Anna Rose, how patient
you were with me
the one known as "Rosie the Ripper"
since I'd have to tear out hem after hem.
Under your guidance and patience
I got so proficient
that next year I sewed for others
instead of doing dishes after lunch.

Mother Patrick as Mistress of Novices,
you were our ongoing director,
adviser and moderator.
You showed us by the size
of your handwriting on the blackboard
in the hall outside your office,
whether we were in trouble
for some indiscretion or violation of the Rule
or else there was a care package from home
waiting for us.

Today, dear Mother Patrick and
Sisters Regina and Anna Rose,
all of you are together again
at the Head Table in the Sky.
I know from my vantage point
in another time and place
that in myriad ways,
I am a better woman
for having known and loved
each of you.

The Foods That Were My Penance

One thing those three Head Table women were keenly aware of was what we were eating. Required to eat a portion of whatever was served, the worst penance came at breakfast when I had to gulp down globs of hot sticky raisins. I detested these immensely because as a young girl I had eaten an entire box of them and gotten sick to my stomach. It's no surprise that I had the following dream.

Eat Me: A Dream

Four huge vats of big black raisins are in front of me. Frozen in place, my eyes are fixed on these shriveled creatures. With sneering expressions on their otherwise empty faces, they keep looking at me and snickering, "Eat me. Eat me."

Eating heaping spoonfuls of the hot or cold stringy rhubarb first thing in the morning was another intense penance. Even a small taste would make me want to regurgitate. We were also served a weird dessert every Sunday at the noon meal - a baked half grapefruit topped with brown sugar. Not anything my Mother or Grandmother would ever have made.

My friend from James Street Sister Bernard Mary and I would squeeze fresh oranges for breakfast. Occasionally, some of us young nuns would be assigned to serve "Specials." These were special and different meals made for the older nuns with health problems and unordinary diets. Some examples would be fish instead of red meat, or only bland and soft foods. To our consternation, some of these women always complained about what we brought them even though we were just the messengers. "Specials" duty was not an enviable chore.

The Letters That Survived

My dear Mom saved a series of letters I wrote home every month after I entered through my Canonical Year. But first I'll share what Mother Patrick sent to my parents several weeks before my first Christmas in the convent. She probably wanted to reassure my family I was doing well. It may even have been a type of form letter sent to every girl's family.

Dear Mr. and Mrs. Engle,

You are both very much present in our Novitiate prayers around the Christ-Child's crib. My own greeting brings you the assurance you and your family have a special place in the prayers of all the Sisters of Mercy for having entrusted your dear daughter to us.

Sister Rose Marie seems quite happy in her consecration to God. In spite of how much you must miss her at home, I'm sure that her happiness is everything to you. Like yourselves, she is counting the days until your Christmas visit.

We have had a happy Advent time preparing for the Holy Child. I think you will be entirely convinced of that when Sister comes to wish you a Merry Christmas on the twenty-fifth.

The Christ Child's blessing of peace and love be on you and yours.

Gratefully in Christ,
Mother M. Patrick, R.S.M.

The Long Letter Home

A month after entering I sent my very first letter home. When writing letters, instead of dates we listed the "feast of the day" as was tradition. Therefore I have noted the actual date in parenthesis where relevant.

Feast of Saint Evaristus
(October 26, 1957)
Dear Mom,

As far as I can remember this is the first letter I've ever written to you. I hope it'll be one of the best. How's everyone? Did you get your new glasses yet? What kind are they?

I've been so busy lately. Everything seems to be coming up at once. Tomorrow, the Feast of Christ the King, we're having Exposition of the Blessed Sacrament and a procession during Benediction. It'll be our first as Postulants.

The next Thursday and Friday we're being host to some 45 Mother Superiors from Mercy orders all over the United States. An education institute is to be held here on campus. We might attend a few sessions. Otherwise we'll be the "Official Clean Up Crew."

Friday night the Novitiate is going to put on an entertainment for all the guests. That Spanish dance we were supposed to do for Mother Superior's Feast day (but didn't - we saw "Twelve Angry Men" instead) will be the Postulants' contribution. The Novices, Sister Josita's in this, (she was the first to enter from our street) are to do a ballet. It's beautiful from what I saw at practice.

A week tomorrow night we Postulants are entertaining the Novitiate with our initial "dramatic" performance. As yet we haven't the program completely prepared.

School keeps me stepping too. I have a 2000 to 2500 word research paper due for English Composition before Christmas. The deadline may seem far off but it really isn't. I've begun the preliminary steps this week. As far as I know, my subject is the question of whether or not the language of the Mass should be changed to English. I also have a book report due the second week of November. Luckily, I've read my novel. (Jess and Maria) already. All I have to do yet is write out my report on good paper. I had a book to read in French 3 also. I've already handed in that report.

We haven't had any homework assignments in zoology yet. We have a test every Friday though. This Tuesday in lab we're going to dissect our first animal a worm.

I'm getting along a little better in sewing now. I finished my four veils. We're starting on our guimps now....

By the way we're also having our mid term exams in a week or so.

The nightgown is simply beautiful and the boots fit perfectly. Thanks for the candy too.

I hope you have a good time at the Halloween Party. How was the Minstrel this year?

I'm glad to hear everyone is feeling fine. I'm back to normal again too. We all seem to be.

When you come next month would you please bring me: a soap eraser, a pair of black woolen gloves, a pack of 5x8 (large size) index cards, deodorant, a strong bristle lint brush, a medium size nylon comb, a college ruled spiral notebook ($.39 Murphy's) and some of that lined but unholed "scrap paper" if we have any left.

I know you won't mind if I say a few words to everyone else now....

Dear Dad,

Everything's fine with me now. Are you keeping up your bowling scores? How's our chance of winning the raffle this month? Did anyone I'd know win last time? When Mom writes again, do write me a few lines too if you have time please. I'll be more than happy to hear from you. Say a prayer for me.
Your loving daughter,
Sr. Rose Marie

Dear Pat,

Well, "Old Girl," how's things? Has Jimmy written? Please ask everyone to say some special prayers every day for vocations we need more ever so much daily. Have you dissected yet? What about pizza? Last visiting Sunday night we had Sister Patricia's Mother's homemade pizza. It was delicious. How's Barbara Ann? How you been out with BG lately? Say hello to everyone for me. Guess what on Mother Superior's Feast day we ate supper by candle light! Au revoir for a little while. Be good and remember those prayers.

You dear "little" sister,
Sr. Rose Marie (Wilma)

Dear Bee,

Thank you for your short but sweet letter. Keep them up. How's school been lately? Have you started diagraming yet? Pray for me and listen to Mom and always be good.

Your 'big" sister,
Sr. Rose Marie

Dear Chuck,

I loved your first letter. Write again real soon, OK. How's altar boy practice? When will you serve your first Mass? Don't forget to send me a picture. Did you see your stamps? Good bye for now. Pray for me. Don't fight with Bee.

Your "big" sister,
Sr. Rose Marie

Well, Mom. I think I better sort of put an end to all this gabbing. I enjoyed "talking" to everyone again. Remember now that you're all in all our prayers here (especially mine.) Please don't forget my Vocation Intention.

Write soon I'll be waiting. Send all my love to Dad, Pat, Bee, and Chuck. Take a big share of it for yourself. You deserve it. Keep up your good work down at the school. Our Lady will remember your efforts. Good bye now. Don't forget the prayers. Two weeks isn't too long a time. Till then you're always in my prayers.

Your most devoted daughter,
Sr. Rose Marie

Sewing Tribulations

Then in a letter in May of '58, I commented on my sewing which was "coming along slowly but surely. Every once in a while, I have a ripping session but not as often as I used to."

A month later I described my work further.

> **Right now I'm working on my charge (work) habit.** As usual, I'm running into all kinds of difficulties. My bottom is uneven. To alter it, I might have to rip most of my facing out. I won't know the verdict until tomorrow. My Reception habit is coming along slowly but surely. Sister Anna Rose took us step by step together on them. I'm trying to make mine as perfect as my 'able' sewing ability will permit.

Yes, once upon a time years ago an unusually sheltered and shy girl said, "Here I am, God. I want to be Yours and only Yours. Do with me what You will." And He did. And now, what now, Lord? I've gone down another road. I've changed. I'm not that same me who couldn't wait for the highlight of nightly recreation when our chocolate fix of the day was passed around. Or the me who could barely stomach hot syrupy raisins or cold stringy rhubarb. Or the me who cried holy tears or depression tears or futility tears most of the time during Holy Hours on Saturday nights from 7 to 8. Or the me, years later, realizing I didn't cry the day I entered the convent and left my parents, sisters and brother. Or the me writing stilted letters home which usually ended with pleas for prayers for vocations. Or the me asking the same, "How's work, Dad?" type of questions every visiting Sunday. Or the me ripping out seam after seam of the many yards of fine stitching at the bottom of my habit.

As I toured the second floor of the Mercy Internationale, I found Mother McAuley's sewing skill room. In those days all garments both plain and elaborate had to be handmade. Catherine McAuley persuaded her rich friends to buy clothing from the Sisters.

Thinking about sewing reminds me that we had to make our habits and other parts of our outfits. The problem for me was a daunting one.

Rosie the Ripper

I'm an eighteen year old nun
required to sew all the various parts
of my "Holy Habit of Religion."
Not on an electric machine
I used at home.
But on an old-fashioned
foot operated treadle.
Thoroughly challenged
with learning how to manipulate it.

For weeks I'd rip out more than I'd sew
leading my Sister peers with glee
to nickname me "Rosie the Ripper."
How patient our teacher Sister Anna Rose

remained with me.

As it turned out,
with my characteristic stick-to-it-ive-ness,
I learned the process so well
that during the next year,
I was excused from dishwashing duty after lunch.

Instead I sewed dominos on the treadle machine.
Dominos were the short black opaque veils
that hung from the top of our heads
to our waists to block the sheer long veils
that flowed mere inches above the floor.

Oh, the Persistence of My Youth.

In another letter to my parents the first December after I entered, I wrote,

> Luckily we didn't get a mark in clothing this time. Maybe by the end of the semester I'll rate at least a F+. Don't laugh. I'm fast becoming the first religious to excel in "professional ripping." Oh well, they say "practice makes perfect" maybe in a few years I'll have the distinction of being 'Head Ripper' at Mount Mercy College.

Letters of Holy Thoughts to My Sister

Last night Father Nene gave a fine talk using Our Lord's words, "I am the Good Shepherd... I know Mine and Mine know me," as the theme. It's hard to explain what I felt. It's as though each little occurrence of the past was only a stepping stone to the present for me here in the convent. The realization of how much God loves me and you and everyone became clearer to me in a few short minutes than in whole days previously. When I look back over all the various incidents of the past, I can't help but see God's hand there connecting each one. As I see it, He's making a chain of events - happy ones, sad ones, exciting ones, dull ones, all kinds of happenings linked together - in this way by His Will He has lead me here. It all works out for Him and for me. He Himself said, 'You have not chosen Me but I have chosen you.' Perhaps in a few years, Pat, when you recall all that's happening to you now in 1959, you too will experience the sentiments I'm trying to explain to you today. I'm sure Mom and Dad and each of you can look back over the years as I have and feel the same as I do. God's always with us and in us more than we are ourselves. As Saint Paul wrote, "To those who love God, all things work together unto good."

In my letters home during my "second year," i.e. Canonical or Enclosed Year, I frequently shared thoughts with my younger sister. In one of them I congratulated her for being "the newly elected President of the St. Robert Bellarmine Sodality" as well as a hint about her also entering the convent one day.

Pat, all I can say is I'll be saying some special prayers that you will be able to carry out every responsibility to the best of your ability. I know you can do it with Mary's help. When things seem to be going all wrong (as they often do) just turn to her with a Memorare. She'll see you through, no matter what. I'm glad to hear you like chemistry. You must have worked overtime to bring up your mark as you did. In case Sister Clement hasn't told you, the world needs good Catholic chemists and lab technicians, that is, if you don't have another vocation in mind. Think about it and pray to Mary about it too. I won't forget to remind her to take care of you as she has so lovingly taken care of me.

MEMORARE

"Remember, O most gracious Virgin Mary that never was it known that anyone who fled to Your protection, implored Your help, or sought Your intercession was left unaided. Inspired with this confidence, we fly to you, O Virgin of virgins, our Mother. To You we come; before You we stand, sinful and sorrowful. O Mother of the Word Incarnate, despise not our petitions, but in Your mercy, hear and answer us. Amen."

Chanting Travails

I n addition to learning how to use the treadle machine, another of my challenges during those early days was learning how to sing. Because every day we had to chant the Little Office of the Blessed Virgin, the liturgical devotion to the Blessed Virgin Mary including psalms, hymns, scripture and other readings. The whole process was a prime penance for me. It wasn't until years later that I was able to change my negative attitude about singing.

My Song of the Crow

"You pick out
your own song from the uproar
line by line,
and at last throw back your head and sing it."
         from "The Sorrow Dance" by Denise Levertov

Wilmerding, Pennsylvania
First grade music class.
The nun lines us up as various birds
by the way we sing the scale.

How well I remember
being the Last in Line.
The Crow.

A long time later

in another time and place,
a new friend who hears my story
sends me a quote about crow's significance
from a book by Carson,
Discovery of Power Through the Ways of Animals.

"Crow knows the unknowable mysteries of creation
 and is the keeper of all sacred law....
 With crow medicine you speak in a powerful voice
 when addressing issues that for you seem
 to be out of harmony or unjust."

In addition to numerous cultures honoring crows,
crows did various good works in the Bible.
They brought bread to hermits in the desert,
defended Saint Vincent against carnivores' attack.
And two tame crows found the corpses
of Saints Boniface and Meinrad.

Today I sing to have been called crow.

Letter About a Dramatic Chant

Unfortunately, during my early days of the convent, I hadn't yet been able to find my voice. My family learned the difficult story of learning to chant in the following letter.

Last Tuesday afternoon was a Red Letter day for me in chant. A few weeks prior, Sister Fidelis told us each to prepare to sing solo one of our favorite chants. First she called Sister Marie Gerard, one of our best if not the best singer. She did a fine job. Then Sister jumped to the opposite extreme and requested that I stand up before the class and make my "professional" debut! I "sang" the chant, "Jesu Dulcis" in Latin. The English translation follows.

Jesu, dulcis memoria,
Dans vera cordis gaudia:
Sed super mel et omnia
Ejus dulcis praesentia.

Jesus, the very thought of Thee,
With sweetness fills my breast;
But sweeter far Thy Face to see
And in Thy presence rest.

When I finally finished singing, Sister had this to say, "You're one person who just doesn't breathe right." For the next five minutes she taught me the correct procedure (I had been breathing incorrectly for nineteen years!) Well anyway, now that I have some idea of how to do it right and how to focus, perhaps I'll have a chance (this'll sound fantastic) to major in voice!

The Charm Course and Cooking

I n this letter I recount working in the chaotic kitchen of the convent. My Mom was a longtime family chef but also the head cook at St. Robert Bellarmine Catholic Elementary School.

Guess what, Mom, I've begun as of last Monday following in your footsteps. After putting on my "new" rubber guimp, I was dressed and ready to start. The former part time cook of the Engle family was then to become for the following month the morning chef at the kitchen of Mount Mercy Convent! Little by little, I'm remembering some of the old tricks you taught me, Mom. Of course cooking for six is just a "shade different" from cooking for 120. Speaking of tricks, I pulled a good one Friday. There I was frying a whole pan of potatoes when I smelled grease. It was from bacon. Luckily, I hadn't started frying all of the potatoes so I just put them all together to use for another day. That same morning I looked through our three big ice boxes for two big crates of cauliflower and just couldn't find them. I knew it was just my lack of looking well so I asked Sister John Berchmans to check for me. Two minutes later she dragged in the crates which I had overlooked. I thought they were cabbages. Now that I think about it, I doubt that I ever saw cauliflower in heads with leaves before. There's always a first time for everything, isn't there, Mom? I'll be finding out a lot of things I didn't know in the weeks to come and, as I said before, using a lot of hints you taught me in our kitchen. One thing I can't wait to learn is how to make ice cream. We have a regular machine for it. Well, at Christmas when I really get to talk to each of you, I'll probably have a million other little anecdotes to tell you. This is becoming quite an experience for me. And I love every minute of it!

The week before last we had the privilege of having another well-known personage on campus - Ann Culkin. She is known across the country for her famous Charm Course. She gave the college girls theirs for five days. Then she gave us her adapted one for nuns three evenings of that same week. We relearned all the basic fundamental principles of good posture, manners and decorum. It was quite a revelation to see one as completely dedicated to this different kind of Catholic Action. In all her suggestions and rules, she bought out the supernatural motive of doing every little courtesy and act of kindness solely for the love of God and His greater honor and glory. And after all is said and done for what other motive should we do anything, except to please God? Remember how many times you used to remind me of that fact? Remember, too, how you used to tell me about saying short ejaculations in between times?

Well, each of these little helps of yours are being explained and elaborated upon now by Mother Patrick in our daily Novice's Directory class. Each day I realize more and more the wonderful foundation you and Dad have given me. I can't begin to thank you for all the big and small sacrifices you've undergone and prayers you've said for me. I hope I don't sound like a broken record when I repeat again, you're always in all my prayers. God love you!

Later in that first year, I told my parents about Profession in another letter.

> All of us Postulants and some of the White Novices are going to be in the solemn procession for Profession Sunday morning. The ceremony is something you never forget. It's most inspiring. One of these days if it be God's will, I'll be on that altar saying "I do" too.

How prophetic those words became six years later at my own Final Profession. I believed I had a vocation to serve God through the people I would be led to meet. I knew I was being sent to work for Him for however long He wanted.

But what did I know about life then? What it meant to be in love. What it meant to express that love fully. Yes, I knew the basic things. But there was much I was wholly unaware of. In particular, many terms from early on were designed to conceal their true meanings.

Early Euphemisms

Growing up in the 40's and the 50's,
I never heard anyone say the word "pregnant."
Only being in "the family way."
Or "getting in trouble."

Words spoken behind cupped hands.
Whispered into telephone receivers.
Hushed comments over backyard fences.
In our kitchen or living room
mumbled in Hungarian by my parents
so we kids could not understand them.

I never heard the word "prostitute."
In high school not understanding
guys' snickered jokes about "Brick Alley."
Only vaguely understanding
it was not a place to go
because "nice" things did not happen there.
One day finally realizing girls and women
do get pregnant without benefit of a piece of paper
and that some give their bodies to paying customers.
Words like "tricks" and "pimps," "hookers" and "whores"
relatively recent additions to my vocabulary bank.

Never hearing anyone say "homosexual."
"Fairy" or "queer" were the muffled terms instead.
Which I wouldn't understand for years.
In eighth grade not comprehending
why the young parish priest was sent away
because he "liked boys."

Learning additional facts of life in the convent
from the novels I read for my college English classes
and being cut down because
of the relative salaciousness
when I shared their plot lines over dinner
with my fellow college student Sisters.

Recalling the day I had to request
a copy of <u>Catcher in the Rye</u>
from the nun Head Librarian.
She reluctantly reached down under the main desk
to retrieve one but only because
I was required to read it for English class.

Why was it such a deal in the past
"to tell it like it was?"
Why did women like my Mom not even know
what would happen on their wedding nights?
What was the Big Secret worth?
Agony and mistrust and denial?
Embarrassed long suffering in silence?

If more information had been forthcoming,
wouldn't women have been liberated sooner,
from their own fears and ignorance?
Was it men who did this to them
or was it the "well-meaning" older women
who hadn't been told anything themselves in advance
and therefore had nothing to pass on to their daughters
except their own disagreeable memories?

Does now knowing more change things in the end?
Are fewer girls raped, shamed and disillusioned
these days without their understanding?
Or are they more mature today
but still unaware of what's happening to them?

Will the young women of today
appreciate what their Mothers, Grandmothers,
Great Grandmothers and all their matrilineal ancestors
had to do to survive in the dark
and learn its secrets by themselves
without benefit of prior knowledge and support?

Will these new women change things for their daughters
so that finally the circle of ignorance and embarrassment

will end once and for all?
Is that scenario even feasible?
Or will "just a girl" and "dumb blonde"
continue to be euphemisms
for women out of touch with themselves and the realities
of lust and love and sex, marriage and commitment?

A Parable

Going to the attic of the Motherhouse was a dramatic process and ultimately a metaphor. Dealing with issues of free will, trust and the elasticity of the memory, going to the attic was also a kind of parable for the plight of women in a paternal world. The poem I wrote about these stairs was published and became the title of my first book of poetry.

The Stairs to the Attic

In the early days we had to get permission for most things
like wash our hair, press our habits and go to the attic.

With no room for our long wool shawls and heavy boots
in the small closets in the dorms where we slept,
we had to go to the dark attic to retrieve those items
from our oversized steamer trunks.

The problem was that every time we got on the elevator
to go to the attic (we always had to have a companion),
a certain old nun was standing in there
with a protruding stomach and deep voice.

She always stared straight ahead and spooked us.
Being teenagers at the time,
Sister seemed like a dirty old man disguised in nun's clothes.
We held our breaths the whole time going up and down.

We believed the elevator was the only way to the attic.

One day an announcement came in the mail
about the first reunion of all of the ex nuns
to be held at the Motherhouse.

We were told to consider the order
our second home that would always be there for us.
(Years later the nuns did provide a short term safe haven
for one of my crowd after she left her threatening husband.)

When the nun emcee announced that we could revisit
the Novitiate floor of the Motherhouse
(since no new applicants were entering,
it was now used for other groups),
I knew this was my chance.

The women in the group, "Innies or Outies"
as we dubbed them,
not aware of my agenda,
thought I was acting weird
when I checked out every nook and cranny
of the halls where we had lived
for the first six years.

Walking down the last hall
past the Mistress of Postulant's office,
I passed the small four bed dorm
where I was assigned to sleep
the Saturday I entered...
Slipping into the white-sheeted single bed
in my brand new long white cotton nightgown,
the clock of the church
down the street chimed nine

and I said to myself,

"Oh my God,
it's 9 o'clock Saturday night
and look where I am."

Across the hall from this dorm
was our old vow classroom.

Next to it was a door with a knob
which turned when I grabbed it.

And Lo and Behold,
There were the Stairs to the Attic.

As a symbolic action, I walked up the stairs
which had always been there,
to give a kind of "hard copy" life to their reality.

When I pondered the significance later,
I realized that the whole experience had been a metaphor
for all we as intelligent young women had willingly given up.

We had never questioned why we had to use
the elevator to go to the attic or why there were no stairs.
We had never even wondered what was behind that door.
We had given up our questions, our thinking minds to God.

And the sad fact of the matter was we had sacrificed too much.
We had given up and away our basic selves.
We had denied ourselves and accepted the belief
we had to do it to save our souls, to be "good Sisters."

And like all the women before us in or out of the convent,
we let ourselves become subservient, non-thinking pawns
in the hands of those in power, whether they be
defeminized nuns in habits or macho men in business suits.

I laugh when telling this story to a new person.
But under that laughter hides a piece of regret
about those early years so long ago
when I didn't "use my head,"
as my Dad had always admonished me,
and accepted it all hook, line and sinker,
losing a part of myself in the process.

(Published in <u>The Critic</u> - Summer 1995)

THE ACTUAL STAIRS TO THE ATTIC

At the next reunion I found *another* set of stairs to the attic in the far hall blocked by a larger than-life statue.

Beyond the Beyond
to the Attics of Ourselves

"Our reach should exceed our grasp
or what's a Heaven for?"
        Robert Browning

Photos of stone stairs to wherever.
To the attics of ourselves?

What is hidden there?
What are we to find
at the end of our climb?

What Mysteries of Life
lay waiting for us
in that cluttered space
at the top of our heads?

Ah, the Stairs to the Attic!
I climb and climb them
up and up and up
while at the same time
go deep and deep and deeper
into the Basements of Myself.

Oxymorons of awareness.
Of discernment.
Of discovery.
All hidden up the stone stairs
to the Attic of Ourselves.

The Silent Retreats

I don't regret the years I lived in that hallowed world. Even during the difficult times of the Seven Day Silent Retreats when we didn't talk at all except to the priest in the Confessional or to the Mistress of Novices. When we ate not just breakfast, but all our meals in silence. When we didn't get to enjoy our nightly recreations with our friends.

Accepting this way of life I was convinced this was what and where I was meant to be "for all eternity." I honored my religious vows with my whole heart and soul. We were repeatedly reminded by our Superiors that, "Your reward with be great in Heaven."

The Early Days Before the Vows

Standing in the attic of myself and looking down at my life, I am drawn back to my pre-teen and early teenage days. The following stories from 1950-1957 are in many ways indicative of the path I would soon take. First and foremost, by being a "good girl," I shied away from crossing lines and committing sins while at the same time doing all the "right" things.

When my parents were away, I'd get my siblings to say the Rosary with me in the living room whether they liked it or not. Later, when I was a teenager, my religious commitment got more serious.

Babushkas, Bangs and Bobby Pins
Growing up as a Catholic Teenager
in Western Pennsylvania in the 50's

Tony Home Permanents.
Peddle pushers.
Crinoline slips.
High heels.
Seamed stockings
attached to girdles.
Veiled hats for Mass on Sundays.
My Mom's big picture hats.
Guys with DA's wearing
pastel-colored pegged pants.
Some even blue suede shoes à la Elvis.

Frequent lines we shouted
if angry with someone,
"OK for you," or
"I'm telling my Mother on you!"

Or "Happy days are here again!"
As one of my friends would say to me
after another friend huffed home
angry with us for some reason.

Then there were "Pittsburghisms"
as I like to call them:
Taking "peepie steps"
in the game "Mother May I?"
Shaping stones on the curb.
Wearing pins and flowers

for our Honor Days once a year.
Drinking "pop" not soda.
A faucet was a spicket.
Wearing identical shirts if dating
for fun days together at Kennywood,
the local amusement park.

Also some odd repeated lines:
"If you don't like it, lump it!"
"That's it, Fort Pitt!"
"Let's red up this room."
"You don't have one iota of sense."
"He's sitting catty-corner from me."

Mass every Sunday no matter what
preceded by Confession the day before.
To ask forgiveness for mortal sins
because I let my boyfriend kiss me.

Never letting my boyfriend
touch my breasts.
Or let him turn me on
which might have led
to getting pregnant.

Uptight and confused.
Indoctrinated and naïve.
Wanting to be loved.
But afraid to let go.
Wanting to let go.
But afraid to be loved.

Churning inside.
Mixed up and distraught.
I stood at the threshold
of my One True Life
wondering,
"Is this all there is?
Is there another way?"

My First Jobs

Since I was my parents' first child,
I helped out with my three and seven
years younger sisters as well as
my only Baby Brother nine years younger.
I changed his little diapers
and watched his chest go up and down
in his crib to be sure he was still alive.

When I was all of twelve,
I officially started working
as a babysitter for an infant
for fifty cents an hour.

Then at fifteen
I got my every Saturday job
for the same amount
at Murphy's Five and Ten.
I became "The Pet Counter Lady"
charged with taking care
of fish, canaries and parakeets
as well as their food and accessories.

One day as I attempted to grab
a parakeet for a customer
out of the wide tall cage
with all the other birds,
one escaped.

Concerned patrons would then
approach me exclaiming,
"Girlie, there's a bird out in the store!"
apparently expecting me
to run through the two floors
with a net ready.

Instead, so as not to destroy
product displays all over the store,

I would wait until the bird
flew upstairs and invariably
into the glass windows
in the front of the building.
Knocked out, lying on the floor,
I would retrieve it
and return it to its cage.
No real harm done.

The other amusing thing
happened when my Dad would pick me up
at 9 p.m. closing time
and some of the women workers
presumed he was my date.

Surprise Sweet 16

Mom told me
to "put lipstick on."
She gave me a surprise party
in the basement of our home.
She baked a red velvet cake.

Sweet 16 in '55.

A Goodbye Party at 18

With my high school friends
again in our basement.
I still have the crucifix
my friend Norma
gifted me that night.
Only three weeks
until I leave home.

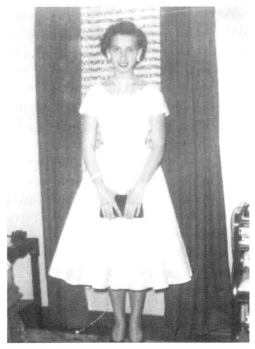

A Superabundance of Love

How meaningful certain prayers have remained for me. My Sophomore year at St. Peter's High School in '55-'56 was when my biology teacher, a young nun named Sister Julia, inspired me to say these words, "Whatever You want, I will be. Give me the courage, the strength and the unselfishness but especially a superabundance of love." I have prayed them ever since those days at the Consecration of Mass. Living prayer helped me come to many important realizations.

A significant awareness began one evening before Christmas during my senior year in high school. Dave, a friend of my cousin, invited me to a college party. The events of this night forced me to face what I might do with my life.

DAVE AND I ABOUT TO GO OUT

The Secret Behind the Green Door

Dave, a year older than I was, was taking me to a fraternity party. My first. It was November '56. I was only seventeen. Nervously, I got out of his new green Chevy in front of the building. From the dark street it appeared to be a dilapidated warehouse, black and dreary and somber. As we stepped inside, the darkness of the small hallway startled me for a minute. I heard rats scurrying about. What's more the pervasive odor reminded me of rotting garbage.

I tried to relax as we climbed the three flights up to the party room. I didn't want Dave to be embarrassed because of me. Since he was in the process of being initiated into the fraternity, I had to make a good impression.

His knock on the tall wooden door sounded like a distinctive knock. Probably someone on the other side had to make certain he was "one of the gang." After a few moments - long, uneasy ones for me - an inebriated and jovial guy holding an oversized beer mug in his hand greeted us, "Welcome! So good of you to come. Hey, Dave, who's your lovely date?"

Dave smiled and complied. "Rosie - Pete." Switching his mug to his left hand, Pete thrust his grisly right out for me to shake. I smiled a friendly "Hi" and shook his, and he rambled on, "Why not come all the way in? This party's just begun now that Lovely Rosie has joined us."

Uncomfortable, I followed him and Dave into the smoky room. I was apprehensive but Dave was a good guy and he was depending on me. Besides, why should I let a macho big shot like Pete bother me?

Elvis' popular song "You Ain't Nothing But a Hound Dog" blared from a stereo set up in a dusty corner. A few couples were on the dance floor. Others were scattered along the sidelines, holding mugs or cigarettes in their hands. Everyone seemed to be having fun laughing, talking, dancing, smoking and drinking.

Still I felt an odd uneasiness. Glancing around the crowded room, I noticed the long old-fashioned windows covered with discolored yellow blinds flipped shut. A stack of chairs, broken and unusable, filled the left corner of the room. A square mock stage stood on the opposite side.

The oppressive atmosphere enveloped me as I heard Pete shout, "Right this way! Right this way! This, my dear friends, is our own bar. A man's best friend his beer is. What did that darn poet say? 'Drink to me only with thine eyes.' What a laugh. Just tell me, how in the world could you drink to me only with your eyes, eh, Rosie? This here's the only good stuff!"

Pete had led us to the far left side of the place. There on a small table pushed partway into a tiny back room was a wide rectangular container with a skinny siphon running from its middle. He patted the thing on its frosty side and bellowed, "Yes, sir, this here's the only good stuff. It just can't be beat! So cool. So refreshing. The Real Thing!"

He handed Dave a gigantic mug with beer oozing over its edges and down its sides. But what could I tell him I wanted? Lemonade? Before my mouth had a chance to respond, I noticed Pete had disappeared. A new knock to be answered. New guests to welcome. I was relieved.

Dave glanced knowingly into my perturbed eyes. "I'll get you a pop, Rosie. You don't mind if I have a beer or two, do you?"

"No, Dave," I said as he left me alone near the beer.

Barely one moment later, Pete roughly grabbed my arm while I waited for Dave to return with my drink. "So there you are, Rosie. How about a dance? Come on, Dave won't mind."

As I was being pulled onto the dance floor without my affirmative consent, Dave came to my rescue. "Hands off, Old Boy! Rosie's my date." Separating us, he handed me my pop in a fire red beer mug. I gulped down half of it pretending to imitate the others and play the drinking game.

"I'm sorry, Pete, but..."

"Sure, I hear you, Dave-O. Have it your way." He meandered over to the other side of the room, grabbed a tall redhead off a chair and swirled her across the floor.

Dave grinned and squeezed my cold hand. "How about a dance with me now that you've turned down good old Pete?"

"Sure, Dave. This is a great Elvis song."

I felt at ease once I was slow dancing with Dave and so glad he was taking me "under his wing." He seemed to understand me. Still I felt as though my Sixth Sense was trying to tell me something. Caught in a web of an unknown kind, I shuddered and Dave pulled me closer to him as Elvis crooned, "Love me tender, Love me sweet, Never let me go." Just being in his arms relaxed me. It was as if I was momentarily entranced.

All the while my head ached as well as my body. When the music stopped, we edged over to the sidelines where an older, sort of distinguished guy was announcing something from the makeshift stage. Dave told me, "That's Ronnie, The Head Honcho."

Everyone gathered around the "stage." Ronnie yelled out, "And now, if everyone's ready, it's time for some songs!" As Dave sang along with them, I listened to the rousing melodies and risqué lyrics with weak attention. But since I felt a little guilty for letting Dave down, I faked a smile and tried to sing. However, my pretending didn't help. I just didn't feel right.

Finally, everyone stopped singing when Ronnie yelled that "Chug-a-Lug" was next on the agenda. Several guys helped him drag a long narrow table to the middle of the room. Others arranged folding chairs around it. Eight couples sat down, a mug of beer on the table in front of each of them.

Out of nowhere, they begun chanting a peculiar refrain, apparently for a drinking game. This while pounding their hands rhythmically on the table and guzzling down the beer, some chugging it non-stop. Fortunately Dave didn't hurry over to join them.

Instead he said, "Let's just watch. It's more fun than getting wiped out. The ones who play usually do."

Again I was relieved to be on the sidelines. Joking around a little, I said "After all, you know what that guy on TV says, 'I'm with you!'" We both laughed, I less than heartily.

The game was now in full swing. Having just swallowed the contents of his enormous mug, Pete held the empty container upside down over a blonde's head. Was she "his girl?"

The players were joking, drinking or swaying. The smell of the beer spilled all over the table and on the chairs and floor seemed to be seeping deeper and deeper into my consciousness. This odor and the "haunting" refrain of the songs everyone was singing off-key became mixed up with something inside me. Unlike anything I had ever felt before.

The room was stuffy and smoke-filled. In my eyes, everyone was staggering around. I tried again to become a part of it all, to laugh with them, but I couldn't. It occurred to me that maybe I was trying too hard.

Losing my patience, I couldn't take it another minute! The overpowering atmosphere and all the increasingly drunk people repelled me. Though I had tried, I couldn't be like them, no matter what Dave thought. An unsettled feeling inside me kept pleading with me to stop pretending and get the heck out.

"Dave, do you think we might leave soon? Like right now?"

"Sure, Rosie. Are you sick? You're pale."

"Could use some fresh air. You don't mind if we go before the party's over, do you?"

"No, Rosie, they'll understand. By the time they're dead drunk and about to be carried out it's no fun anyway." He started to speak in a quieter voice as he added, "The truth is I don't want to join their frat house."

Dave motioned to Ronnie, "Say Old Man, we're going to be on our way. Rosie is a bit under the weather. I hear something is going around."

"Sure thing, Dave. Glad you two came, though. Take it easy."

Ronnie's "send-off" sounded like the sweetest medicine would taste. Despite my mood I could have flown down the rickety steps and plunged into Dave's car in a flash.

As we crossed the deserted street, the cool November breeze cleared my head a bit. When we first got in the car, it was chilly so a sense of refreshment swept over me. Switching on the radio, I sighed a subdued "At last!"

Leaning back against the soft passenger seat, my weary eyes automatically closed. But the odd feeling that had bothered me all evening continued to assail me as I dozed off.

Startled awake by a familiar song called "Green Door" on the radio, I heard....

> "Midnight, one more night without sleeping
> Watching till the morning comes creeping
> Green Door, what's that secret you're keeping?
> Green Door, what's that secret you're keeping?
> There's an old piano and they play it hot behind the green door.
> Don't know what they're doing
> but they laugh a lot behind the Green Door...."

Last summer, Dave, his friend Ted, Faith and I had gone out to dinner together. It was several nights before Faith left to enter the convent. On our way to a drive-in theater to see "A Summer Place," we were crossing a bridge as the same song "Green Door" played on the radio.

Ted didn't know Faith was becoming a nun because she never told him. All she had said was, "I'm going to college in Oakland." Although it was unsettling for me that there was this elephant in the room, I decided that if she didn't want to tell him, I wouldn't either.

As I relived that night heading to the drive-in, the refrain of the "Green Door" kept replaying through my mind. It was such an appropriate song for Faith - going away to search for "The Secret."

Still here I was, waiting and wondering, continuing my own attempt to find That "Secret Behind the Green Door." Except now it was a different Saturday night as Dave and I crossed a different bridge as I listened to the same song from that unforgettable night a year ago.

It was uncanny the way Dave acted. Never had I mentioned the connection between Faith and the song. Yet it seemed as if he was reading my memories and thinking about her as well. As the song played, he blurted out, "Wow, was I blown away when I heard about Faith. I could have fallen through the floor."

"Everyone was shocked. I promised I'd never tell anyone. How'd you find out, Dave?"

"At a recent party I asked my buddy's girl who goes to Mount Mercy College if she knew a Freshman named Faith. Janet seemed puzzled and said, 'Faith? Yeah, she's that nun in my bio lab. I don't know her, but she seems OK.' Well you could've knocked me over with a feather. Faith a nun? No way! Always wrapped up in black? Never dating again. Never getting married. Only praying all day?" At the wheel, Dave was swerving a little as he excitedly flailed his arm for emphasis.

"I haven't had a chance to visit her, but her Mom did tell mine that she's doing well. She's the second to enter the convent from our street. Joanne was the first last September," I added.

I'll never forget the question Dave then asked me. The exact words he used. He must have understood something about me even before I did.

"You wouldn't happen to be thinking of entering too, would you, Rosie?"

For a long frantic minute I didn't know what to answer. I wasn't thinking about entering the convent, was I? Yet subconsciously I was pondering the possibility and thinking about it, wasn't I? Perhaps that was why I was so uncomfortable and disconcerted at the party. Why I knew I couldn't, didn't, wouldn't ever fit in that world.

This question about my future was why something was lurking somewhere within my uneasy sense of unrest, of not belonging, of feeling out of place. It had been hiding within me all along. Two words were all I could answer Dave, "Who knows?" Promptly changing the subject after that, I added "But thanks for taking me out tonight. The music was nice."

But Dave's question haunted me, scared me, challenged me, yet intrigued me. Without realizing it that night, it pushed me out on my own "Search for the Secret Behind the Green Door." A search that less than a year later would lead me to leave my family and friends and the world. I would follow Joanne and Faith to that Other World of vows and penance and, most of all, that continued searching....

5, McKEESPORT, PA., FRIDAY EVENING, FEBRUARY 22, 1957

Book Week Stresses Written Truth

—A Daily News Photo

Christian books as "heralds of truth" are receiving emphasis during Catholic Book Week, which opened on Feb. 17 and will close on Saturday. Seen here are four members of the St. Peter's High School Library Club as they looked over one of the lists of books recommended for reading. Seated is Norma Jean Similo and standing are, left to right, Patricia Lundis, Patricia Goettler and Rose Marie Engle.

Observance of the week is sponsored by the Catholic Library Assn. as a force in the struggle to "promote the reading of good literature in this day of over-emphasis upon the seamy, the materialistic and the degenerate side of life."

Several book lists have been prepared and the Library Club at St. Peters is promoting distribution and attention to the lists among the students. Sister M. Ricarda is the Moderator of the club, which plans a special program each year for Catholic Book Week.

The Senior Prom and Convent Visit

That Spring of '57 I had another peculiar experience when I asked a friend to go to the Senior Prom with me. What I didn't intentionally tell him in advance was the requirement that we girls and our dates were required to go to the convent beforehand. The nuns had to check out our gowns to make sure they weren't cut so low as to show cleavage. No doubt the holy Sisters also tried to put the fear of God into our dates so they wouldn't try to take advantage of us in any way that evening.

My date, Paul, was so disconcerted as he stood in the convent foyer that he kept his hands respectfully folded as he watched the line of nuns on the stairs peering down at us. One of the older nuns ominously turned to him and asked, "Are you praying, young man?" He could only avert his intimidated eyes, not daring a response.

When the time came, he was more than relieved to hurry out of that old building. As we got back into his Buick, he wiped the sweat from his brow and practically squealed out of the parking lot James Dean style.

Despite my Mom's friend Goldie doing up my hair and my buying an elegant white flowing gown for the event, the Prom was a disappointment. When my self-proclaimed theme song of those days, "The Great Pretender" by The Platters was played, I laughed to myself at the ironic significance of its lyrics. "Too real is this feeling of make believe // Too real when I feel what my heart can't conceal." It was difficult even pretending to enjoy the evening. My date didn't dance well and certainly didn't seem to enjoy the Prom after his unpleasant experience at the convent. The last time I saw Paul was when he dropped me off at home at midnight and disappeared up the street into the foggy night air.

The Blue Dell Pool and Getting Dunked

There were long nights waiting for phone calls. I was just beginning to get "boy crazy" as a teenager in the mid 50's. Stretched out across my single bed in the room I shared with my two younger sisters, I'd be swathed in Noxzema, my skin scarlet and tender from the previous day under the sun.

I had spent the afternoon at Blue Dell, the local swimming pool. There I would purposely back float into roving bands of guys who were known for whirling girls through the air from the five feet deep section into the eight. Two of these guys I facetiously called "Lazy Lump" and "Rat Face." Invariably I'd swim in their direction, hoping to get picked up and tossed. Then coming up for air only to go down again. Attention starved always wanting more. More times being grabbed and thrown into the deep end. More plunging, more being dunked down over and over.

Then on edge for hours waiting for calls about dates for roller skating, square dancing or movies. Preoccupied with thoughts about who'd be at those events, what would happen, what would they think of me. Continually wanting more and more and more attention.

The Sixth Commandment

The anguish about breaking any of the Ten Commandments, particularly the Sixth, "Thou shalt not commit adultery," plagued me. It was interpreted to prevent sustained kissing and positively no petting or anything beyond that. When my two sisters and I arrived at that "certain" age of long phone calls in the night, excitement over dates and dances and fancy dresses, my Mom would always admonish us, "Just don't let him touch your breasts." As if he wouldn't try anything else.

All mortal sins. All leading to damnation. Hell and fire never to end! As an understandable result, agonizing about letting my boyfriend steal a kiss at the end of a date. During the week afterwards waiting scared for Saturday afternoon. Then in the dark of the Confessional Box, I could once more become safe and secure, off of the road to Hell. Brainwashed to believe that we would end up there if we died before confessing our sins.

Holding off my high school boyfriend Brian when we were sixteen. "I can't. No, I can't. No!"

"Kissing inevitably leads to more serious sins," maintained the priests at church and the nuns at school. I wasn't sure what they meant happened between a guy and a girl in the back seat of their cars, but I accepted what they said in my innocent naïveté. It was despicable behavior.

This type of fear-based indoctrination also affected my Mother as a young girl. As any good Catholic girl, she went to Confession regularly.

Confession: The Sacrament of Penance
(From the-latinmass.com)

"Make the sign of the cross as you say, 'Bless me Father, for I have sinned, it has been (state how long since your last confession) since my last confession, and these are my sins.'

Tell the Priest your sins.

When you have finished confessing your sins, say, 'For these and all the sins of my past I am truly sorry.' The Priest will give you a suitable penance, and he may give you advice.

Make an act of contrition. 'O my God, I am heartily sorry for having offended Thee. I detest all my sins because of Thy just punishments, but most of all because they have offended Thee, my God, who art all good and deserving of all my love. I firmly resolve, with the help of Thy grace, to confess my sins, to do penance, and to avoid the near occasion of sin. Amen.'

The Priest will say the prayer of absolution. At the end of the prayer, say 'Amen.'

The Priest will say, 'Your sins are forgiven, go in peace.'

Than say, 'Thank you Father.'

Perform the penance you were assigned by the Priest."

Sodality: A Religious Guild

One of the stepping stones of my spiritual preparation was becoming a certified member and practitioner of the Sodality of Our Lady. The aim of a Sodalist was "to foster ardent devotion towards the Blessed Virgin Mary" and "To sanctify self... to sanctify one's neighbor... to defend the Church."

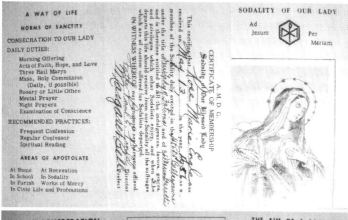

CARD DETAILING MY DUTIES AS A SODALIST

St. Peter's Students Named to Honor Society

Seven seniors were initiated yesterday as charter members of the newly-organized chapter of the National Honor Society at St. Peter's High School. The ceremony was conducted by student members of the chapter from St. Xavier's Academy, Latrobe.

The society recognizes students for character, scholarship, leadership and service, signified by the letters on the placard held here by two of the seven new inductees. This is an enlargement of the pin which they wear now as members. They are seen as they receive certificates and congratulations from the Rev. Leo A. McCrory, pastor of St. Peter's. Left to right, they are Patricia Lundie, James King, Father McCrory, Richard Kront, Rose Maria Engle, Robert Charney, Alberta Zewe and Richard Uhar.

Eggs and Kisses

"The more things change, the more they remain the same."
        French Proverb

My Mom tells the story
of watching a chicken lay an egg
when she was little
then hurrying off to Confession
because she had been told
it was a sin.

Was this in the same ballpark
as what happened to me
as a tense teenager
making sure I got
to that same dark box
to confess my mortal sin
of letting my boyfriend
barely touch my lips?

Discussion About
"The Mortal Sin" of Kissing

My beliefs wouldn't let my boyfriend kiss me for longer than a second, let alone allow him to do anything else. Not surprisingly, he was frustrated with this denial.

"What's the matter with you? What's the matter?" he'd keep asking me.

"We're not allowed to. You know it's a mortal sin. I'll have to go to Confession. If I die before I do...."

He would moan and answer something like, "Come on, Rosie. You can't believe in all that stuff about damnation? All I want is a damn kiss."

I never followed up with, "You'll go to Hell too if you kiss me and don't get to Confession before you die."

He would have replied, "Forget it all, Rosie. At my school there's no nuns and priests. No one even tried to tell us this nonsense about hell and kissing."

As a result of my repressed Catholic upbringing in a puritanical society, I hadn't allowed the natural blossoming of my sexual self. In hindsight one of the reasons I entered the convent at eighteen was to escape this burgeoning sexuality. Understandably, I had no viable way to handle or deal with my hormonal evolution.

BRIAN AND I POSING BEFORE A DATE

Brian of the Elvis Smirk

Every Sunday I would watch his family
parade into the old St. Aloysius Church,
he behind his parents
leading his three younger siblings
in a line down the aisle.
This was when I first saw him
when I was eight in the late 40's.

One day when we were both fifteen,
(our birthdays were one day apart,)
I was officially introduced to him
when his parents invited my family
to dinner at their house.

What struck me at first
was the way he could twist words
and make ordinary ones
cleverly different and unique.

Most of all, he had that "certain look"
that grew from the edges of his mouth
into a snide smirk Elvis style.

He drove an old beat up
light green Chevy pickup truck.
Friday nights he'd run into a bar
called the Wilmerding Café
and buy us fried fish sandwiches
with cod overflowing the sides.
I waited in the truck.
It wasn't right in those days
for a girl to go in a place
that sold beer and wine.

Thinking about our friendship
from the vantage point

of age and maturity,
I've realized Brian
cared and maybe even loved me more
than I did him in those early days.

He used to introduce me as "my fiancée"
which I wasn't and didn't like him calling me.

How well I recall his "Waterloo" with me.
I loved going dancing
at a place called Bert's Glenn.
One night my Dad drove
my younger sister and me
there for the evening.

At the hall I was having an exciting time
dancing with a lot of cute guys.
One in particular was a smooth operator.
I was laughing as he twirled
me around and around
as I enjoyed every minute.

Then, as though he was transported
in from another planet,
Brian was standing in front of us
yelling at my partner
about dancing with "his girl."
(My youngest sister must have told him
where we went.)

Before I could grasp the situation,
the two guys charged away in a huff
to "have it out."

Thankfully, a security guard intervened.
They never came to blows.

From that night on
I refused to date him

because he was too possessive.
The girl he had considered
to be his future wife
was not having it.
I was fighting to be
"My Own Person."

When in the spring of my senior year,
I announced my decision to become a nun,
he was devastated by the news
as he stood in our kitchen.
My sister tried to reassure him
that if it wasn't the life for me,
I could come home
during the first six years.
His response has never left my memory,
"If I know how stubborn she is,
she will never leave."

He still tried to convince me otherwise,
saying he "needed me and
I could save my soul in the world."
But I was adamant.
My mind was made up.
No one could unmake it.

Months later when my family
came on Visiting Sundays,
my Mom would tell me
Brian was dating a girl
with a ponytail like the one I used to wear.
Her name was also Rose.
Later I learned they married.

Then six years later
the day before my Final Profession,
I was walking down the hill
on the Motherhouse grounds
in deep meditation,

when I was distracted momentarily
by a curly haired, black bearded man
getting out of a pickup truck
in front of the college library.

The next morning
after our solemn ceremonies
when we could talk at breakfast,
one of the women in my "Crowd"
jarred my mind when she told me,

>   "I met someone you used to know.
>   I was meditating behind the library
>   when I realized the guy working on the roof
>   kept moving closer and closer to me.
>   Finally, he broke the silence to ask,
>   'Do you know a girl named Rose Marie Engle?'
>   When I answered, 'Yes.
>   She's Sister Raymond now.'
>   He quickly corrected me emphasizing
>   the 'Mary' in your name,
>   Sister Mary Raymond."

So Brian and I had passed each other
as though strangers in the night.

Part Two

"To God the Joy of My Youth"

Coming of Age in the Convent

Those cool breezes,

those wondrous flowers,

those refreshing waters,

did they all lead us inside the convent walls?

EIGHTH GRADE MAY PROCESSION
AT ST. ALOYSIUS

My Sexual Self

During the late '50s I began facing my latent sexual longings despite my Vow of Chastity. But looking back even further, I didn't have any context to comprehend my first stirrings. There were no sex education classes in the Catholic schools I attended. Even worse, the word "sex" was virtually never uttered.

My Preteen Highs

Visiting my grandparents,
going into the bedrooms of my young
thirty something aunts.
Lovely curtained four poster beds, all white.
Dressing tables with oversized mirrors
with fancy jars of perfume on top.
Barb and Olga used to save empty ones
to give to my sister Pat and me.

Wandering alone
into the expansive living room
reading True magazine articles
filled with accounts of illicit affairs
and other sexual information
I wasn't aware of then.

But feeling a fine high nevertheless
from reading about dating and guys
in the magazines I had never
been exposed to.

Not realizing until years later
what was happening in me.

Spin the Bottle

Later in eighth grade I felt all "squishy" and turned on inside when hearing Ronald's changing voice. As a Sophomore I played the infamous "Spin the Bottle," in the basement of my house no less. Wanting so desperately to fit in with the "with it" kids, I even broke the record for the longest kiss with a guy named John. I wasn't even slightly aroused.

The fact that this ever happened is amazing considering the fear of hell instilled in me by the priests and nuns. What's even more remarkable is that I didn't dutifully go to Confession and confess my sin to the priest.

By design, these teenager games were all "hush hush." Our parents and our priests could never learn about these long "sinful" kisses.

Christmas Visits in the Convent

Circa 1957-1960

Trying to stay away from the window.
We Postulants and Novices
were not allowed to look out to see
who was coming to visit.
Waiting anxiously for the telephone call
that my family had arrived.
Hurrying over to Saint Joseph's Hall
to be with them for an hour or two.

But not allowed
to open the gifts they brought
while in their presence.
Having to wait
with all the other new nuns
and open them
in the long room across from the Novitiate Chapel.

Not permitted to keep
scented soaps and powders
or anything with any color on it
including stationery.
Not allowed to eat the "goodies" Mom baked
 - her red cake and nut rolls and nut horns -
until 8 p.m. in the Novitiate at recreation time.

Trying to keep a conversation going
with my parents and two sisters and brother
about the classes I was taking in college
or the habit I was fine stitching,
or the girl who had just entered.

Laughing about the day after Christmas
when Sister Marie Gerard and I were sent
to go to the Pittsburgh department stores

to return all the "lady" presents
us Sisters weren't allowed to keep.

Getting on the street car,
putting the shopping bags
down on the slushy floor,
snowy and wet from the
wintry weather.

Minutes later
having to retrieve
all the bars of scented soap
and boxes of perfumed powder
that fell out of the bottom
of the disintegrating soggy bags
cascading this way and that
around the crowded street car.

Spending that whole afternoon
in one department store after another
trying to return a certain
long black lace silk slip,
only to find out finally
from an astute saleslady,
"Sorry, you can't return this
because it's homemade."

Also thinking it could've been
the infamous lacy black slip
I took from Pat D.
the day she entered
which she continues
to kid me about.
Wondering later
if one of the "Old Girls"
got to wear that slip
and if it made her feel sexy.

Sister Alma and Picking Apples

During occasional halcyon days, Sister Alma, the elderly nun with arthritic fingers in charge of the kitchen, was like a substitute Grandmother to me. We young nuns helped her with chores like peeling apples, slicing potatoes and shredding carrots. It's no wonder I've often thought about her and imagined our conversations.

"Sister Alma, you were in my dream last night. You were a trim young woman with black hair but not wearing the habit. Why was that?"

"My dear Sister Mary Raymond, even I at one point wore regular clothes. We are all women even if we strive for something more."

"I want to thank you for the homemade desserts and freshly baked bread you made in the Motherhouse. And it was truly a gift when you got us out of the Mount for a day trip. Did you know how liberating that was for us teenagers?"

"Were you having second thoughts about being in the convent, my dear?"

"I never had a thought of going AWOL or jumping ship in those days. I was convinced that I was doing what I was meant to do. That I had a vocation. No one, even my high school boyfriend, could convince me otherwise."

"You were so sincere, so conscientious, so serious. What bothered me was how uptight you were. It took you a long time to loosen up, to take things in stride when things go wrong or go bump in the night."

"Dear Sister Alma, you were like my Convent Grandma. I loved you. My own Grandma died when I was twelve. You were the proverbial Godsend to all of us. And I loved your homemade ice cream."

"You are most welcome. May you find joy in your search."

Picking Apples with Sister Alma

A fun day away
from our religious community
for us nuns-in-training.
Riding on a long bus
with Sister Alma,
our surrogate Grandmother
and cook at the Motherhouse,
who had large knotted hands.

Traveling on this bus
way into the country
to pick apples at Saint Xavier Academy,
an Infirmary for the aged nuns.
Being able to see
the back porch Dad built
on my house on James Street
as we drive by Park Terrace on Route 30.
Maybe the driver even slows down a bit
for me to get a better look.

After picking bushels upon bushels of apples,
several of us slip away out of sight.
We remove our starched headpieces
then take off our floor-length black veils
and stretch out in the tall green grass.

In those days the little hair we had
was covered all day and night.
But that day after we took it all off,
ah, the exquisite feeling
of the fresh air on our heads.

The Canonical Year
and Religious Classes

I n the following three letters to my family in '58, I wrote about picking fruit, school, dancing as well as new girls entering. The first two letters are when I was still a Postulant. The third letter is after I received the Holy Habit of Religion and my white veil, thus commencing my Canonical Year.

We didn't attend regular college classes during that year. Instead we earned six college credits from classes in the Novitiate - Christology, concerned with the theology of Jesus the man; Dogmatic Theology dealing with truths of faith related to God and His works; Gregorian Chant; and Music Appreciation, my personal favorite, with an emphasis on classical music by Beethoven, Chopin and Bach. Finally, there were classes on The Life of Mother McAuley, Novice's Directory and the Ascetical Life. During the Canonical Year we prayed many times a day and didn't have visiting Sundays with our families.

Vigil of Pentecost   (May 26, 1958)

Dear Mom & Dad and Pat, Bee & Chuckie,

On Mother's Day evening we had our Novitiate May Crowning. The youngest (the most recent to arrive) crowns. My "Possie," Sister Patricia Anne, thus had the honor this year. We Postulants led the procession, followed by the Whites, the Temporary Professed and the Superiors. As we walked around the back circle, we said the Rosary and sang two or three Marian songs. I suppose you've never seen the life-size statue of Our Lady in the back circle.

Oh Mom, last night the voice and piano students of the college had a recital. Sister Josita played. Altogether six Novitiate sisters sang or played. One of our newer postulants, Sister Marian sang. She has a beautiful soprano voice.

Chuckie, I just love you altar boy picture. Have you been serving lately? Are you still playing in the Little League?

Mom, the cherry pies were simply too good to describe. We appreciate your wonderful cooking.

It doesn't seem possible but we only have four more days of school left. We have Memorial Day off and then begin our finals on June 2.

I gave my final speech on Wednesday on devotion to the scapular. I made an A.

My sewing's coming along slowly but surely. Oh by the way I'm learning how to starch in a few weeks.

You're all in all my prayers every day. Keep praying for vocations. I love you all very much.

Your sister in Christ,
S. Rose Marie

Fourth Sunday After Pentecost
(Jun 23, 1958)

Dear Mom & Dad and Pat, Bee & Chuckie,

It's my guess that none of you can imagine
what I was doing and where I was last Tuesday. I'll
give you a hint - you and I were doing it together in
New Jersey about this same time last year.
Swimming, you think. No. (That's an ordinary
occurrence for me. I've been there 3 times since
school's been out. I have you all beat!) Riding in a
red convertible? No. (It was an orange bus.) Well,
rather than prolong the suspense, I'll fill in the
details. (Speaking of swimming, though, I just now
got back from a quick dip. I was teaching Denise
how to swim and back float. She's a wonderful
student.) And now back to those details.

I was up in a tree at Saint X's picking
cherries! All of the Possies, Canons, some of the
senior Whites and Mother Patrick went. We picked
both sweet and sour ones. You can guess what kind
I picked and how many I ate in the process. We
certainly had a fine time - climbing the trees, eating
our "picnic" lunch in the grass, riding the swings
and see-saws and taking in all the sun we could get.
(I never thought I'd get burned again but since we
could roll up our sleeves for easier picking, we got
sunburned arms as well as faces.) We picked about
a bushel of sour cherries and strawberries, and
about four times as many sweet cherries.

Tomorrow we start summer school with
metaphysics, the philosophy of being. I'm also
going to try to spend some time every day
practicing my typing. I'll need some skill in it for
when I teach. Sister June Elizabeth's going to help
me with the margins and letters work.

Oh, Mom, please don't forget to send Sheaffer's ink (blue black), black thread, a toothbrush, and a 6 inch round mirror. I think they're not more than a dollar in the five and ten.

On July 27 we're having the social for the prospective Postulants. I helped to write the invitations. So far twelve seem to be set. As yet no one from our vicinity has applied. I know, though, that if we pray doubly hard to Mary, she'll send us some candidates. Maybe you could offer your rosaries for this intention.

I received a nice letter from Norma the other day. You know I can't help thinking she should be here. Perhaps you all could say a little prayer for her and Alberta and Sylvia too.

Right now I'm working on my charge habit. I'm running into all kinds of difficulties. My bottom is uneven. To alter it, I may have to rip most of my facing out. I won't know the verdict unit possibly tomorrow. My Reception habit is coming along slowly but surely. Sister Anne Rose took us step by step together on them. I'm trying to make mine as perfect as my "able" sewing ability will permit.

These past two Saturday mornings I've been starching. S. Bernard Mary was my initial tutor.

Tomorrow morning we are singing the High Mass for the opening of summer school.

Don't forget I'll be writing again around the 16th of July to tell you my new name. Please pray for me especially beginning Wednesday evening when we go into Distant Retreat.

Time is passing so very quickly. Before I realize it, it'll be August 26th already.

Remember you're all in all my prayers always.

Your loving daughter and sister,
S. Rose Marie

Feast of the Exaltation of the Holy Cross
(September 16, 1958)

Dear Mom & Dad and Pat, Bee & Chuckie,

We, all the Whites (we wore white veils for
two years after our First Profession), went to St.
X's last Wednesday. This time we picked apples.
The limbs were so loaded down that we could just
casually stand and pick or even sit down (that is if
we could take sitting on jagger bushes!)You should
have seen me, Pat. Why it was like one of our old
blackberry picking days to get to the trees from
which we wanted to pick. S. Miriam Francis and I
had to plow through three feet high 'worn out'
blackberry bushes. My legs got a little scratched up,
but I didn't care. After the picking fun, we had a
picnic lunch - hot dogs, potato salad, grape drink
homemade cookies, peaches and all the trimmings.
Going home we said Vespers in choir on the bus.

Speaking of Office, this is my week to be
Antiphonarian (give out the responses for the
psalms.) I said them for the first time at noon today.
I have to call on all the choirs of angels to sing for
me (my voice has yet to improve.)

Our Novitiate family, as of last Sunday, was
increased by 14 new Possies. Getting their clothes
and dormitories made and in order was really quite
a job. But finally all was ready on time and they all
arrived safely. Incidentally, I'm the sister from
Duquesne's Angel. Her name is Barbara
Clougherty, and she's a graduate of the Academy.
Don't forget to pray for McKeesport vocations.
Maybe some girls will enter in February. If all the
ones come that have made arrangements for
February, this 1958 crowd has a good chance of
being the largest yet. Keep praying for more

vocations and also for the perseverance of the ones who have already made the big step.

Oh, Mom, I have good news! I want to clear up the question of letter writing. You (each and every one) can write me as often as you please. I'm the one that can only write one letter each month. Then I receive all the letters you send on the second Sunday of each month.

We just had an outdoor picnic supper, kind of held by us, Canonicals. At 8 we're going over to St. Joseph's Hall probably to dance, play ball or skate.

Tomorrow we Whites and the Possies and Mother and two other professed Sisters are going on a real picnic at a farm about a 45 minute drive from here. This time we're going in cars rather than the bus. From the description we've heard of it, it sounds like it's quite a farm with orchards, swimming pool, show horses, and ponies. Next month I'll tell you how the day turned out.

Chuckie, how's you batting average? Do you think you'll make the Pirates? I hear they're in 2nd place.

Next week I'm on bells. I'll really need that watch then. Oh guess what, Norma sent me a Saint Raymond Nonnatus medal with her card for my feast day.

Remember each of you are in all my prayers always.

Your loving daughter,
Sister Mary Raymond

What is a Nun?

In terms of Etymology and wiktionary.org, the word nun originated from the Old English "nunne" (nun, priestess) and the ecclesiastical Latin "nonna" (nun, tutor). The Latin word for monk is "nonnus." In French and German, nun is spelled "nonne." Interestingly, in Italian "nonna" means grandmother or granny. Which means older nuns would look like "nonnas." Likewise, in English, grandmothers are sometimes called "nana," a term of endearment.

Also, in many Semitic languages, nun is the 14th letter of the alphabet. In Aramaic, nun means fish.

I feel a greater appreciation for being a nun after learning how the term came to be.

The Sisters Who Abused Me

Not all of the nuns were so dear and kind to us as Sister Alma. The Sisters of Mercy were all human beings and could still be unkind and obnoxious. Trying not to be affected by them, I focused on prayer and meditation. One day while reading the Bible in Chapel by myself, I came across a line in Psalms 73:9 which described these unhappy nuns. "They place their mouths in heaven and their tongues walk on earth" could have been an epigram for my next poem of remembrance.

Tongues That Hurt

Some nuns acted
like problem women
out in the world:
acrimonious, mean, hateful
jealous, vindictive and
secretive backbiters.

My long-time Jewish friend can hardly believe
that any women in religion would act
so similar to their counterparts in the lay world.

However some nuns did share all the same foibles,
they had all the same feminine wiles.
But were trapped by their hormones.

Particularly at menopause,
they had no proper care or treatment.
Which could be why some mistreated
and even physically abused young students
or were mean to Postulants and Novices.

When certain nuns became "Superiors,"
they acted like the worst kind of men
sacrificing their sensitivity and femininity.

Recently the ones who are still able
have been instructed that
they have to work until the age of 75.

Hopefully, none of the senile ones
continue to be told to teach
7th and 8th grades
as they were routinely assigned then.
The Worst Decision
for the hapless nun and her students.

It's no wonder

through these years
that I was overcome some days
with Bile in My Being.

It was more of a bad taste
in my mouth and stomach
which came and went
un-summoned and unannounced
rather than an actual event
that happened once.

It was a nauseating,
rancid taste in my mouth
of being put down
by my inner accusers,
the shaking "no-no-no!" fingers
of my inside critics.
Thankfully, they are now only
anorexic memories.

But when did these critics stop
disturbing me, upsetting me?
Stop being stretched over me
like an inner black pall
making me feel small
and worthless to myself.

It reared its ugly face
during my teenage years
as well as during my twenties
when it occasionally returned.

Was it when I felt
homesick,
lovesick,
life sick?

The slender memory of it lingers.
Revisiting me in different ways

as a feeling of being ignored,
un-esteemed and unacknowledged
by my peers,
but in particular by my inner ones.

Slender Memory,
painful bile of feeling a kind of
misbegotten,
star-crossed
homesickness
for someone or some place,
I know you haven't fully left.

You come back to me
disguised in myriad forms
from being glanced over
for acknowledgment,
being ignored or dishonored
or patted patronizingly on my back.
To never being enough.

And even cut down
for supposedly "running around town,"
when I was doing God's work.

Repulsive Taste of my Being,
slightly recalled
yet lurking there,
why can't I just learn
be satisfied with who I am
and love and honor that person?

Why do I always want,
expect and hope
for someone else
to honor me?

For me certain memories
are less than sweet.

Playhouse 101

It stood in Lois' backyard,
one house down from Barbara's
and one house up from mine.
Built by my dad,
square and wooden,
with two windows,
one on each side
of the one room
with front porch.

We divided the inside
down the middle.
Left side for Lois.
The right for me.
Barbara got the porch.

All preschoolers then,
we decorated our special place
with mismatched curtains
and rickety furniture
from our parents' basements
that fit in the small spaces:
odd chairs from discarded kitchen sets,
a lone small square table,
several handle-less pots and pans
and an assortment of jelly jars.
Especially my little green tea set
Santa brought me
the Christmas I was three.

How many hours
we three enjoyed
playing house there!
Setting our little table
pretending family life.

Wrapping my little sister's hair
in big clothes pins.
Covering it with a lamp shade
to simulate a hair drier.
Dressing up Barbara's
tiny black lapdog Daisy Mae
in a baby outfit
with a ruffled hat
we tied at her chin.
Pushing her around,
our living doll,
in our baby buggy.

Then one sad day
Disbelief!
Horror!
Tragedy!

Lois' older sister and a friend
ransacked our little house.
Ripping down curtains.
Throwing out the furniture.
Destroying all we had created.
Devastating us.

Our house was never the same.
Playing in it was never the same.
We were never the same.
Those mean girls
had forced the three of us
to take the First Test
in The School of Life:

Playhouse 101.

(Published in my book of poetry, Stairs to the Attic)

Toiling Away in the Laundry

As I walked through the lower level floors of Mercy Internationale in Dublin, memories flashed back to me about working in the basement laundry at the Motherhouse. During these hours there were unmistakable moments of surprise, humor and sadness.

Saturday Mornings in the Laundry
Circa 1957

Folding sheets with exact precision
with the Mistress of Novices.
Feeling the warmth of the area.
Later sitting at the take-up end
of the wide presser
as long thin pieces of cotton
with little ties at the ends came through.
With difficulty, following the Rule
of not looking at anyone.

Also, catching large square pieces of muslin,
not knowing what they were for.
Again, not permitted to talk
or laugh or look at anyone.
Not allowed to ask anyone
since it was a Time of Silence.

What Was That?!

F inally, at lunch I could ask a Senior Novice some pertinent questions. After some small talk about our meal and the weather, I broached the topic on my mind....

"Sister, some odd stuff was coming off the presser this morning."

"So?"

"First, there were long narrow cotton pieces. What were they?"

Cracking a smile, she answered, "You're describing what the old nuns wear instead of bras. They're called binders - to hold down their you-know-what's."

"There were also some big square pieces of cotton or linen I folded."

Very quietly the same nun looked around embarrassed and then explained, "Well, Sister, those are for... you know... their monthlies."

I gasped thinking, "How gross." Then, feeling squeamish even thinking about it, I asked softly, "Do they rinse them out before putting them in the laundry?"

The older nun, slightly exasperated, replied "We hope so."

A Happy Break Out of the Heat

Recalling how my Mom finagled
an unscheduled visit with me
on my twenty-first birthday
after I finished my assignment
working in the dry house that morning.

Explaining to her in the living room on the main floor
what working in the dry house meant:
loading up, pushing in and pulling out
the long-wheeled contraptions which resembled
the racks bakers use to carry shelves of baked goods.

On tin trays I would flatten out
the newly starched coifs and guimps
so they could dry in the extreme heat.
The professed older nuns
wore these items on their heads
and over the top front of their habits.

I had to be meticulously careful later
when taking the wearable firm forms,
called guimps, off the trays when dry.
Because if not, I could tear one across the middle
making it unsuitable to be sewn or worn.

And worse, the "Old Girls" would be very upset
since their name tags were on each piece
and they would know what happened.

Off on Our Merry Ways: A Dream

Seeing our prim and proper Mistress of Postulants
walk her inimitable and proper ladylike way in front of me.
Then, so sure no one was around,
she skipped her merry way off
through the rest of the back rooms
off the laundry of the Motherhouse
as I had never seen her or any nun do.

Realizing through Jungian dream study
since everyone and everything
in a dream is a part of the dreamer,
I realized she represented me
wanting to "skip my merry way off"
beyond this revered place and life.

A Creative Writing Assignment

In the world of the Motherhouse, I felt penned up. Yet I was beginning to see through my idealistic and false notions of what being a nun meant. Starting to wonder, albeit only on an unconscious level, I asked myself a series of questions:

"Why must we?"

"Why do we have to do this this way?"

"Why can't we try another way? A faster way? A more creative way?"

"Why does it have to be done at all?"

It's no wonder then that I would write a story in which these feelings surfaced. It was a first person narrative for my creative writing course as a junior at Mount Mercy College in '61. It concerned a convict obsessed with waiting for the day he'd get out of prison. Sister Aquinas, the head of the English Department who taught the class, was discombobulated by my disturbing creativity. She couldn't understand what in the world had inspired me to write this story.

I realized months later it came from somewhere deep inside my psyche as my discontented feelings surged and gushed out onto paper. Since I couldn't yet speak my mind, I had to hide behind the fictional man in the story.

Vigil

Tomorrow is for getting out... Tomorrow. Yeah, tomorrow's for going back - back. One more hell of a long endless night - the last.

Nine... Nine black long, thin, iron years... But now at last getting out ... Out! Yeah, nothing else is real anymore. Everything so far away yet right here. So loud and yet so quiet.

Nine years... nine... pacing up and down up and down... And now, by God, it's... almost... finally... time... time! Time. What is this thing time anyway? Just living with the nightmare that started so long ago and won't end?... Nine unending years. Yeah and now it's time to be getting out of here but when? When? Answer - Crisp, cool, jaggy, sharp...

"Sunday, Mister. April 1. Easter, you know. Suit and tie. That'll be real nice, eh? Well, see you around, Mister." What a hell of a slob that guy was making up such a dirty rotten joke about me getting out on Easter Sunday morning. Just a damn April fool, that's what I am. It's just like I'm going to rise from the dead to die no more...

But who will be waiting for me? Would anyone be? Damn you anyway, man!... Everything is quiet so damn quiet here... so damn quiet but no matter I hear roaring in my ears.

Come off it, Jess. Just get some shut eye to get ready for your big day. Your grand slam Resurrection scene. Your

Easter. And just think it's like as though this rock hard bunk here is your grave and tomorrow you're just going to get up from it and rise. What a damn laugh.

Tomorrow. Yeah, only tomorrow's left now. Only tomorrow. Just wait, old man, old God, old world. Jess will show you all tomorrow. Tomorrow I'll turn over a new leaf. Yeah, that's what I'll do. I'll be a real guy again with heart and feelings and memories and dreams and... nightmares.... nightmares....

All too real and too clear as though they happened yesterday but won't stop today or tomorrow or any other night or day. God, why can't I forget just for tonight. Just this once. But no. Damn you, Lord. I can't! Nine years of it. Miserable, iron hell years in this place. My God, my God, my God will it never end? Not even tomorrow or tomorrow?

To hell with all that. I don't give a rat's ass about it. Just roll back that stone, lovely ladies, Jess is coming through with changing colors to show the world his act.

He's rising or else... Tomorrow... Tomorrow!

THE END

Did I realize in my inner self that I was the man in the story? He was my animus (in Jungian psychology, the male part of a woman), waiting and agonizing to start anew, to leave the way of life I'd chosen years before. This story was another indication that perhaps I didn't belong here forever.

The person who lived an abused and ignored semi-existence within my body pleaded for attention, screamed and clawed for it, but no, I couldn't or wouldn't acknowledge her. There was no way I could stand up during those early years and announce, "It's over. I can't go on. I have to get out." My false pride, my "Introverted Puritanism," as the head of the English Department phrased it, wouldn't let me give in or up. I had to keep on, stay in and play the game.

Each time things got bad, I held on and out until the tide invariably turned and things improved. If I waited long enough - if I suffered long enough - a break would come. Like when I'd get permission to go to a local house to help out over Spring Break and live like a normal person with some friendly professed nuns. Or I'd be asked to be a companion for a fellow nun to go to the dentist or the doctor. Or I'd get to take a thought provoking history class from the bearded professor who was a renegade on campus. Or maybe I'd be challenged with an interesting term paper and happily earn another "A."

Or sometimes it was a visiting Sunday with my family, which could be a problem instead of a help. Sometimes my sister wouldn't want to come visit. She thought I didn't treat my high school boyfriend right and felt sorry for him when I entered. Although this was unpleasant, it was still a distraction from the heaviness weighing on my heart.

Finding the Humor in It All

Even though during those early convent years life was hard, there were funny events which relieved the tension. What welcome reliefs they were for the otherwise frustrating and irksome days.

When we were new nuns only nineteen, Sister Mary Louise, my classmate from St. Peter's who entered with me, and I were asked to help out in the Infirmary of the Community at St. Xavier's out in the country in Latrobe, PA. Our first assignment was to help an elderly nun put on her oversized stringed corset like the one I saw years later in "Gone With the Wind." Our problem was we couldn't figure out how to do this. As a result, we were cracking up like the silly teenagers we were. Since Sister was senile, she didn't yell at us for attempting, as we finally realized, to put her corset on backwards. No surprise we were never told to help one of these older nuns again.

The saddest of the nuns in the Infirmary would stand at her cell door crying out for her son. We never knew if she had given birth to a child long ago or if she was just lost in some fantasy world.

The Holy Water Escapade

One evening a friend and I decided to play a joke on our friend Sister Barbara. First we put a prie-dieu or individual kneeler in her cell which we could do with ease because we didn't have locks on our cells. But we decided we also needed a bottle of holy water to put on top of it. Since neither of us had any, we knew an older holy nun, Sister Emmanuel, surely would. Since it was after the 9 p.m. Grand Silence, we could only stand in the doorway of her cell. Without a question and probably thinking, "What holy young nuns these two are." Sister gave us the holy water. Then we laughed to ourselves as we scurried across the hall to complete our plan.

Convent Hijinks

When assigned to clean the altar in the main Chapel, we had to go down the stairs to the work room for the cleaning materials. While there one day, Sister Eleanor secretly tied the ends of my long veil together as a joke. I went out on the altar doing my work not realizing how my veil looked. The holy nuns in the pews would have been upset if they saw my veil that way. No one ever said anything so Sister didn't get in trouble and didn't ask for a penance.

The Breaking of Dishes

The Rule was that we were required to take a piece of whatever dish or object we had broken in to the Mistress of Novices. Once there, you asked for your penance which could be anything from not eating candy at recreation or enjoying dessert at dinner to saying several rosaries or a mix of other prayers. In my Crowd Sister Geraldine was always dropping things, especially the family-sized earthen crocks our hearty foods were served in at meals.

One day while we were in Chapel, we knew that Sister Geraldine was helping Sister June Elizabeth in the sacristy. All of a sudden we heard a roar of a noise combined with a scream. Sister had leaned against a large square marble shelf and promptly knocked it down. How we had to force ourselves not to laugh.

Speaking of Sister June Elizabeth, she got in trouble once for wearing her Church Cloak in a recreational skit without permission. Our Church Cloaks were only to be worn at special occasions like Professions. They were long off-white cloaks buttoned at the necks and worn over our habits. The Mistress of Novices handed down a swift penance.

Another one of my crowd was a procrastinator. Every time Sister Patricia would break a dish, she would purposely or otherwise forget to take a piece in to the Mistress of

Novices to ask for a penance. One evening while we were performing our chores, the Mistress of Novices happened to do a check of all the Study Hall desks and found Sister's filled with the multiple pieces of pottery she had been saving. For her penance she had to kneel in front of the life-sized Pieta statue in the main hall for fifteen minutes every morning for the next week. How nearly impossible it was for the rest of us as we walked by on the way to our college classes not to burst out laughing. "Custody of the Eyes" certainly came in handy during those mornings.

What Did My Mom Think of Me?

I have imagined many times how my Mom must have reacted the afternoon I left home to enter the convent. The following story is partly from her perspective. I'm the nun in the beginning and at the end of the story recounting the actual routines of those days. As I wrote earlier, I had been nicknamed "Ree" because early on my younger sister and brother couldn't say Rose Marie. My Mom's thoughts and feelings are based on long talks I had with her later in life.

The Joy of My Youth

A 5:30 a.m. knock at each cell is accompanied by a high-pitched chanted prayer announcement by the nun Greeter, "Lord Jesus, preserve us in peace." From inside each room a barely audible "Amen" response was expected. Then hands search through white cotton sheets for a white cotton night cap taken and tossed off in the night to be replaced atop a close-cropped head. Floor-length black crinkle-crepe robe slipped over a long white cotton granny gown. Black slippers - soft and noiseless ones - pulled out from under a single bed. A plain white spread folded neatly at its foot.

I, a young woman of twenty-one, hurry down the long, high-ceilinged hall to the bathroom. There I hear no sounds except the gurgling of water running in the outmoded toilets, the dripping of water in the sinks or the occasional gulping of the old, overused pipes continuing to swallow water for over a hundred years.

Several of us young nuns are lined up waiting for a cubicle or a sink. No one speaks. No one even peeks out of a window. All of them are tightly shuttered and closed anyway. No one looks directly at anyone else. No one puts on makeup or perfume or checks out her face in a mirror. There weren't any mirrors anyway so the temptation to sneak a glance in one was futile.

Scuffling quickly back down the hall to my cell, my morning ablutions complete, I know I only have fifteen minutes left. I recite each of the required prayers as I put on each part of my religious habit. The long black serge pleated from-the-yoke-to-the-floor habit. The wide black leather cincture with the large rosaries hanging from the circle attachment at my right side to the hem of my habit. The rounded, heavily starched white guimp that covers my bodice and just about flattens my breasts. Then the coif, a heavily starched headpiece with a short black under veil. Finally, the nearly floor-length, sheer black veil.

At that point I would need to be kneeling in my pew in chapel ready for the extended series of morning prayers led by the Mistress of Novices. After that the opening thoughts for the morning prayer before the half-hour meditation. Then Mass and the Little Office of the Blessed Mother. All followed by a family style breakfast eaten in silence with the other young nuns.

Within the twenty minutes from the wake-up bell, the knock at my door and the five-minute warning bell for meditation, I, a Senior Novice, would be on my way to the Novitiate Chapel. Others quicker (or was it that they were holier than I was?) would already be there, dutifully kneeling in place saying their private prayers before the Office of the Blessed Mother we sang in choir with the Community.

For me meditation meant half an hour of trying valiantly, though typically unsuccessfully, to stay awake. Dealing with such sleep-inducing factors as the overly warm temperature, the soft lights of morning as it dawned and the hour of 6 o'clock, I tried every way I had read or been told about to stay conscious. Wetting my handkerchief, one of the regulation large white men's type we used, to wipe my face every few minutes to stay alert. Writing in tiny letters in my notebook so I would have to concentrate more. Trying to do spiritual reading for the half hour. Kneeling instead of sitting. But since I swayed back and forth in this position and distracted the others with concern that I'd fall out of the pew, the Mistress of Novices insisted I discontinue this method.

However, most mornings no sooner did I spread my veil apart and flatten out the pleats of my habit behind me before I sat down, I would drift off and travel to some dream world far away from the convent chapel and the morning's meditation. My eyes would slowly shut, my head would invariably fall forward and a wondrous sleep would gently, but assuredly, overtake me. It was an exception of a morning for me to stay conscious even through half of the thirty minute period. Some mornings I even slept fitfully through part of the Mass and the Office, only be jolted awake when I inadvertently dropped my Missal or office book with a crash.

I'd usually only manage to stay awake for the few embarrassing seconds to retrieve the item. All of this was a grave trial for me, to be sure, since I was so serious about following The Rule and so firmly convinced of my vocation. But I knew God loved me despite my weaknesses, my shortcomings and my inadequacies, no matter how humiliating.

Some mornings my dreams would follow me from the narrow single bed of my room to the straight back seat in the Chapel pew. Dreams of green grass under my bare feet, dreams of wandering through orchards on a summer afternoon with the wind in my uncovered hair.

Dreams of other people and their perspectives. I'd journey back into a world of someone I'd left behind in the outside world. More often than not this would be my Mom, who would speak to me through an imagined stream of consciousness in my mind....

My Mother's View

"It's hard to believe Ree was just a year old when we moved into this house. A tiny little bit of a baby with a few strands of blond hair and such soft smooth skin. Watermelons. The day before she came into the world I thought it was just an upset stomach coming on from all the juicy pieces of watermelon I ate on that Sunday picnic in the mountains. Our first she was. And the first girl on Charlie's side of the family in a quarter of a century.

When I was sixteen, I wanted to be a nun and join Sister Cordelia, my close friend. But everything changed when I met Charlie. How embarrassing when I spilled soup all over him at that church supper. How I missed him later after we started seeing each other and he left for Florida to work at an orange orchard to help out his Godmother. What romantic letters he wrote to me while he was gone. But when he came back, the Ferris Wheel ride at Kennywood and his question at the top which changed everything. Remembering it all in the quiet of the night.

The quiet of the night. What thoughts run through a person's brain in the quiet of the night? Taking Ree when she was six to meet Sister Cordelia. The locket she gave her. How she seemed to set her aside for God even at that early age.

Ree was a good girl. She went to Mass every morning and made all those visits to Church after school and at lunchtime. One of her little girlfriends told me about them. She said she even saw her saying the Rosary as she walked around the football field during lunch. And then... And then... That Day I can never forget.

What a beautiful Saturday morning it was. Ree up early as usual to attend Mass. She went and came back home trying to be nonchalant. As if nothing out of the ordinary was going to happen that afternoon. Yet I knew. A Mother always knows, doesn't she? She didn't want to upset me and Charlie and the kids.

After all, little Chuckie was going to third grade and Bee into fifth. How could they understand what their big sister was about to do? Did they see what was happening around them as they ate their lunch and played with their toys?

Did they know Ree was packing last-minute things to take to that place on a hill an hour away? They couldn't comprehend that she wouldn't step foot in this house ever again. As if they could realize what it meant for her to leave us and her home and give up a future life with a husband and kids. As if they would ever get to know her. They'd only see her on visiting Sundays once a month. Each time more a nun. More changed. Less a girl. Less the daughter and big sister we all knew.

What did I know for that matter that sunny morning? Did I realize how utterly different she'd look coming down those long marble steps at the Motherhouse? Dear God, how I nearly broke down. This was my little girl. My baby. My first. Her hair covered up under a short black veil with ruffled edges around her face. And that unflattering long black pleated skirt and cape. Those black shoes and heavy black stockings. Was this the same young girl who only moments ago had kissed us all goodbye and walked up those same marble stairs?

No, something happened to her up there in that nun's world of darkness and prayers and penance. Something happened to her up there so she would never be the same again. Never sit down to eat supper with us. Never pace up and down the living room waiting for her boyfriend to pick her up. Never knock on the front door after babysitting when she couldn't open it with her own key.

Never talk on the phone to her girlfriends for hours on end. Or fight with Pat over some boy. Or study chemistry late into the night at the kitchen table. Or work on math with her Dad. No, now she seemed so pale and different.

Through that second year, their Canonical one, when we weren't allowed to see her at all except at Christmas and Easter. Through birthdays when I'd try to finagle an extra few minutes' visit from the Novice Mistress, a little dried up lady who seemed to be forcing a smile for all the parents. She would say how sweet our daughters were as though she knew them, our little girls, better than we did. Yet, I guess she did know them better as the months and years passed and they got into their twenties and went to college and got their habits....

What a day that was. A lovely ceremony with the nuns' heavenly chanting. A long slow procession into the Church. In turn my first baby going up to the altar to get the long black habit and the white veil and white cloth covering most of her face. She became an Angel that day. It was nearly worth the missing her, the crying for her, the regretting that she would never give us grandchildren to love and care for...."

WITH MY MOTHER

Back From Imagination and in Chapel

In the other world of Waking Reality, I continued in vain to stay awake. One of my Sisters beside me shook my arm as the ringing of three bells announced the priest's entrance on the altar. Like out of a trance, I stood up for the beginning of Mass, the stream of thoughts from my Mom tucked away between the pages in my meditation book. Tomorrow and tomorrow and the next day other worlds of the other people I'd left behind would come back to me and take me away again for a while back to other places and other times and other people. The ones I had left behind along with my Other Self. The one I would never be again. The one I had given away to God forever.

"I will go to the Altar of God, to God the Joy of my Youth," the words flowed automatically out of my mouth as the priest began the daily Mass. For a while I could stay awake. For a while....

Yes, it was difficult for my Mom to say goodbye to me when I entered the convent. However, I imagine how her Mother, my Grandmother, said goodbye to her Mother, my Great-Grandmother, years before... when she left her home in Hungary for the last time and traveled a world away to come to America.

Leaving Home and Letting Go

"To live in this world
you must be able
to do three things:
to love what is mortal;
to hold it
against your bones knowing
your own life depends on it;
and, when the time comes to let it go,
to let it go."
                    Mary Oliver from "In Blackwater Woods"

I'm remembering my leaving home
eighteen years after my birth
to enter the convent
another world away.

Imagining seeing my new self
as my Mom did
as I came down the wide marble stairs
in the front hall of the Motherhouse
shrouded in black from head to toe,
her oldest daughter another person
in a strange world with strangers.

And how difficult it was
for my Mom to say goodbye
believing she would never see me again
as a regular person.

Yet her Grandmother had faced
something even more extreme
when her seventeen year old daughter
at the turn of the century
left her home on a farm
in Hungary outside Budapest
for a new life worlds away
in Braddock, Pennsylvania.

Who's to say which Mother endured the greater loss?
For each and all the goodbye was Goodbye.
The flesh of her flesh and bone of her bone
would never be home again
no matter what or how or when.

Never walking in the house again,
never back for dinner on a holiday
and never staying the night.
No, it would never Be the Same.

Still and all I can't help believing
it had to be the hardest for my Great-Grandmother
to say a forever goodbye to my Grandmother.

There was a finality in their leave taking
which went beyond time and space.
As I've said to my high school students,
it would be like leaving their families
for Mars and never going home again.

One day soon before she passed on
Grandma told her youngest daughter
that the day she left her family
she knew she would never go home again.

Did her Mother know that as well?

(Published in The Mercy Newsletter, October 1995)

Note: The Mercy Newsletter is written by The Sisters of
Mercy of Pittsburgh, PA.

Mother Irenaeus on Her 90th Birthday

When I was a Junior in high school in '56, I wrote an essay about Mother McAuley for a contest submission. Afterwards Mother Irenaeus, the esteemed retired nun living at St. Peter's convent, asked me to read it to her. What an honor that was.

Then, several years later in a letter to my family about Mother Irenaeus, I wrote,

> On April 6th we celebrated our dearly loved Mother Irenaeus' 90th birthday and her 71 years in the convent. Mother was a Superior for some 20 years. She was Mistress of Novices when our present Mother General was a Novice. She was Superior at St. Peter's when I was a sophomore. Do you remember the speech I gave about Mother McAuley that year? Well before I said it here at the Mount, I had to go over to the convent to say it for Mother Irenaeus. I'll never forget how wonderful she was to me. The evening of our celebration this year, the Possies put on an entertainment for the Community. Sister Lorraine played her vibraphone. She was a grand success. A few of the others sang and some played the piano. Needless to say, Mother loved every minute of it.

In our Canonical year '58-'59 after receiving the white veil, I recall a certain class lecture where we got an inadequate explanation of how to reconcile Free Will with the Will of God. Also during that year we'd have "Recreational

Singing" once a week which I truly rued. Thankfully, I got permission to sew for other nuns during that hour instead. "Rosie the Ripper" had all but disappeared at that time with the incense at Benediction.

Living Long and Prospering

T he schedule we were required to live by was strict. Eating, sleeping, recreating and all other activities were regulated and managed by our Superiors. This had its advantages in the long run. With a steady and sufficient amount of food and sleep, our bodies were protected from the ravishes of hunger, fatigue and most other maladies of the modern American.

We wore no makeup that could damage our faces over time. There were no hair perms or toxic coloring dyes on our hair. Going on a diet or becoming an anorexic was prevented by the watchful eyes of our Superiors monitoring us at meals. We did not worry about home mortgages or paying off car loans. Never giving birth, we were free from the incredible concerns of child rearing. Our days were pre-planned so stress was not a primary concern of ours. And since we typically entered the convent straight out of high school, we moved from our safe and protected parents' home into the safe and protected home of the Motherhouse.

As a consequence, many nuns routinely lived longer than their lay counterparts. The fact that very few nuns drank or smoked was not insignificant either.

The Demanding Early Days in the Community

I n my first year in the convent, I attended Mount Mercy College run by the Sisters of Mercy. During this Freshman year I became enthralled with Egyptology in all its mystery. If I hadn't become a nun, I might have become an anthropologist or even an archeologist.

As young nun students we were like non-entities forbidden to talk to the other college girls, the "seculars." No talk of clothes or dates or dances as those students would invariably banter about. Only hurried words to other Sisters about exams or the recreation we had to plan or concern about how high our names went up on the blackboard in the Novitiate. Their sizes could mean trouble.

We were not allowed to seal the letters we were mailing home. The Mistress of Novices had to check them out to see if we had written anything reprehensible or unacceptable like a note to a former boyfriend or various "heretical" thoughts. Also any letters we received could be opened. We made our Christmas and birthday cards using holy cards and wrote holy thoughts like "May the Holy Virgin Mary love you and protect you in this happy Christmas season."

Oh, Saturday night Holy Hours when my knees burned and my head rang with all kinds of weird and wild thoughts. How holy I was being. How my prayers would help to save the world from sin and damnation. How my tears were tears of acceptance of my Vocation to be a Sister of Mercy regardless of the cost. How all my pains and heartaches were to be offered up so that my joy one day would be boundless in Heaven. How I would become a saint and somehow be a part of saving the world.

Exaggerated "Holy" thoughts about my life as a nun. I realized later that my tears were not all "Holy" tears but more so sad homesick tears.

My feet would hurt. The Novitiate had been given a supply of surplus black laced shoes. The pair I had to wear was too narrow for me and caused problems for years.

My Crowd, the girls who entered the day I did, were always there for support and understanding. The nine of us were each going through our own challenges adjusting to our new life, but our collective camaraderie helped us through all the stages of our lives in the Community.

Sister Miriam Francis, the only nurse in our Crowd, and I were walking one day back to the Motherhouse from our hospital. While on our fifteen minute stroll, a homeless man on the sidewalk called out to us, "Stop. Stop, Sisters! I want to be a Christian." All we could do was continue our walk, unable to face the poor soul. Later we recounted what had happened to our Mistress of Novices who, without hesitation, said, "You did the right thing, Sisters."

That same friend had an especially horrific duty one morning precisely because she was one of the few nurses. There was a dead body....

The Mystery of the "Fallen Nun"

On an otherwise ordinary morning, a middle-aged nun was found lifeless. Supposedly she had fallen over the bannister and down two floors. Was it a horrific accident? Or did she jump to her death that day?

Her brother was a pharmacist and may have been giving her drugs for depression. Did she take too many or not enough? Or did she have an interaction with another medication? Or maybe she suffered a heart attack and tumbled over the banister while trying to call out for help.

It was inconceivable that she could have been pushed. What nun could contemplate or act on such an impulse of destruction? If she did have enemies in the building, the rumor mill was mum. Some things are not meant to be spoken of. I, for one, was not going to stick my head out to inquire further.

Because she had to take care of the nun's body, Sister Miriam Francis probably knew something. Were there lacerations around her neck or was there evidence in her pockets, perhaps some telltale residue on her shoes? Yet it was her duty to be silent - as she was surely told not to never speak of it. By a fateful series of decisions, the woman's body was not removed until the afternoon so we had to pass by it on our way to kitchen duties. It gave us teenagers the creeps.

In retrospect, maybe this noticeably thin nun was just depressed and gave up on life. Whatever was the true story, the whole event was pushed under the rug and made all "hush hush." The Mother Superior didn't want the nuns, especially us youngest ones, to have nightmares about the tragedy or talk about it to our families.

Glory Be

"Glory Be to the Father, and to the Son, and to the Holy Spirit. As it was in the beginning, is now, and ever shall be, world without end. Amen."

Doxologia Minor
Latin Version of Glory Be

"Gloria Patri, et Filio, et Spiritui Sancto. Sicut erat in principio, et nunc, et semper, et in saecula saeculorum. Amen."

Dialogue With Myself

A lthough I had taken the vows of Poverty, Chastity and Obedience, I never quite grasped what I had given up by my vow of Chastity. My pre-convent sex education and subsequent sexual experiences had been so slight. My only understanding of celibacy was as an up-in-the-clouds concept. Now I wonder as though in a hazy vision of another life....

"Who was that girl(?) that woman(?) shrouded in black? Who was that person no longer of 'this world?' Who was that 'good nun' in my mind's memory show?"

"It's not me," one part of me replies.

"You're wrong," the other part corrects.

"No, it's me. I was there. I did live it all. I did believe in it and want it and intend it once."

But the Mysterious Adventure into the Green Unknown, an integral part of every day we really live and love, was about to lead me elsewhere.

My Vocation as a Teacher

Continuing my tour of Mercy Internationale in Dublin, after viewing Mother McAuley's bedroom, I walked into the International Room. It was the first classroom of the newly founded Sisters of Mercy where about two hundred students were taught in shifts throughout the day. Currently, it's a meeting room representing all of the nations served. Standing there, I was caught up reliving....

My Lifetime Career

From the time I began
at age five "teaching"
all the stuffed animals
my two best girlfriends
and I could collect
and position on chairs.

From the time all the kids
my age on James Street
became my students
in our basement
or out on the cement wall
next to our house.

From the time I was in fourth grade
at Saint Aloysius Grade School
when Dominican Sister Fidelis
asked me to watch the first graders
while she ate lunch
and I showed the little ones how to make words
on top of their desks with tiny letter squares.

From later that year
when that same nun asked me
what I wanted to be when I grew up,
immediately answering "Teacher."

In my mind's eye
we're still standing in the first floor hall
outside the fourth grade classroom.
A tall young woman/nun
wearing the long white habit of her order
and a skinny ponytailed nine year old girl.

From the mornings on the bus
riding to grade school
when the non students
would beg me
to give them my homework
while I would try instead
to lead them to their own answers.

From all the telephone call
appeals for assistance
throughout high school
for composition ideas
or information on homework
as well as answering
my younger sister's questions
as we did our homework
together at the kitchen table.

From Freshman year in college
tutoring two nuns from India.
Shakespeare's ideas about women
the most challenging for me to translate to them
across religion, language and cultural barriers.

From happily volunteering
to help out at local grade schools

over college breaks
at Easter or Christmas.
Especially one third grade class
where I taught the eight year olds
how to walk carefully and quietly
so that they wouldn't break the eggs
I got them to pretend
were strewn all over the classroom.
How wonderfully silly they looked
attempting to lift their little feet
up as far as they could to tiptoe over the eggs
they imagined were there.

From being in the first "Crowd"
in the convent to get our BA's
before going out to teach.
The nuns before us
in only summer school classes
studied for decades to get theirs.

From being the only one
in my "Crowd" to student teach
in both my Major English
as well as in my Minor French.

All the beginnings of my lifetime career.

He Who Knows
A Persian Proverb

"He who knows not, and knows not that
        he knows not, is a fool; shun him.
He who knows not, and knows that
        he knows not, is a child; teach him.
He who knows, and knows not that
        he knows, is asleep; wake him.
He who knows, and knows that
        he knows, is WISE; follow him."

The School for the Blind

P rior to my first year teaching, I was assigned to teach a religion class once a week to junior high students at the Pennsylvania School for the Blind in Oakland. The students were typical silly early teens despite their situation in life.

One evening I heard the most vivacious girl in the class ask everyone as she bounded into the room, "Did you see that funny movie last night?" Immediately, the most outspoken guy in the group, a pudgy thirteen year old, responded with the jab, "We didn't *see* anything!" The reality was that all the students talked using "see" as any sighted person would.

Working with these teens taught me a vital lesson. To be appreciative every day for all the abilities I had, in particular my eyesight. Several of the students had been blind from birth. Others had suffered various accidents that robbed them of their sight. None of them bemoaned their lack of sight in my presence.

Several months after my evenings teaching there, I was invited to a performance of one of the students from that class as he played a fantastic trumpet solo. His hearing and dedication were top of the line. He didn't let his situation in life get the better of him, but instead used it to his advantage.

The Juvenile Detention Center

Never knowing what my next assignment would be, I did my best not to worry about the future. Thanks to my Vow of Obedience, I didn't raise any questions when my Superiors instructed me to work with "the Wards of the State" at the local Juvenile Detention Center.

I'll never forget the morning I met three darling little sisters ages six, eight and ten. The oldest girl told me they were sent there because their Mother, now in prison, had put their baby sister on a hot stove. What a traumatic experience. I have often wondered whatever happened to each of them. How long were the three of them Wards of the State? Did their baby sister survive? When did their Mother get released from lockup? Why wasn't their Father taking care of them? Was he dead?

I also substituted for a fellow nun attempting to teach Religion to the nine to eighteen year old "rough and ready" delinquents at the same center. The class was followed by Mass. At the door of the classroom and on the way to the elevator down to Mass, a stern policeman routinely stood guard. Both of these places were within walking distance of the Motherhouse as was the Presbyterian Hospital where I visited patients to comfort them.

Graduation From
Mount Mercy College

May 1962

Dear Mom,

I have enclosed the reserved tickets we received for Baccalaureate Mass (June third) and Graduation (June fifth.) There are two reserved tickets for the Mass. But of course any one else can still come. It's to be at St Agnes, the Church where "Pat" was received. The important thing I have to know by at least next Wednesday is how many will be coming to the brunch after the Mass (It costs 75 cents and will be served in the college dining room. I'll be able to be with you too!) Let me know, then, the number who'll be coming to it - you and dad and Bee and Chuckie and maybe a few others. Oh yes, and if you can, Sister would like to have the money by Wednesday also.

If you noticed, too, you have five white reserve seat tickets for downstairs in Antonian Hall and two in the balcony for Graduation. I doubt if any more than seven come, there will be seats. Possibly, there might be some extras though.

I'm really getting anxious about everything. I can't wait to see all of you. I have two more big tests yet so say a little prayer for U.S. and Pa. History (Saturday) and Physical Science (Monday.)

Write as soon as you know how many will be staying for the brunch. Send my love to all.

Your loving daughter,
S. Mary Raymond

Epiphany

My first full year teaching in the classroom was during the '62-'63 school year. Still a Junior Professed nun, I hadn't yet taken my final vows. I taught seventh grade at Epiphany Elementary School, an old three story brick building on the edge of the Hill District of Pittsburgh. Every morning and afternoon we nun teachers on the staff took a twenty minute cab ride in between there and the Motherhouse.

During the early part of that school year, the professed nun who taught eighth grade and I became good friends. We would meet on breaks and talk, enjoying each other's company. However, for some reason one day she announced we couldn't do this any more. She even told me that I was also not to talk to any of her eighth grade girls whom I had been friends with. The Principal probably thought we were having a "Particular Friendship," the nuns' euphemism for a lesbian relationship. Therefore we were forbidden to be friends anymore.

Because I wasn't yet a Final Professed Sister of Mercy, I was not permitted to talk to any of the Professed nuns back at the Mount after school, including my friend just mentioned. What if I needed help on a lesson plan after hours?

THE GREEN THAT NEVER DIED

**MY SISTER PAT AND I
IN THE NEW HABITS**

In fact, even when my younger sister entered the Community three years after I did, I was not permitted to talk to her. Because she was in a different time of religious training than I was, the Rule forbade me from conversing with her or anyone else in her group. I did see her at Visiting Sundays and on the "QT" at unique social events.

The Nuns' Day Outings

Two such occasions where I could talk to my sister Pat were the Nuns' Day at the Ice Capades and the Nuns' Day at Pittsburgh Pirates baseball games. These special events were free of charge and the entire stadium or arena would be reserved for nuns exclusively. Such orders included the Sisters of St. Francis, the Sisters of Charity, the Sisters of the Holy Ghost and the Benedictine Sisters. Both the ice skating and Pirates games were not exactly my cup of tea, but I got to see and interact with my sister so it was a welcome change of pace. I have a fuzzy memory of Alice in Wonderland being performed by men and women in fancy outfits on the ice.

In another special outing I got permission to visit St. Robert Bellarmine Church in my hometown. There I proudly saw my little brother serve Mass for the first time as an altar boy.

In the convent there was no way I could share any of my dreams or nightmares with anyone. This is why it feels so liberating to acknowledge them here.

Taking It All Off: A Dream

At a place away from where I live. Studying and teaching. Before the end of the afternoon, I take a walk. Then I get on a crowded student bus to the edge of campus where I get off. To graduate I need to pass an important history test.

Realizing the test is about to start, I hurriedly walk back in the oppressive heat. Asking a student whether the left turn at the corner will take me where I want to go, he says yes. I'm nervous because I don't feel prepared, not knowing the fine points of the subject. I pass a kid giving someone a piece of candy.

Getting back to my room, I settle myself down before the exam. Several others are there. I decide in a flurry of action to take off my veil and habit and then all the rest of my clothes. What took me so long? Taking it all off with great relief, I finally leave the convent.

Having Our Teaching Positions
Threatened

At Epiphany Elementary there was drama in the air. It was '63 when the sixth grade teacher, another Junior Professed, and I asked our Superior, Sister Regis, for permission to visit Mrs. Oleander in the hospital. She was the PTA president of the school and had just given birth.

Sister Regis said we could go, but when we happened to mention that fact at lunch, our Principal, a nun of roughly the same age as our Superior, indicated her very different beliefs. She announced emphatically, "If you go, you don't have a job at this school." Needless to day, we didn't dare go. This nun thought it was inappropriate for us to socialize with a woman who had just delivered a baby because it might lead us to hanker after Motherhood ourselves.

A girl in my seventh grade class that year wrote a story which still takes my breath away. Lorraine showed in her well-written psychological study that she understood how a small child could thoroughly manipulate her Mother.

In that same class I taught a short blond-haired student named Larry. Every day as he started to bound down the three flights of stairs at dismissal, he would turn around with a Dennis the Menace twinkle in his eyes and call out to me, "Night, Sister. Have a good weekend!" Over the years I've tried to take his advice and revel in the joy of my free hours each day after work.

LORRAINE AND LARRY

The Quest For Perfection

I t was virtually a sin to laugh or smile in the convent or to show any positive emotion. As a result, I became a stone face, typically wearing a severe look. I wholeheartedly bought into the "striving for perfection" script of mental conditioning. As the aim of religious orders, it was such a high and mighty objective. Certainly in those early years behind the Convent Wall, I tried to be perfect, but once I was "in the habit" was I any closer to the day of actual perfection? Could I actually ever achieve that exalted goal?

Fortunately, beyond all the Novitiate and Juniorate conditioning and some time after my Final Profession, I realized that this so-called perfection was an unreachable goal. Even striving for it was a daunting challenge. I realized I could never be God, the only one who can be Perfection. How could anyone even imagine reaching up to His height? Nevertheless, during most of those first six years of convent training, I was convinced I'd ultimately arrive at that point. Somehow. Someday.

MOTHER MCAULEY MEMORIAL

Dorms and Cells

Walking into Catherine McAuley's bedroom during my visit to Mercy Internationale in Dublin, I was struck by its austerity. This is the only room with the original pine plank floors. All the other areas of the house have had wood rot and were replaced. Catherine's desk and writing tools are on display here. In this very room she died on November 11, 1841 at the age of 63.

As I walked around this humble room, I was reminded of the various places where I slept during my early days in the Novitiate. First, I was assigned to a four person dorm, each area surrounded by bars that left several feet open to the ceiling. On these hung heavy linen curtains. Inside each area stood a single bed and a small dresser. We were only allowed to open or close these curtains at certain times in the morning or evening. What a little unreal world they enclosed. No one was allowed to talk in the dorms. If our Superior found out we did, we would be given a penance - maybe to say an extra Rosary or to refuse a piece of chocolate at recreation for a week.

One of my "Crowd" used to take out her frustrations by shaking these divider bars. When she did, the whole room reverberated. Naturally, some tried to muffle their chuckles, others groaned and yet some holier ones prayed for her. The largest dorm had twenty of these curtained off areas. All the sounds of every nun resounded through the room - breathing, coughing, sneezing, mumbling, crying, not to mention audible reactions to dreams or nightmares.

Then when I was a senior in college, I was assigned to a cell in an area that had originally been a large room for library or recreation activities. This was a hastily sectioned off place for five nuns because with additional girls entering more quarters became necessary. Up a step stood four sinks, always testing our patience by being clogged or noisy, then two more cells and a row of closets. Again every noise was magnified. Though there was more privacy in this situation than in the twenty person dorm, still it was less than ideal.

MY WHOLE FAMILY WITH
OUR PASTOR, FATHER BAILEY

A Local Convent instead of the Motherhouse

I n '63 I was told to teach seventh grade at Cathedral Elementary School, a short distance from the Motherhouse. This was the first "local" convent I was assigned to live in. My cell on the second floor of the brick house convent was smaller than one I would have shared in a college dorm. A stark white-sheeted single bed, a modest dresser, a small desk, and a chair barely fit in it. But I shared the room with no one else and appreciated the stillness, the quiet serenity.

During this '63-'64 school year I was a young professed nun in my mid-twenties living in this convent with only twenty other nuns instead of at the Motherhouse with several hundred Sisters.

Was it a mere coincidence that a girl I grew up with an hour away on James Street was also living in this local house? We had double dated in our previous life.

And Then There Were None

Dedicated to the Four Nuns of James Street:
Sisters Josita, Bernard Mary, Mary Raymond and Josepha

From '55 through '60
four teenage girls
from my hometown street
entered the Pittsburgh Sisters of Mercy,
each after her graduation
from Saint Peter's High School.

From down over the hill from my house,
Joanne left first in the fall of '55
and became Sister Josita.
Faithy, who lived across the street from her,
followed her in '56
and became Sister Bernard Mary.
And from about twenty houses up the street,
I left next in '57

and became Sister Mary Raymond.
Three years later my younger sister Pat
decided to grace our ranks
and became Sister Josepha.

Then in the early '60's Faithy was the first to leave
for greener pastures and a husband.
My sister Pat followed her a short time later
before she made her Final Profession.
And then by the summer of '70,
Joann and I had also climbed over the walls
on our own searches
to find ourselves on the Other Side.

Did a mystical something
in the air, ground and water
of our street -
Idealistic breezes of Dedication?
Tantalizing perfumes of the flower of Sacrifice?
Captivating waters of commitment to a Cause?
Did this lead the four of us to become
Sisters of Mercy?

Those cool breezes,
those wondrous flowers,
those refreshing waters,
did they all entice us to go
inside the convent walls?

A Screwdriver and a Dresser

As the youngest women in the house, Sister Bernard Mary, Sister Naomi and I were assigned the every Saturday night chore of scouring the industrial-sized institutional stove in the kitchen. Afterwards on the QT my "old" friend would invite me to come to her cell where she had a thermos filled with the transparent joy a lay gym teacher had given her. I would pour out a few inches of this vodka and then swirl it with orange juice I had carried upstairs from the kitchen after working. This bright concoction made me feel calm and relaxed once a week and brought me the best experience of "creature comfort" I would have for years. (We were not permitted to drink alcohol then but when we could only on special occasions, I would watch older nuns slip cans of beer in the deep pockets of their long black slips.)

Other than that weekly respite, my only other escape was to climb up on top of the rickety old brown metal dresser in my cell. From that perch I could gaze out of the tiny window above it to the street below. There I would fantasize what it would be like to be a "secular" or a regular person out in the world again.... I'd be walking on the sidewalk beside a handsome man. Or perhaps pushing a stroller or holding the hand of a darling little toddler. Or maybe I'd be jogging in the early morning sun without a worry in the world.

Would I have been admonished if one of the Professed nuns ever found out about my "Special Place?" Without a doubt. We weren't supposed to look out the windows because if we did, we were supposedly hankering after the world we had left behind.

I never told any of the other nuns what I drank on Saturday nights. I never revealed anything about my secret perch where I watched the world. Fortunately, it was a violation of the Rule to burst unannounced into another nun's cell. A Sister would have to knock first and wait for the other nun to open the door. This meant I could slip down quietly from my private perch and no one would be the wiser.

Praying for the Repose of JFK's Soul, November 1963

Across the years I kept a warm place in my heart for the solace I found sitting on top of the brown metal dresser. It had been there for me particularly during those tragic days in November when we first got the news at school that we couldn't believe. Our first Catholic President John Fitzgerald Kennedy had been assassinated in public for the world to see. When that sad fact was verified, we accompanied all of our students across the street to St. Paul's Cathedral Church to pray for the repose of his soul. Camera men from the various Pittsburgh TV channels took videos and pictures of us in all our grief and spirituality.

The hours and the days afterwards flash across my memory as a blur of incomprehensible horror played out over and over through the devastating images on the flashing black box in the Community Room. Hours passed as the twenty of us nuns living in the Cathedral convent sat sobbing in front of the TV. (Two years before we wouldn't have been permitted to watch television.)

The myriad nightmares we had after those harrowing hours watching JFK's funeral haunted us. The image of Jackie Kennedy trying to be strong as she held onto her little son and daughter has never left my memory. We prayed for them and held them in our hearts.

My seventh grade students were rightfully numb with cynicism and disillusionment with the adult world. How was it that someone could pull a trigger and murder a young handsome President blessed with all the charisma of a King from Camelot? How did I maintain my own belief system that God was in Heaven taking care of us? I wanted to become the Best Sister of Mercy I could be to help change the devastated and diseased world.

In terms of helping make things better, one thing we didn't do was vote for President. Being apart from the world, we didn't see ourselves as active participants in the political selection process. Furthermore, public office and women were practically mutually exclusive in those days. Women's Suffrage had only been effectively enacted in 1920 by the Nineteenth Amendment to the Constitution. Forty years later in 1960, the U.S. Congress was still 97% male. By 1970, it would be 98%. Even to this day, Pennsylvania has never had a female governor or U.S. Senator.

Disbelief

How could such a tragedy happen
to our first Catholic President
and maybe the last?

Hearing echoes of the nuns asking,
"What is this world coming to?"
"Where were the Secret Service?"
"Were the godless Soviets behind it?"
"What's going to happen now?"

The assassination of his supposed assassin
did nothing to quell our questions.

My Special Place

How did I manage to remain in that way of life? With the help of my seat atop the dresser peering out into the world. The world that kept coming back to torment me through the problems of my young students, the ongoing hassles of the "Good Sisters" in the convent and the disturbing events of the turbulent 60's.

No matter what, my "Special Place" was always there for me. Even if the world went down the drain with the kitchen's dirty water, sitting on that perch looking out always brought me a degree of respite and peace.

V-J Day and The Crisis in Cuba

In addition to those traumatic days after JFK's removal from office, there are other events of world significance indelibly etched in my memory.

August 14, 1945

My sixth birthday.
V-J Day.

I organize a group
of my friends

and we parade
up and down the sidewalk

outside our houses
in steel town, Pennsylvania

pounding pots and pans
with wooden spoons

as trucks filled with soldiers
standing in the back

careen through the neighborhood
laughing and hollering.

The Prayers of Innocents

One afternoon in the early 60's
we young nuns were called to Chapel
at an unusual time and told to pray
about a global situation.
No mention of what it was.
No questions from any of us.

We weren't allowed to read newspapers
or listen to the radio.
Watching TV was not permitted,
even for the news.
In fact, there wasn't even one TV
in the Novitiate.
So we never were told
what we were praying about
or whether or not our prayers
were answered.

Years later
several of us
who prayed together that day
figured out over a friendly dinner
that we must have been asked that afternoon
to pray that the world didn't end
as a result of the Cuban Missile Crisis.

Could it have been that our virginal prayers
all those eons ago made some kind of difference
and kept the world safe from annihilation?

Perhaps the prayers of nuns in the early 50's also helped save the world. This time the threat was from Communism during the Korean War. How overwhelming that five million soldiers and civilians lost their lives in that conflict - preceding the division that exists still today between "North" and "South" Korea.

The Chimes of the Bells

When I think back to the first night I entered the convent, I still hear bells and chimes and somber noises. This awareness would lie fallow inside me but would surface over and over again. It would ultimately lead to the genesis of this memoir, The Green That Never Died.

Locked in My Memory

My first night in the convent
was weeks after my eighteenth birthday.
As the Church Bells Chimed Nine
on September 7, 1957,
I said to myself as I curled up in bed,
"Oh my God,
it's 9 o'clock on a Saturday night
and look where I am."

Which should have been the first indication
that I didn't belong in that hallowed world
of pleated long black serge habits,
white, heavily starched breast and head pieces,
black cotton stockings and stringed granny shoes,
frequent prayer, penance and self denial.
And especially the countless arcane rules
in the cause of Salvation.

Nevertheless it was years later
that I lived the realization of this awareness
and climbed out of the white sheeted beds of that life
onto the multicolored ones on the other side
as the Church Bells continued to chime nine
during my vivid memory of that first night
I fell asleep as a new Sister of Mercy.

A Voice in the Dark

"He will give his angels charge of you
to guard you in all your ways.
On their hands they will bear you up,
lest you dash your foot against a stone."
            Psalms 91:11-12

It's 1958. I'm nineteen.
A Postulant.

I can't wait for a companion
to go with me to the college building.

So I leave alone that evening
to be the first in the pool

where we weren't permitted
to talk while changing or swimming.

There's not a soul there.
It's pitch black in the hall.

Can't find the light switch
in the absolute darkness.

I pat the wall on the right for one.
Then move to the left wall

where I feel a cold metal knob
that turns easily.

Opening the door,
I hear an inner voice advise me,

"Don't take one step."
Thankfully, I heed this command.

Finding the light switch,
I flip it on, my eyes temporarily blinded.

As my eyes adjust and focus,
I gaze down a flight of stairs to the boiler room.

Where if I had taken one step in the dark,
I wouldn't have survived.

My Guardian Angel had protected me
Lest I dashed my foot against a stone

Or fell headlong down the stairs
Onto the concrete floor of the basement.

To perish would have cut short
My life's mission to serve God.

Danger and Lies

It would be in the mid 60's when I was a Speech and Debate Coach at Saint Xavier's, an all girls' boarding school, when tragedy nearly struck again. Along with four teenage students I was on the road to a speech competition an hour away.

Did my daily prayers help me survive as I faced perils and pitfalls?

Near Deaths on the Ice

One winter morning I was sitting
in the passenger seat
of a car with one of my students,
Marianne, at the wheel.
The nuns in my Community
were not yet permitted
to get our driving licenses.

Marianne was driving
three speech club participants
and me who was to be a judge
in a competition in the city.

That morning the roads
were ice covered
in that hilly Pittsburgh area.
Ironically, as a disc jockey on the radio
asked facetiously,
"Are you slipping and sliding?"
our car hit a stretch of black ice,
twirled out of control across the lane
and stopped, stuck fortunately
in a snow covered grassy area
of the divided highway.

Had we spun all the way out
onto the opposite lane,
we would've been "sitting ducks"
directly in the path of a trailer truck
barreling down the hill.

The Truck Would Have
Not Been Able to Stop,
Hitting Our Car Head On,
Killing All of Us Instantly.

This stark possibility
assuredly registered with me
while four husky men
heaved our car
out of the snow bank
and turned it around
to face in the right direction.

Then one of the burly men
stuck his bearded face
in the window and bellowed,
"Good Luck, Ladies!"

Saved from certain disaster, my student Marianne continued the drive to the competition, knowing the tires on her brother's car were threadbare. Yet many events were yet to happen later that day, into the night and beyond.

The Secret of Marian's Tavern

Somehow - someway with our five Guardian Angels' protection and help, we made it to the speech competition at a public high school in the city. After I finished judging and while the girls were delivering their speeches, I watched more and more puffs of snow fall and fall. How we'd ever get back safely to the academy was beyond me. Calling Marianne over, I asked, "Will you be able to drive us back in this weather?"

"I don't know, Sister. The tires are close to bald. That's probably why we kept skidding."

"We'll need a plan. Let's wait until everyone's finished, then we'll decide what to do." In my mind meanwhile, I frantically kept searching for one such plan as I noticed the roads kept looking even worse.

The competition ended without any of the girls winning a trophy. But the lack of awards was far from a concern as Cindy asked, "Oh, Sister, how are we getting home? You aren't going to make us return in Marianne's car, are you?"

"It depends on our driver. What do you think, Marianne?"

"Well, I didn't want to come here in the first place in this weather. Now it's worse. I don't want to drive all those miles...."

Out of nowhere, Nan interrupted and blurted out, "Hey, I just thought of something. There's a girl in our class whose sister owns a nearby restaurant. They have rooms upstairs. I wonder if she'd let us stay there tonight."

"That might be a plan, Nan. Do you have her telephone number?"

"Ummm." She looked through her purse for a tense minute while the other four of us stood nervously watching her. "Yes! Here it is, Sister. She gave it to me just in case we had time to stop by. I'll go call her."

When Nan came back, she had a Cheshire cat smile on her face. "She said it's fine to stay there. Only there's just one teeny, tiny problem. The rooms are above her restaurant called Marion's Tavern so we'd be sleeping right above a bar. Is that OK, Sister?"

At that I felt backed into a corner. I didn't have any money with me thanks to my Vow of Poverty. In fact, none of the girls had enough money for all of us to stay overnight in a hotel. And there was no way Marianne could drive another fifty miles in this snow with old bald tires. So I realized I had no other choice but to agree that we'd stay at this tavern. Since I was one of the youngest nuns at the school, there would be problems to face if any of the nuns found out what I'd done.

While they watched me for a decision, I finally answered, "I don't think we have any other option. I'll call school and let them know...."

"Wait," Marianne interjected. "You aren't going to tell the Principal where we're going to stay tonight, are you, Sister?"

"I'll say I decided we'd spend the night with friends in the area because of the bad weather. She doesn't need to know we'll be sleeping over a bar."

Later we traipsed through six inches of snow with me in my now wet floor-length habit. As we then trudged into the building and made our way upstairs, I noticed a group of rowdy men drinking and singing loudly in the smoky bar area.

I kept saying "Hail Marys" to protect us all the way up to our rooms.

Then before we collapsed for the night, I in my own room on the right and the girls across the hall, I called everyone together. As we sat on the floor in a circle, I spoke softly, "Look, girls, I have to ask you a special favor. Under no conditions can you can tell anyone, not even your closest friends, where we're staying tonight. If this gets out...."

I didn't have to finish my sentence. All of them realized how vital keeping quiet about this was. We all made eye contact as they shook their heads in agreement without a second thought.

The next morning Marianne's brother, Harold, came to drive us back to St. Xavier's. Fortunately, by then the roads were essentially dry. But the adventure was not over. We breathed a sigh of relief, happily moving along in the car but we then got a flat tire. As we stood on the side of the road in yesterday's clothes, we watched Harold change the tire in his good Sunday suit. I silently thought, "Glad this didn't happen yesterday. Our Guardian Angels have truly been working Double Overtime."

The girls all must have kept their lips sealed tight because no one ever found out where we stayed that fateful night above the bar at Marion's Tavern. Some time later it was demolished to make way for a road.

Leaving my Coif, Guimp and Veil Off: A Dream

I'm in a Church in full habit but have known for some time that I'm going to leave. At some point I just take off my head pieces. The person beside me is somewhat surprised.

We get outside. I'm standing on the left. Then from the middle area a car drives up from an underground parking area with another woman at the wheel. The car is filled but she can't maneuver left so she stops. As the car turns, I take her place in the driver's seat. Where am I headed?

Out But in the Habit: A Dream

I'm at the Mount, the Motherhouse, officially out of the convent but back there for a visit and wearing the habit. Some realize this and I overhear them comment about the fact in a derogatory way, which I disregard. Looking in the cells in search of someone (Someone I left here, the person I was or used to be?)

My Life at St. Xavier's

What a singular school St. Xavier's Academy was. How thankful I am for the four years I taught English, French and Religion there. Thankful for being able to coach the Speech and Debate Club, taking the place of an elderly nun. (In high school I had been active in Speech and Debate.)

I have fond memories of my four years at St. Xavier's. Anticipating after school hours and guitar music, movies and plenty of talking with my best nun friend. Enjoying Saturday night midnight snacks during Lent when we could eat treats. Tiptoeing with "Mebi" through long dark hallways to "our" TV room. Drinking Mountain Dews on the "QT" in the school store at odd times of the night. Taking long walks through the countryside with several nun or student friends.

Nevertheless, during those days I faced a lot of deep wondering and searching. Stirrings inside, unaccepted yearnings for a different life. The life I had renounced was still on my horizon. As I ask at the end of this next poem, how can we ever separate what we become from each of those who were so much a part of that becoming?

To All the SXA Girls Now Women

A new teacher of two years,
a Final Professed nun for only as long,
I smiled the first time Judi,
a senior in my English class, asked me,
"When are you going to leave?"

Later another student Margie
remarked to me out of nowhere,
"You should have been a Mother."

How could she and Judi
have foreseen the future?
Ah, the insights of the young.

It was a unique place, St. Xavier's Academy,
Working with you girls, now women,
helped to change my life.
For that I'm eternally thankful.

Remembering a certain April Fool's Day
when I walked into my English class
to find the girls had turned all the desks
in the opposite direction facing the windows.

On the spur of that awareness,
I taught the class in French.
The nun they nicknamed
"Puff, the Magic Dragon"
beat them out at their own game.

How can we ever separate what we become
from each of those who were
so much a part of that becoming?

Through the Mists of
Saint Xavier's Academy
'64 - '68

Walking through the mists
surrounding the hundred year old
castle-like girls' academy
and nun's retirement home.
I'm in my mid twenties
meditating outside.
So pleased to be alone
strolling beyond
the old red brick building
and its ten foot ceilings.
Passing the tall windows of the boarders' rooms
where snow would blow inside each winter
leaving an inch across the sills.
Passing the long wooden side porch.

All the while
the morning fog enveloping,
caressing and soothing me.
I imagine as if it's the hands
and arms of an exquisite lover.

The building decidedly female.
Alternately:
A Giddy Teenage Girl.
A Sour Middle-Aged Bitch.
A Fun Loving Young Woman.
A Walking Dead "Old Girl."
A Babbling Biddy.
A Prayerful and Mindful Nun.
A Thoroughly Modern Woman.

Thriving on meditation like this
at peace alone and apart
in the silent solace
of the misty morning.

But eventually having
to return to earth
walking out of the mists
back into the clear of the day.
Renewed, revitalized
ready to go on to whatever.

Deeper emotional growth.
Acceptance of love/hate.
Jealousy/approval.
The ups and downs of each day.
Fortified to persist
standing up for my beliefs
despite being put down
for doing that very thing.
"Mebi" and I being "On the pan"
as the elderly Superior of the House
called it when she told my friend and me
she knew what was going on.

How certain older nuns
showed their disdain
and jealousy of us
for being friends with the girls.
They were mean unhappy nuns.
Did they not have any love in their hearts?

Our acute shock
when the "List,"
the announcements
of where each nun was
to teach the next year,
was read
in the Refectory.
Hearing that every one
of the whole group
of older nuns
who had openly attacked us

had each been reassigned
to different schools!

Relishing each moment
of this misty walk every morning
wide awake and aware
of all the thoughts
flowing from my heart.

The movement out.
The separation from.
The time alone and apart
because despite my gregariousness,
realizing that in many ways
I'm a contemplative at heart.

ST. XAVIER ACADEMY

Oh Birds, Breeze and Green

Oh birds, chirping for dear life,
for all the life you know, for the life you are,
teach me to sing, to flow and to fly free.

Oh bird of myself out on a limb and waiting,
fly me to my next limb, my new nest, my new piece of sky.

Oh limb that I fly to and rest on while I wait,
teach me patience during the in between times.

Oh breeze, cool and inspiring,
give me numerous ecstasies of inspirations.

Oh Green of Hope and New Life and New Harmony,
grow inside me even in the darkest winter of myself.

Sing a sweet song for me, Birds.
Blow a buoyant breeze for me, Breeze.
Go on greening and growing my life and spirit, Green.

Berries, Roses and Giggles

The strawberry patches.
How I loved picking quarts
of the succulent red berries
for lunch during the four Junes
at St. Xavier's Academy.

The grapevines as well
bulging with dark purple balls
edging the somber pebble path to the cemetery.
And the long winding driveway
through the flowing arms
of the towering old trees
where swings once
dotted the shaded grass.

In my mind's eye
I watch a Graduation
as each young woman
dressed in a long white robe
carrying a dozen red roses in her arms
walks in procession into the Chapel.

And I smile about the ironic significance
of the "Do Not Enter" sign
on the door outside the Chapel
which lead to the convent area
knowing that few young women do anymore.

Next seeing the "parlor" across the hall
where the dead nuns were laid out.
Recalling my first year teaching
at the all girls' high school.
Having to take my Freshmen
down to pay their respects
to a newly deceased nun.

The girls not wanting to go
Detesting being made to.
Terribly afraid to sleep
in the same building
with a dead nun
laid out in a room
with no flowers.
Only a soft lamp left on
even during the day
by the top of her plain black casket.

Reliving one morning
at the cemetery
for another nun's internment.
From the other side of the fence
in the neighbor's field,
a cow mooing each time
the priest uttered a word.
All of us young nuns trying so hard
to hold back hysterical giggles
at the absurd incongruity of it all.

Fire ultimately destroys this lovely building.
Only the nun's humble cemetery remains
and the unattended apple orchards
of our summer and fall outings.

What remains is a historic marker
on Route 30 in Latrobe, Pennsylvania
to honor Saint Xavier Academy's
once regal beauty.

Mists.   Separating.
Fog.   Protecting.
Shadows.   Embracing.

Can only go so far for so long away.
Have to come back to reality out of the mists
as from the Elusiveness of Dreams.
The mists surround and envelop.
And invariably dissipate.
Escape comes and goes and is gone.

Reality invites me to return.
Through the mists of SXA in my mind,
the Feminine Spirits of the Building
wait for me at the open door
or sit with me on the rocking chairs
on the long wooden side porch.

A relevant prophetic dream comes back to me...

Being in the mountains
right before I am to drive down.
An encompassing fog comes in
and I think I'll have to stay longer.
A street car goes by but does not stop.
Suddenly the air clears.

A Happening

One enchanted evening in the auditorium at St. X's, my students and I held an event called a "Happening." For this multimedia performance we put together many types of art work and played popular music from the 50's and the 60's. Then we moved in a free-flowing dance in ever widening circles. Undoubtedly, an unforgettable night. Everyone from the elderly Sisters to the youngest Freshman girls were side by side with a number of male students from St. Vincent's. I was ecstatic that it turned out to be a true Happening, particularly memorable because the old nuns danced with us in circles to the music of freedom.

Fundraisers and Dancing on the Sly

Since funds at the Academy weren't forthcoming for Speech and Debate Club travel to events, I organized a series of regular Rock n' Roll dances to raise money. We played music on a classic reel-to-reel magnetic tape player. Students at the academy would pay fifty cents to attend. Young men from St. Vincent's across the highway would come to be their dance partners. The nuns insisted that each boy wear a tie; I kept a selection of them by the entrance, some of them castoffs from my Dad.

It was hard for me to watch all the kids dancing but not dance myself. When I could slip away, my friend "Mebi" and I would hurry upstairs to her first grade classroom directly over the auditorium where we could hear the music. Flipping on the lights, we would fast dance together to our heart's content in front of her desk to songs like "Red Rubber Ball" and "Hang on, Sloopy."

The Political Machinations of '68

During the last year I taught at St. Xavier's Academy, one of the phrases we nuns lived by - "in the world but not of it" - hit full force when we learned about two assassinations in two months. First, on April 4, Martin Luther King's and then on June 5, Robert Francis Kennedy's. My "holy" prayers as well as those of all the Sisters couldn't keep these two deaths from happening. We spent extra hours after each premeditated murder praying for all involved - the families and friends left behind as well as whoever from whatever group was responsible for the two shootings, never truly pondering the motivations for these two political acts.

One woman in my Novitiate walked with others in Selma, Alabama in solidarity with those denied voting rights. Alabama Archbishop Thomas Tollen reacted negatively about an unknown number of nuns joining as least forty priests and numerous lay people in this demonstration. He criticized the priests and the nuns in particular believing they had no place "in such an environment." But as Barry McGuire sang in his oh so memorable and still so relevant song, "Eve of Destruction,"

> "Think of all the hate there is in Red China.
> Then take a look around to Selma, Alabama.
> You may leave here for four days in space
> but when you return it's the same old place."

Over the years I've wanted to talk to priests who were always saying, "We need to go back to the Bible." To each one I'd say, "Yes, let us go back to the Bible. Wouldn't Jesus have been in such demonstrations standing up for the downtrodden, the prostitutes, the gays - anyone considered less than a human being by 'the holier than thou' folks? As Jesus said, "He who is without sin, cast the first stone."

Our "Adventures" in Asia

Even when a TV would have been available in the mid and late 60's, I wasn't watching the evening news. Instead I was working with my Speech and Debate students and involved in other extracurricular activities in service of the Community such as home Masses for shut-ins and Ecumenical Bible Groups. Though I knew about our "war" in Vietnam, I was not privy to the ever changing gut-wrenching statistics of the conflict. At least 58,000 American men and 67 of our country's young women would be killed there before we gave up and came home. To say nothing of all the other ravages of our involvement in Southeast Asia, particularly the secret wars in Laos and Cambodia. During this nightmare I prayed for those who died, I prayed for those who were hurt, I prayed for an end to suffering and strife. For as nuns our duty was to pray for peace.

A Heavy Conversation With "Mebi"

On one of our long Sunday walks beyond the Academy buildings and through the fields of the countryside, I had a conversation with my good nun friend, "Mebi." I had given Sister Marietta that nickname because I used to kid her that she had an amoeba memory.

"Mary Raymond, what is your take on all that's been happening out there in that world we left behind?"

"You mean the war? Or Dr. King and the riots?"

"It's all Terrible, isn't it? We should be thankful we're away from it and protected here."

"Come on, Mebi, don't give me all that stuff about being in the world but not of it. We're all affected by what's been happening out there beyond our little convents."

She paused for a moment, taken aback by my assertive comment. But she did then add, "Maybe you're right. My cousin's friend was killed in Vietnam. Another came home crippled."

"It's horrible. Good men being killed. Others permanently wounded. The women on both sides we don't hear about."

"Yes, all the wives and Mothers and others dealing with these tragedies."

"Let's pray for all of them."

Part Three

"Green, Green, It's Green They Say
on the Far Side of the Hill.
Green, Green, I'm Going Away
To Where the Grass is Greener Still."
The Fireballs

Approaching the Beginning of The End

'64-'69

Reach for the stars

and they will come down

and bless you.

ALL MY PARENTS' CHILDREN

The "Waiting for God" Poems

I n order to stay awake during early morning meditation time in '64-'65, I would write in my Meditation Journal with unusually tiny handwriting. Significantly, I composed the following series of poems I called my "Maranatha Poems," related to the theme of the words engraved on my ring "Come, Lord Jesus." I signed each of then as "SMR."

Until He Comes

I wait
        impatient, impulsive.
Another day
        quietly yet listlessly
Past.

I search
        impoverished, impassioned.
Another hour
        fled yet not gone
Away.

I call out -
        Where is He?
        When will He come?

But the answer's
always the same.
He's here now.
Just blinded to me.

Almost Home

The night is inky
            sullenness.
The day crystal
            doggedness.

Yet somewhere
            amidst
the Rose of Dawn
and the Vermillion of Dusk,

I see ahead.
Yes, I'm almost home
and He's there waiting.

Presque Arrivé

I am restless.
I am weary.
I need someone
so sincerely.
Where to turn?
Where to run?
I cry out
so forlorn.

Life is pleading.
Time is passing
  But
He is coming
to take my hand.
  Yes,
We're nearly home.

Maranatha

The Lord comes.
He is within me.
I search beyond;
He is not there.

I look for solace
Mysteriously given.
I cry fulfillment
Lovingly bestowed.

Oh God, Oh God,
why have I forsaken You
within me?

Come, soul of mine,
He is right here.

Eternity

Waiting is for ever
but once ever has passed,
Fulfillment is for eternity
for Love alone will last.

Going to Kansas

I
n the summer of '63, the year after I graduated with a Major in English and a Minor in French from Mount Mercy College, I was awarded a grant for the study of French at Kansas State Teacher's College. I traveled by train to the six weeks' program taught exclusively in French. We were also expected to speak French on breaks and listen to news in French at lunch. The only time I could speak English was during several hours after lunch in the air-conditioned bedroom I shared with two other nuns in the program.

One morning at a break, the elderly woman who headed the group commented to me, "Ma soeur, au commencement de ce programme, vous etiez si silencieuse mais vous avez changé."

To which I responded, "Ce n'est pas possible pour moi d'etre silencieuse toujours ansi j'ai parlé Francais."

She said that I had seemed so shy and quiet initially, but that I've changed. I told her I couldn't stay silent all the time so I had to speak French. By the end of that summer, I had become so fluent that when a stranger asked me a question on the train trip back to Pittsburgh, I responded to him in French without a second thought.

FIRST SUMMER AT KSTC WITH THE
DIRECTOR OF THE FRENCH PROGRAM

The next summer of '64, another nun from my Community also received a grant at the same college and we flew to Kansas together. On a jet plane for the first time, I sat beside a man in the Air Force who had only flown on small two-seater military planes. He was shook by the jet engines and especially by not being in control. So much so that he couldn't eat the full meal served to all the passengers. However, I ate it calmly and with flourish.

At these summer French classes I felt so upbeat and alive. Partly this was because I was wearing a pair of black slip on shoes I had recently bought, not the regulation clod hopper black stringed ones. It was the first time since entering the convent I had comfortable shoes.

Also I was wearing a habit which I made out of a rather thin material. I felt kind of sexy, for the little I knew of sexiness, sitting in the last row of the 7 a.m. class each morning. Fittingly, beside me was a laid back guy who wore the casual outfit of sandals, khakis and a t-shirt. Meanwhile, up in front of the room, sat the other "trois Soeur Catholics" as they were referred to.

How could I forget the handsome forty-something professor during those early morning classes who kept repeating "Si vous voulez" ("If you wish") every other few lines in his lectures? One morning I counted the times - thirty in the hour. The gossip was that he was having a fling with the twenty-something blond woman in the class. The circumstantial evidence was minimal but they did talk together on breaks.

After that summer I spoke with two brothers from Lyon, France who were part of the program. Sharing my concerns about teaching French, they reassured me that I would do well. And I did from Day One in the classroom.

THE LATROBE BULLETIN
Thurs July 5, 1965

At Institute

SISTER MARY RAYMOND, R.S.M., of St. Xavier Academy visits with Miss Suzanne Plasse, a native of France, who is assisting in the French Institute at Kansas State Teachers College of Emporia, Kan. The institute is sponsored by the college in cooperation with the U.S. Office of Education and the National Defense Education Act. It is being held to assist high school teachers increase their knowledge of the French language and its culture. Sister Mary Raymond teaches French at St. Xavier.

The Semisweet Trip to France

With only one week's notice in the summer of '65, I was told to chaperone eight teenage girls on a trip to France. Three weeks in the Normandy area and three weeks in the Paris area. All because the older nun who had arranged the trip became ill. When originally planned, the group was scheduled to be in England but like my assignment, that changed at the last moment. So in my mid twenties, I became the youngest in the Community to be a chaperone abroad. True to my vow of Holy Obedience, I never questioned this mission with all its attendant responsibility.

The week before I left home, my Mom took me to one of the department stores in Pittsburgh to buy a black sweater. While we were there, of all the people in the world, I ran into my high school French teacher from the Community. She didn't seem at all pleased that I was going to France before her. In fact, I don't think she ever did travel there.

The first disconcerting experience of the trip occurred when we took a needed restroom break. It was during the bus ride from the airport to the French school where we would be staying for the first three weeks in the Normandy area. To our surprise and consternation, we found that the bathrooms were coed. Culture shock was no excuse to not use the facilities so we all adjusted our conventions and took care of business.

Being an inveterate writer, I sent a series of letters to my family back home.

July 10, 1965

Dear Mom, Dad and Chuck,

Sunday morning 9:30 - Post Office strike in town - several strikes of plane mechanics - I don't know when this will arrive. Call Sr. Magdalen or if she's not there Sr. Kathleen to let her know all's well. I will write as soon as possible but many problems of stamp buying, Traveler's Checks. The night of the telegram sending was unique... It was the first evening here at the school in Caen where we finally arrived after about a 7 hr. bus drive (breakdown and all) from Le Bourget, the Paris airport. I have been so grateful for my French despite my accent and pronunciation problems, the people understand me and I them the first time without repeating!

Yesterday was our first full day and in the afternoon we had several hrs. on our own in Caen. I spoke to the clerks at the train station, the only place we could cash Trav. Checks because the banks are closed on Sat. But they ran out of cash and we couldn't wait. Then after we window shopped awhile, and several of the girls (I have 8 now- they replaced the one from St. X who couldn't go) went into a department store (a cross between a big 5&10 and Hornes) where I saw exactly the kind of purse I wanted. (In NY we spent several hours looking - I finally bought one for $# at Woolworth's which pulled apart already) it was 50 francs reduced from 70 (about $10 reduced from 14) made in Italy. I asked the lady if I could cash a Travelers Check,

---

she directed me to another counter and then upstairs where I showed my passport identification and the lady filled out a green slip which I returned downstairs. Then the saleslady came up with me and another slip and I received the purse and change. It cost only about 8 something. The amazing thing is I did all this without even a word of English. Then I even asked a lady who sold flowers on the walk near an ancient church St. Peter if there was anywhere to throw the straw inside and she understood me and took care of the bundle. After that I got these few stamps at a Bureau de Tabac (something like a bar soda pop magazine store) talked with the woman about where we were from and ordered Pepsi colas without any problem.

At 5 all of us were driven to the key part of town for the celebration of Caen's liberation in WWII. It seems we bombarded the city to protect it from the Germans and then returned to rebuild it. The most impressive part of the short ceremony with a group of former Army young men, firemen and WWI veterans was the playing of "The Star Spangled Banner" and "America the Beautiful" by the small band. I suppose our group of 100 outnumbered the French there. A little old lady stopped me after it was over and we had a talk (naturally again in French) about who we were and where we were from. Then we were to have a film first night but it didn't arrive because of the Post Office strike.

The food is very good. The most unique things so far - about 9 inch Boiled fish with heads on, yogurt (all palatable with lots of sugar) and a delicious apricot pastry. Meals are 7:45, 12:30 and 7:00. Today we're going to the coast of Cherbourg. Tomorrow classes start. I won't be able to get regular French ones. There aren't any on campus but I'm hoping to get into some homes and in town to talk. I hope you can read this. To Bee and Pat too. Once I can get to the band or the Post Office, I'll be able to write. Love to all and keep praying for us.

Sister Mary Raymond

July 28, 1965

Dear Mom, Dad and Chuck,

Probably by the time you get this (especially the way the mail's been slowed down) if all goes well, about six girls and myself will be going by train to Rome. According to the information I was able to get in Caen here, it'll cost about $50 round trip and take about 20 hours. I think we can depend on at least $1\frac{1}{2}$ days to sightsee, I just hope my money'll hold out if the figures I've been given differ when we get to Paris. We're leaving tomorrow morning for Versailles (new address on the envelope) which is about 12 miles from Paris.

How's everyone? I've been wondering why all of you haven't written. Have you gotten my postcards?

In the past few days we visited Rouen where Joan of Arc was burned at the stake and Lisieux where St. Teresa entered the Carmelites. We saw her habit, shoes, her curled long hair and her discipline. Then on to Falaise where there is a chateau in which William the Conqueror lived 1,000 years ago.

Unfortunately, I haven't been able to swing Lourdes. Since we didn't tentatively plan for it before we left, we don't have enough money. Beside that we just don't have another weekend to take the long trip. However, I did manage to give a Sister whom I met all the Mass intentions etc. for when she goes soon. She is bringing me back a postcard so I can let Goldie know how the intentions are set up. There are just too many possible things to do but time and money don't permit them.

We're hoping to be able to attend a ballet and an opera in Paris for reasonable prices.

Love,
"Ree"

Dear Mom, Dad and Chuck,

We arrived here in Versailles about 7 miles from Paris Friday afternoon. The school where we're staying is quite nice with lots of huge, beautiful trees surrounding it like St. X. Here the Sisters are on a different floor from the students. Four of us are rooming together on the top floor. We have high good hospital beds, fine plumbing facilities and lots more peace and quiet then we had at Caen.

Recently, the girls have been much more agreeable, probably some of the cultural shock had to wear off. I hope these last weeks are smoother.

Yesterday we had a bus orientation tour of Paris - Eiffel Tower, Louvre, Notre Dame, Place de la Concorde etc. We'll be having numerous tours of individual centers of interest in the days to come. We stayed in the city after the tour to shop a bit in a huge department store - Galleries Lafayette. I bought Bee some perfume - we got a 36% discount because of paying with Traveler's Checks. Would you like any special kind of souvenir? Otherwise, I'll find something.

This afternoon we're going to see the fountain displays at the Chateau of Louis XIV here in Versailles for the evening and magnificent fireworks. I can't wait!

I'm really hoping you make the Pirates, Chuck! My own baby brother.

How are the fair plans coming, Mom and Dad? What are the dates? Anything different this year?

It's rainy and cold here as it was in Caen. I never wore a sweater or a raincoat so much in my life. We won't know how to act in Rome it'll be so warm. Or for that matter when we get home.

Did you get my postcards? I've been trying to do so much in such a short time that I hope I fit everything in with the right stamps etc.

Send my best to everyone. I can't wait to see you at the station in the 18th. Be careful about the mail after the 10th or so. You see, we're leaving here for Geneva on the 14th. If mail comes then, it'll be sent back to the States. We don't have an address in Switzerland.

Love and prayers,
"Ree"

Group Composition & Quirks

The makeup of the group I chaperoned those six weeks consisted of five girls whom I taught at St. Xavier's Academy and three others who joined the trip from other schools.

One of the girls who had never been away from home before cried for her brother each night. Another one never wanted to go on the extra excursions, happy to write long letters to her boyfriend instead. The first night at the school where we stayed, the girls were repulsed by fish served with the heads still on. They refused to eat them. When not eating on the campuses of the schools where we stayed, several of the girls always ordered spaghetti in every restaurant believing they got the most for their francs that way.

An overwhelming day trip of the first three weeks was a visit I took to Normandy Beach with several of the native French teachers of the program. On June 6, 1944 the mission here was dubbed "Operation Overlord," the Allied invasion of western Europe during the second World War. When I saw all the rows upon rows upon rows of stark white crosses on that calm clear beach, my heart overflowed with pain. Can anyone, especially women who have never been in combat, truly understand what it means to put his/her One Precious Life on the line every single moment?

The Train Situation

As the weeks passed, I experienced numerous ups and downs dealing with the group of teenage girls in my care. Prior to our ten hour trip from Paris to Rome, I had to complain in French to the Conductor that we didn't have the right arrangements for our ticketed place on the train. Since the situation was not remedied (C'est la vie), I shared a place on the train with several of my girls. On our long trip back to Paris, I removed my veil to be able to sleep. One of the teenagers managed to slyly snap a quick picture of me in this unusual state. As far as I know, she never showed it to anyone when we returned.

The Best Laid Plans in Rome...

My plan in Rome was to arrange for lodging at the Customer Center at the Roma Termini Station, one of the largest train stations in Europe.

When to my consternation I found it closed, it was a make or break moment. Looking around the train station, I felt lost and on the brink of a crisis. But fortunately Sophia, a woman I met on the train, had told me she and her husband always stayed at a particular pensionne, or small boarding house. When I called this pensionne and mentioned Sophia's name, our reservation was accepted. My girls and I hopped a bus across the city and arrived at the place twenty minutes later - a rather small hotel named "Due Torri" in the middle of a narrow cobblestone alley.

The owner took care of us as if she were our French Grandmother. One situation did cause her extreme concern however. Several of my girls were staying in a room with a balcony which they enjoyed going out on to breathe in the air and watch the locals. But when our dear pseudo-Grandmother found out, she quickly alerted me that the girls should not go out on the balcony because it was tantamount to inviting men up into their room. Laughing to myself, I thought, "When in Rome, don't do as the Romans do." I instructed my students to follow what the woman advised and beware of the Italian men.

The highlight of the whole six weeks for me was that weekend in Rome. How marvelous I felt standing in the middle of St. Peter's Square feeling a deep awareness of My Vocation as a nun. I would have loved to have arranged an audience with the Holy Father Pope Paul VI, but he was out of town. He was the first pope since 1809 to officially leave Italy. He was also the first pope to visit the Western Hemisphere, on a one day visit to New York City on October 4 of 1965. There he gave a speech at the UN General Assembly in which he appealed for peace, "No more war, never again war. Peace, it is peace that must guide the destinies of people and of all mankind." In addition, he sent a goodwill message to Apollo 11 which supposedly is still on Earth's Moon... "To the Glory of the name of God who gives such power to men, we ardently pray for this wonderful beginning."

Early Spirituality

When I was in third grade in the 40's at St. Aloysius School in Wilmerding, I'd head outside after lunch. As I walked alone up and down the bleachers of the public high school down the street, I'd say the Rosary at noon. An innocent girl in a flowered dress, my light brown hair was plaited.

I'd also make visits to the church, kneeling to pray at each statue. Most importantly, though, I would be having My Visions. Yes, Visions! When did they start? I'd be kneeling in a pew when I'd see religious scenes taking place on the window of the right sacristy door. What did they mean? I don't think I ever tried to figure them out at the time. I just knew what I saw was out of the ordinary. I asked my girlfriends if they saw them too. Some said they did but I didn't believe them.

MY FIRST COMMUNION OUTFIT

My Visions

What I Saw
in Old St. Aloysius Church.

What were these "Visions?"

Instinctively I "knew"
I saw people from the Bible
walking across the frosted glass
to the right of the altar.

I was eight,
an excessively devout and quiet girl,
walking around the church
every day at lunch time
praying at the foot of each statue
of the Blessed Mother, Saint Joseph,
and the Pieta among others.

And each time I knelt in a pew,
I saw these holy people
walking across the Sacristy door
to be with me.

I didn't question or wonder.
I just saw and accepted.
And knew I was blessed.

Candles Light Mt. Mercy Campus for Mary's Day

TRANQUIL GLOW—Their serene faces limned by candle light, some of the nuns and Catholic students from the Tri-State area who took part in the annual observance of Mary's Day last night at Mt. Mercy College are shown above. Sponsored by the Pittsburgh Intercollegiate Federation of Catho- lic Student Organizations, the ceremony started in the campus theater with an address by the Reverend Howard J. Ford. A candlelight procession to the hilltop followed and Bishop John F. Dearden gave the benediction. After the crowning of Our Lady, students recited consecration act.

The May Day Messenger

More visions would follow and be as real or as mysterious as these early ones. They would continue and be meaningful even if I didn't seem to understand them. And somehow they'd be linked with Green. The Green That Never Died through and despite all of the questions. Indeed they would persist....

May Day, '58. Early evening. All of us Postulants, Novices and Junior Professed who lived on the third floor of the Motherhouse formed a procession. With lighted candles in hand, we walked up the hill of the Mount to the Front Circle, which was outside the main door of the Motherhouse. As we stood there assembled under a stunning spring sky honoring the Blessed Virgin Mary, a dog barked and barked and nuzzled at the bottom of the priest's vestments and continued barking.

Caught up in all this, I imagined that animal to be a messenger telling me that I would persevere in what I was doing. I would be firm in my intent and become the best Sister of Mercy possible. Lines from Francis Thompson's "The Hound of Heaven" ran through my mind. How I, too, had fled Him, up and down through the haze of my days. How He had subsequently followed and found me and I had finally followed and found Him. Yes, I knew that night that I was assuredly where I was supposed to be. Somehow the dog barking in the spring darkness and Thompson's poem meshed together and spoke to my spirit. Yes, I would continue to follow Jesus and evolve to whoever I was to become.

My Mission

Noon Saint Peter's Square Rome.
August '65

Church bells
Ringing! Ringing!
I stand surrounded
by thousands of people.
Yet feel alone.

As the sun then shines
on me and through me,
something happens.
I experience a palpable
Sense of Mission.
Of being sent to help
all the people I can
as a Sister of Mercy.
A tangible sense of all
I am meant to be and become.

Permeated with these awarenesses,
I stand awed.
Moments pass beyond time.
My Sense of Mission vibrating
to the beat of my heart.

Later I board the tourist bus
with the teenage girls I'm chaperoning
and return to the everyday world
as though nothing of importance
had just resounded
into the core of my being.

Visions - Mysteries - Meanings. Every day we really live and love is a Mysterious Adventure into the Green Unknown. The Green Unknown always with me. Right in front of me in the unknowns of every day. The challenges. The adventures. The new days. The new beginnings. The going where God has led me in the past and continues to lead me.

Postcard From Rome

On August 7 I sent my family a postcard with a picture of Saint Peter's Basilica on it and these words...

Another fascinating chapter in my Great Adventure abroad! Rome is so beautiful, sunny and hot. We've been extremely lucky having been able to arrange four tours on the spur of the moment which cover all the highlights of the city. Next week this time we'll be on our way to Geneva, Switzerland and then HOME! I can't wait to see you.

The Sites of France

As part of the tours in France, we visited the "Notre Dame de Paris," or as it's known in English, "Our Lady of Paris." French Gothic in style, it was built eight centuries ago. Adjectives like "impressive" and "awe inspiring" don't do it justice with its beauteous Rose Windows. The girls called it "out of sight!"

Another cathedral was Chartres, or more specifically, the Cathedral of Our Lady of Chartres. It was also Gothic and built in the 13th century with flying buttresses and intricate stained glass windows. They were painstakingly taken out piece by piece to be saved and protected during the bombings of the second World War. It also had a labyrinth and Rose Window.

No trip of even a weekend could leave out the Louvre. With over a million objects including the renowned Mona Lisa of da Vinci and the Greek statue of Venus de Milo, it is a remarkable museum, the most visited of all. The grounds are magnificent as well, kind of like an ongoing living and growing work of art.

A "Touch and Go" Bus Ride

Another time my girls and I were standing smashed together on a crowded bus when I noticed a man attempting to take advantage of the sardine-like situation. He was what I call "a Lizard Man," a sleazy tall guy in his 30's who tried to "inadvertently" cop feels from my teenage girls. Since none of them could speak French, I made up a language accentuated with relevant body language to direct them to get off at the next stop. As we jumped off the bus free from the packed crowd, it felt like we won the game.

That weekend in Rome we toured the Catacombs. Even though because of my life choice at eighteen, I didn't become an archeologist or anthropologist, I still felt like one, especially as I was led down into the historic depths beneath the city. Speechless by what I saw. The ancient burial tunnels containing half a million bodies including the crypts of Popes and martyrs as well as third century frescoes. How I would have liked to explore the area further, preferably during the day with strong men protecting me.

Even though I was wearing the long black habit of my Community, whenever I walked down the sidewalks in Rome, bold Italian men would surprisingly attempt to pinch me on my behind. A disconcerting experience I never had at home in the Pittsburgh area.

Meeting a French Couple

Back in Paris I was walking down a sidewalk with an older nun chaperone from a different community when I dropped my long black raincoat. (When my students back home would see me wearing this, they'd call me "Zorro.") An elderly French woman picked it up for me and I thanked her in French. This short exchange led to an extended afternoon getting to know her and her husband who drove us all around the area to places we wouldn't have seen otherwise. To top off the afternoon, she served the other nun and me tea and cookies on the balcony of their second floor apartment.

The next day several of my students needed to get money at the American Express Office. As I walked through the building with them, I ran into a woman from the Kansas State Teachers' French Program who was on a trip to celebrate completing her MA degree. What were the chances I would see someone I knew from another hemisphere within a ten minute window?

Pilgrimage to Lisieux

Theresa, one of my students from St. X, took a side trip with me the following day. We had our tea and breakfast and hopped on a train in Paris to visit Lisieux, the second largest place of pilgrimage in France after Lourdes. What stands out in my memory of that day is going to the museum and seeing the long beautiful hair of Saint Theresa in a glass case. She was a Carmelite woman who died of TB at the age of 24 never having founded a religious order or performed fine works. Yet today she is known as "the Little Flower" and patron of the missions even though she never went on one. She did, however, care about the people with her whole heart. Along with St. Francis of Assisi, she is the most well-known saint who Pope Pius X called "the greatest saint of modern times."

Mt. Blanc and Monte Carlo

Another notable trip of those six weeks was traveling up the Alps to the ski resort Chamonix at the foot of Mt. Blanc. This highest summit in the Alps is at the junction of France, Switzerland and Italy. On the way Theresa sang "Climb Every

Mountain" and "Edelweiss" from the film "The Sound of Music" released about six months earlier. We also walked through the infamous Monte Carlo, although it was not "in session" at the time. In other words, no one was gambling so we toured the maze of empty rooms.

The Geneva Connection

Our group spent the last two days of the trip in Geneva, Switzerland, a splendid city. In the middle of town was a picturesque lake with the famous Jet d'Eau, one of the largest fountains in the world. The first water jet was installed in 1886. The present one inaugurated in 1951 to pump lake water instead of city water using a partially submerged pumping station. Beside glorying in this beauty, I recall window shopping at all the marvelous clock and watch stores. What works of intricate art those time pieces were.

There on August 14, my Quarter of a Century Birthday, I was walking down the street with several of the chaperones when a group of revelers passed by tapping us on our heads with small plastic hammers. It was part of some festival and an odd yet amusing way to celebrate my birthday.

The Final Crisis

As though at the last blow of the horn, at the end of an otherwise rather exciting, informative and calm six weeks away, a final problem with two of my girls evolved. Every student in the program had been told in advance that under no circumstances were they to drink any wine even if they visited a French family's home. If it was found out they did, they would be sent home immediately at their parents' expense. As far as I knew, none of mine did imbibe during those six weeks.

At 8 p.m. in Geneva on that final night of this momentous trip, I checked in on my girls in their room. Excited to be leaving Europe and returning to their families, they were dutifully packing their belongings and souvenirs and chatting about what they'd do back at home. After that I was thrilled to be able to relax in my room listening to classical music on my transistor radio. The other chaperones had invited me to a concert that night, but I had no interest in attending it. I was anxious to return home and be done with these six weeks of considerable responsibilities and occasional loneliness. Ah, what a wondrous peaceful sleep I enjoyed that night which thankfully prepared me for the trauma of the next days.

The next morning at breakfast I overheard a conversation which duly upset me. The evening before, two of my girls, kind of "hippies" before the word was in common parlance, took themselves over to the college students' hotel after I said good night to them. There they managed to get drinks and proceeded to get drunk and had to be carried back to their room. Needless to say, I was distressed at this development.

Back in New York to Deal With the Fathers

When I returned to New York, I called both girls' Fathers. The Father of the girl I had taught at St. Xavier's came to see me and profusely apologized for his daughter. However, the other Father never bothered responding. Since he was in the management of the sponsoring organization, he may have told his daughter to wait until the last night to drink since she'd be coming home the next day. The real issue for me was that if those girls had gotten into worse trouble thanks to their reckless behavior, I would have been called on the carpet and the Community could've been sued. The two girls did survive their ordeal with no lasting repercussions so I was most grateful. Their Guardian Angels were certainly keeping watch.

While I was thoroughly relieved to return home after dealing with all the responsibilities of those six weeks in France, I faced a new situation. In France I had worn the long serge black habit for what was to be the last time. While I was away, the Community changed to a shorter, softer gray material habit. Now I had to sew a new habit for myself which I did with proficiency.

Applying for a Master of Arts Degree

During the next year of '66, I received a letter from my Superiors instructing me to apply to Duquesne University for my MA in English. Again there was no question about doing that because of my vow of Obedience. Attending this nearby university meant I would still live at the Motherhouse and not have any real freedom. Not a welcome letter.

Wonderfully, before I could even apply for my transcript, I received another letter which essentially said, "Forget Duquesne University and apply to the University of Notre Dame instead." I had no idea at that time how this turn of events would irrevocably change my life forever.

Thinking now about another nun receiving a significant letter, I'm remembering a conversation I had with Sister Carmen when I was teaching at the Cathedral School in Pittsburgh. She taught eighth grade and one day was standing in the hall outside my seventh grade classroom. Walking up to her, Sister Carmen proceeded to then tell me she had just gotten a letter instructing her to apply to a graduate school out of town. She admitted to me on the verge of tears that she didn't want to go. However, she too had taken a Vow of Obedience so she dutifully did what she was told. What then happened as much as walks right out of a tale of fiction. While at this school she met a man. As they got to know each other, they fell in love. When she announced to the Mother Superior that she was "leaving the convent to marry him," the old woman was taken aback. Looking her sternly in the eyes, she proclaimed, "I guess I shouldn't have sent you away to school." I felt that was tantamount to saying, "I should have kept you locked in your cell so nothing like this could happen."

A Getaway on the Jersey Shore

Before heading to Notre Dame University in the summer of '66, I was told I could go to the Community's New Jersey "house" at Sea Isle City. There we were permitted to walk the block to the beach in our long full-body cover ups, take them off at the edge of the water, swim a bit and then reverse the process. In other words we couldn't sit out on the beach and enjoy the warmth of the sun on our virginal bodies. I sent two postcards to my family that summer. One the day before my birthday on August 13, the other a week later.

I wrote the following on the first postcard, which had a picture of young women holding little children at the edge of the water,

> "Superb. Fantastique. You wouldn't believe all we've done just the first day - Bonnie and Clyde, bike ride, a motor boat ride, dip in the ocean. Sun, sun, sun. A bit of shopping. (Watch for a treat in the mail - a taste for everyone, probably taffy.) By the way, don't these little tikes remind you of some people? Do write."

Then on the other one with six sailboats,

> "Bonjour!!! I won't be making it out on one of these boats but the water, sun, shore and Sisters here are 'magnifique.' I'll be browner than brown by the 27th!"

Diversions at Notre Dame

In the summer of '66, after arriving in Notre Dame University in South Bend, Indiana, I made the most of my opportunities. In between taking classes, I had the use of a canoe....

My Glorious "Indian" Summer

By a wondrous mix of events
at Notre Dame University,
I was thrilled to have the exclusive use
of the biology department canoe
for the six weeks of the summer session.

Each afternoon after class
I'd carry the paddles
stashed in my room
down to the lakeshore
where I opened the lock for the boat
and dragged it into the water.
Then I hopped in, taking with me blank paper
for my new creative writing class stories
and my drama text for American Lit.

Though I was a nun in my twenties,
some curious onlookers presumed
I was a professor's wife.

Shoving out from the shore
for the next several hours,
I would read and write
docking whenever I wanted to
to jump in and swim.
Relishing the beauty of the lake,
the scenery and the free flowing fun
during those warm afternoons in the sun,
I was ecstatic.

Green Waters at Sunrise

The lake stretches out its lazy arms
to morning and sun and life reborn.
Across the horizon the green waters glisten.

I stand alone and watch the colors
shimmering, glowing, sparkling,
laughing with the rising sun.
Little waves lick at my bared toes;
they tingle at the coolness.
I squirm them deep into the white sand.

I long to lunge forward
and challenge these waters,
green and beckoning.

I want to stay here forever
and satisfy my need
to be sea and sand,

Life and Love,
Sun and Ocean
and all the Glory of Morning.

Green and cool the lovely waters wait
for one still defying the Night
to embrace this new Day,

knowing that Life
mysteriously begins
with Green Waters at Sunrise.

Sunbathing on the Roof

At Notre Dame I lived in a single room in a three story building during my summers on campus. That first summer a group of us nuns found out that we could go up on the roof and sunbathe. (Despite initially getting sunburned, I worked assiduously to get a tan. One of my Crowd remarked when she saw me just back from Notre Dame one August, "Were you really away at graduate school?")

We wore modest one piece bathing suits. That is, until the afternoon when we read a note on the now locked door to the stairs. It said, "Sisters, you may not go up on the roof anymore. You are distracting the men working on the opposite building."

Such a simple respite denied outright ending our days tanning in the sun. Did the "distracted" men know we were young nuns? Or how did our Superiors know we bothered those workers? Older nuns were typically jealous of the freedoms we younger ones displayed.

Interactions with Priests and Nuns

O ne afternoon at lunch in the campus cafeteria, a nun friend and I met two priests our age. After some socializing and cultural discussion, we agreed to go to a movie called "The Glass Bottom Boat" with them the next evening. Outside our dorm we rendezvoused with them while wearing our long habits and, of all things, long white gloves! Did the two priests have a good laugh later about our strange formal appearance? One of them eventually married a nun he met on campus and they became my friends Dick and Jane.

That summer I would go to breakfast daily with several older nuns of the Community. What aggravated me was that if one of us wanted a second cup of coffee, the nun who would get it would hold out her hand for the dime to pay for it. To me that was a violation of our Vow of Poverty so I stopped enjoying breakfast with them.

Back in Pennsylvania and Depressed

T hen during the '66-'67 school year at St. Xavier's before my second summer at Notre Dame, I became quite discombobulated and depressed. Tossing and turning during the bitter cold winter nights when the snow would even cover the inside window sills. Though I treasured my close nun friends, on some deep level of my being, I yearned for a man's body to solace me. How I suffered through those interminably long nights fantasizing about sitting across from a handsome man in a candle lit Supper Club like in old 1930's movies I had seen. He'd be looking at me lovingly as we toasted each other and then he'd passionately kiss me right there in public. The closest I got to the supper club fantasy was when I drank the apple cider that had fermented on the windowsill of my cell.

One certain extremely down and out night, I soaked in the bathtub for three hours trying to resolve the issues plaguing me. Questions about leaving or staying in the convent I had just started to seriously face for the first time. Weighing, measuring, wondering. Lining up all the pros and cons. Thinking through each one as objectively as possible. Confronting all my pent-up human needs. The incessant demands of my body and spirit that had been plaguing me for years, repressed and silenced, hidden away deep within my being.

Finally a resolution. I decided that the next summer at Notre Dame would somehow make the difference and be the answer. When I lifted my water-logged body out of the tub that night, my mind was at peace.

The Notre Dame Summer That Made "The Difference"

And so it was that the summer of '67, my second one at Notre Dame, truly did "Make All the Difference." In fact, what I couldn't have known is that it would change the entire course of the rest of my life. As though I was driving down a road and the only way to go was not on the straightaway but to veer off to the right. Wonder of Wonders, that summer became "The Fairy Tale Summer of My Life," when I met Earl and fell in love with him. Though at the time my mind made me think it was just infatuation, it would take years of maturing insights for me to realize and admit out loud that I did, in fact, without question love him and always would. With him for short periods of time or away, I would love him. Whether he could or would or wouldn't return that love, I would always love him. In the following poem I recounted our story. As Rod McKuen sang, "We had joy. We had fun. We had seasons in the sun."

Still to the Ends of the Earth?

"Love consists in this -
that two solitudes protect,
and touch, and greet each other."
            Rilke

We met in graduate school
in the summer of '67
I was a nun
and he a priest.

After some time, I knew
I would always love him no matter what.

I'd always tell one
of my women friends,
"If he'd turn up at my door,
I'd go to the ends of the earth with him."
He was the first adult male
to accept and love me
as an adult woman.

He had asked me during the last night
of that summer (his only one there)
"Can you go back to the convent
after all that has happened?"
and I replied a too quick,
"I think so."

But that was then.

What had helped me most
during our times of separation
was his belief that when two people
sincerely love each other
and connect with each other

on a deep level of themselves,
they somehow manage
to see each other again.

Did it matter
that our times together
were limited
by the demands of his priesthood?

It did matter to me.
There never was enough time.
And our relationship
always remained platonic.

Yes, it did all matter.
But I came to terms with the reality that
if he ever left the priesthood,
it wouldn't be for me.

Nevertheless, in the back of my mind,
a fantasy about us as a couple crouched.
A fantasy that someday someway
we would be together.
Even if I had to wait
until the world beyond this one.

He has an engaging charisma.
A delicate blend of macho and sensitive.
A Hulking Heart he is.
Has anyone else
ever painted him that way?

After all,
he has changed my life.
He continues to be
the Main Catalyst of My Growth.

To a Man I'll Always Love

It's not just because you were the first adult male
to care about me as an adult woman.
Treating me as more than a nun.

It's not just because you were
a kind of male midwife
during my birth at thirty
at the Roofless Church in New Harmony.

It's not just because you do something to me
that I've struggled to explain or understand
yet simply know is real.

It's not just because hearing your voice
does wondrous things to me.

It's not just because
you know me on a level
few other people
in the universe do.

It's not just because
"I don't need to touch you to feel you,"
as Streisand sang.

It is just because I love you.
And I always will.

Joellen, my main woman friend from those summers at Notre Dame, was a nun my age. And like me, she was on the precipice of deciding whether to move on to a life beyond the convent walls. We have remained close over the years just as we have with both Earl and George. In fact, we call ourselves "The Notre Dame Four."

Our Halcyon Days
for Joellen

"Those were the days, my friend,
we thought they'd never end.
We'd sing and dance forever and a day....
For we were young and sure to have our way."
       Mary Hopkins

It was the mid 60's when we met
at graduate school at Notre Dame,
a time that changed our lives.

We were two young nuns then
on the verge of returning to the world
flowing with each other's growth.

Joellen and I had met these cherished friends
in the basement of a dorm one Friday night
over a hassle about who would get
the one last piece of pizza.

Remember how you
began to care about George
and I, his friend Earl?

Where would we be
or better who
or what would we be
if we had not met
and become friends
with each other
and with those two dear men?

In the Grand Picture
we have all been blessed
beyond measure.

With a number of other
young priests and nuns,
we would sing at St. Hedwig's,
a former convent in South Bend,
and dance in a group.
So happy to be alive together.

JOELLEN

Several notable song lyrics
still ring in my ears
across the years.

> "Green. Green.
> It's green they say
> on the far side of the hill.
> I'm going away to where
> the grass is greener still."
> (The New Christy Minstrels, early 60's)

> "Bottle of Wine. Fruit of the Vine.
> When you gonna let me get sober?
> Leave me alone. Let me go home.
> Let me go back and start over."
> (60's folk song by The Fireballs)

As you and I and George and Mike
ultimately decided to do
"going where the grass

is greener still"
while Earl remained a priest.

All those times we sang them
with Mike's guitar accompaniment,
how could we have realized
those words would prove prophetic.

Unveiled and Free

At an afternoon break from classes
on the way to Lake Michigan,
I relived the joy, the release, the semi-orgasmic high
of my hair, finally uncovered and as long as I wanted it.
As I leaned way out the passenger window like a dog,
I felt it coming alive again as it fluttered in the breeze.

Flashes of Memories:
Notre Dame Summers
Circa '66-'69

At Graduate School in the Summers When We Were Nuns
(For Joellen)

You call, dear friend, in early April
saying it's a belated Christmas card
over the airwaves.

And I am taken back to
Notre Dame days and nights
of fun and love
growth and change.

To you and George.
To me and Earl.

To St. Hedwig parties.
To a Dunes Mass.
To dinners in town.
To movies together.

Slithering off campus, you and I,
to go on mini shopping sprees
for regular clothes in South Bend.

Coming back laden with bags.
Laughingly refusing to show the men
what new outfits we had bought
no matter how desperately they pleaded.

Hearing an older nun from my Community
announce to me one day, "TA's on campus."
Which was a reference to Sister Thomas Aquinas,
our Mother General at that time.

Knowing the nun meant,
"Go put your habit on."
But I didn't because it would have been
hypocritical, and nothing happened.

Going to the Lake Michigan Dunes
on the Fourth of July,
a group date of priests and nuns
in the sun and on the sand with each other.

Playing "War" on the backs of the men
in the cool water
squealing and laughing like teenagers.

"Playing College Library,"
as Mike would dub it.
George "in state" on the first floor,
his long legs propped up,
assorted books opened around them.

Dancing the Bunny Hop,
singing folk songs
accompanied by Mike on the guitar.
Laughing and drinking
thoroughly having fun together,
all at St. Hedwig's.

Watching with glee and delight
as "Patriarch" George dances Zorba
with all the sensuality of a true Greek.

The two of us being separated purposely
by George and Earl
so that we could have a "date date"
on our way to a certain evening at St. Hedwig's.

An outstanding wish Earl sent my way one day,
"May you have good peace, hope and humor."

The Joyous Guitar Masses

We attended unforgettable guitar Masses in the campus chapel, ones altogether different from the depressing, somber, holier-than-thou Masses that otherwise were prevalent. Joyous singing in the style of folk music and wonderful celebratory guitar music would fill the air. My friend Mike was one of the guitarists who would play for the hundreds in attendance. I'd even play the bongo drums on occasion. The flowers on the altar seemed more colorful, the light flowing through the stained glass seemed more spirited, everything seemed more charged and alive during those vibrant Masses.

Vatican II

My friends and I were invigorated by the prospect of long awaited reforms within the Catholic Church. The Second Vatican Council, known as Vatican II, was formally opened in '62 and was the first ecumenical council in about 100 years. We were thrilled with the revolutionary proposals put forward, including calls for greater dialogue among Christian faiths.

One day several of us talked about arranging a demonstration on the Notre Dame University campus.

"Shouldn't we do something to celebrate Vatican II? These reforms are much overdue."

"What do you have in mind?"

"How about staging a demonstration in its honor."

"Yes, but Mike has an uncle who's a Bishop."

"This could cause trouble for him, couldn't it?"

"It's a real possibility. We should drop the idea."

"It would have been great."

The Dune Mass

The absolute highlight of that second summer took place on the top of the tallest Lake Michigan dune. A group of us had traveled there together and gloriously spent the afternoon basking in the sun. Like something out of an idyllic fantasy, we celebrated a "rebel" Mass together on top of the monumental dune. It was a slice of time that we could never recapture.

**GEORGE WITH ME AT
LAKE MICHIGAN BEACH**

To Be Young and Innocent

It's the summer of '66.
A group of us
twenty something nuns and priests.

This afternoon we're on
a one of a kind outing
at the Lake Michigan dunes.
Sharing food, friendship
and good conversation
in a true community.
And most of all,
a Mass Mike celebrated
atop the highest dune
under the glowing sun.

We exchange The Kiss of Peace
in warm embraces.
High on Life and Love
and the Glory of each other.

Later all stretched
out on a blanket,
we look up through
the green branches
of an enormous tree
into the deep azure blue sky.

At the end of this delightful day,
all of us are reluctant to leave.
We know this is a moment in time
that we will never have again.

Teaching at St. Elizabeth's and the Extreme Response

After that summer at Notre Dame, I was assigned to return to the city during the school year of '67-'68. There I would teach at St. Elizabeth's High School in Pleasant Hills, a short drive from downtown Pittsburgh. I taught five classes of senior English and particularly bonded with my Honors Class of only fifteen pupils. A far cry from St. Xavier's in the countryside.

During that year how did the four of us - all young nuns under thirty - muster up enough courage to put ourselves in such a vulnerable position? Our transgression? We wrote our infamous letter to the Mother General requesting to be able to wear regular clothes, but only in the convent after hours. Would we have sent it if we had known how her reply would devastate us? We had risked everything by asking permission for a small trial program to wear regular clothes after school - a skirt and blouse instead of the now short habit.

How stunned we were at the response we received. Were we so naïve to have thought it would go exactly as we hoped it would? The Mother General's reaction wrecked us. What a disgrace we had brought on ourselves. How we had misused our college educations the Community provided. How we had thrown all our training to the wind. To imagine wanting to give up our "Holy Habit of Religion" for even a part of the day within the privacy of the convent walls. To wear shirtwaist dresses or skirts and blouses after school just in the convent. What a despicable request.

Priestly Advice

The scathing reaction to our well-meaning and innocent request forced me take some sort of action. I called George, one of my close priest friends from Notre Dame, then pastor at a small parish outside Cleveland.

"You only have one choice," he said. "To face her. To go and tell her what you think."

"But I don't know if I can do that..."

"Yes, you can. Just consider her like any other woman in her slip and bra."

Then I responded, "But I don't think she wears a bra," recalling the binders I had watched coming out of the huge presser in the Motherhouse laundry when I first entered.

That short conversation gave me the nerve I needed to confront the Mother General. (That name with all its overtones and undertones of significance, though no longer used, continues to rankle my psyche.) However, when it came down to the wire to go to confront the woman, only one of the other nuns who signed our unacceptable proposal showed up with me. The three others chickened out, probably deciding that optional habit wasn't worth the fight and that the Mother General was too formidable an adversary.

But for the two of us brave young women the issue went beyond wearing regular clothes to a deeper issue of excessive control and denigration of our basic selves. We had to stand up for ourselves or become less than women in our own right.

Over the intervening years I wondered why change was so traumatic for the "the Old Girls." Why did the young ones have to fight for it tooth and nail? Why was that limb so secure when we had each other's support but so wobbly when threatened by our Superiors? Why did it take the young ones so long to stand up and be counted? Yet in the end the real issue always came down to the same question, "Why did it take *me* so long?" By this time I had already been in the convent twelve tumultuous years.

I had bought into the indoctrination I had been subjected to from Day One. I had accepted the authoritarian power plays which robbed me of my basic dignity, not to mention my own ability to think and reason and stand up for what I believed.

Guest at the Prom and Locked Out of The Convent

My senior Honors English class students invited me to attend their Prom that spring, not as one of the chaperones, but as their guest. My friend Sister Joann drove me and Sister Celine to the dance but couldn't pick us up afterwards. We assured her that we'd be able to get another ride home.

One of the students asked me to dance with him that night, something I could only refuse. Around 11 p.m. my nun friend and I accepted a ride home with the two young assistant priests who lived in the Rectory next door to the convent. It was a short and pleasant ride back, the two of them sitting in front, we nuns in back.

As soon as the car pulled up in front of the house, I realized with a jolt to my whole body that we had an immense problem before us. It wasn't just that we were getting out of a car with two men at that late hour. No, it was that the nuns locked the door at 9 p.m. like a bank vault and we had foolishly forgotten to bring a key with us. In fact, I'm not sure we even had one then we could use.

We said goodbye to the kind priests and got out of their car. My first plan was to throw little stones up at Joann's window to get her attention, but I wasn't a good shot and she wasn't in her cell at the time anyway. As we stood there staring at the old building, the crickets sang their song and the moths fluttered around us.

Increasingly nervous, we knew there was no other choice but to ring the doorbell. This would do more than raise a few eyebrows at the midnight hour. And Lord Byron's words from so long ago rang out, "Tis strange but true, for truth is always strange, stranger than fiction" when the worst possible nun in the house, who happened to live at the top of the front stairs, was the one who answered the door. "Mon Dieu!"

She was an older nun who steadfastly refused to discuss any controversial issues at meals. Being that it was hours after the Grand Silence of 9 p.m., she didn't utter a word. But I will never forget the volumes of venomous thoughts she flung at us as she stared at me in particular. I still feel her piercing eyes of contempt and judgment. She never asked either of us where we had been and why we were coming home so late, instead presuming wherever we'd been or whatever we'd done was improper and unacceptable. All too often, I was unjustly condemned behind my back, never to my face. Always the smiling scorn. The hesitation or outright refusal even to sit with me at the dinner table. The head shaking disapproval in corners, at end of halls, in doorways.

In the midst of these hassles, I enjoyed joining a group of my students each month to attend a play at the Pittsburgh Playhouse. Seeing the "The King and I" stands out in my memory. Also, I found my students' class song particularly relevant.

"Ev'rybody Get Together"
by the Youngbloods

"C'mon people now.
Smile on your brother.
Ev'rybody get together
Try and love one another right now

Some will come and some will go.
We shall surely pass
When the one that left us here
Returns for us at last.

We are but a moment's sunlight
Fading in the grass.

C'mon people now.
Smile on your brother.
Ev'rybody get together.
Try to love one another right now."

A Long Way To Go

That Spring my Notre Dame friend Earl came to town for a notable Priest Conference I had told him about. One of the assistant priests covered my classes so I could take the day off. Signing out the convent car, I drove away and picked him up at the airport. We then had a fine drive to the Allegheny Mountains. As I was about to leave him there and drive back to the convent, he turned to me and made a prescient statement, "You've come a long way, but you have a long way to go."

The Summer of '69

How could I ever forget a particular experience of world significance in the bellwether year of '69. I was reveling in a summer afternoon at a lake near Notre Dame. Later, when all of my friends were gathered together, the tension in the room was palpable as we sat mesmerized by what we watched on the TV facing us.

Full Moon Over
Mt. St. Francis Lake in Indiana

It's the afternoon of July 21, the last summer of the 60's.
A group of us young nuns and priests
from graduate school at Notre Dame

as well as six visiting theologians from Europe,
representing a sort of Community of the World,
sit in a small crowded room together

watching Neil Armstrong apparently walk
on the same moon that I commune with
when it shines in an orange ball above me.

All of us gathered in friendship first
for a break at the lake that summer day
swimming and waterskiing and feasting.

But how much more earth shattering was
the momentous event we shared in awe
as we listened to these words:

"One Small Step for Man!"
"One Giant Leap for All Mankind!"

The world was forever changed yet again.

A Letter About a Day in the Mountains

One Christmas I received an unexpected gift from my "baby" sister which both startled and pleased me. Wrapped in sparkling green and red paper were two letters, one from April '69, the other from September '69. I had sent them from Pennsylvania to her in Japan where she had recently moved to marry her Navy man. Will she ever realize what keeping and returning those letters meant to me? It was a time-traveling experience to read them again, reliving the emotions....

April 15, 1969

Dear "Baby Sister,"

Around the time when I was deep in the midst of creating your box of "prizes," I came across an article about a Clergy Conference for Inner City Priests to be held at the William Penn the 8th and 9th of this month. Just for the heck of it I decided to send it to my best priest friend from Notre Dame grad school last summer. He's about 32 and an all round great person. Needless to say, over the summer we seemed to have a real meeting of minds. It was particularly hard to say goodbye to him the last night since he had said then he wouldn't be going back and he wasn't a letter writer.

As things turned out, he surprised me with a call at Christmas having heard from another friend about how down I was. Then I returned the surprise about a month ago. It's just so wonderful to know someone cares about me.

On Holy Saturday he called to tell me he was going to attend the convention that he wouldn't have known about if I hadn't sent the clipping. It was just too unbelievable! He asked if I'd make sure he'd have a room at the William Penn Hotel and if I could maybe come to the airport at 11:30 Thursday morning to pick him up. As he remarked later, he knew by my voice that no matter what I'd be there. Can you imagine with my license hardly five months old, I rented a car! I can't tell you how fantastically exuberant I felt; I winged 60 all the way from downtown to the airport. It was simply unbelievable to see him get off the plane (the first time I ever saw him in his clerical clothes) to meet me, to get in "my" car for the day and take off for a glorious day from his hotel check-in, to lunch together, then to a spur-of-the-moment trip to Laurel Mountain, 182 miles round trip.

It was so lovely - a special person to talk to, to laugh with, to be just me with, from driving along "sans" veil, to walking the ski slopes "sans" shoes, to just breathing the mountain air together.

Goodbyes were hard again but somehow I know we'll get together over the summer although it's as far from his place at the other end of Indiana as it is from here. But he thinks he'll be dropping in at Notre Dame on a visit to his brother in Chicago. I hope so.

One main point he's tried to get through to me is that I did come a long way over the summer (he thought I was extremely naïve at first) but that I have far to go though the only way is up. Also he insisted that I have to start to stand up and fight the head ladies of the community instead of just staying in my secure corner.

A special thing he shared with me was his "Love Circle." If one is loved, he is secure, then can relax and go out to others and thus be able to love. How much this applies to me and how much it can have bearing on everything. Love and Loved is at the top of the circle at 12 o'clock, Secure at 3 o'clock, Relaxed at 6 o'clock and Go Out to Others at 9 o'clock.

I've hardly done justice to this whole wonderful happening. For now, though, it'll have to do. Do write again soon. It seems spring is here to stay. By the way I did a green collage on the back of my bedroom door with the words "GreenGreen is a God Color."

Love,
Ree

What excitement and joy that letter brought back to me. Had all of that happened that Spring? Over the years I had forgotten some of the details of this Prologue with my ongoing concentration on the coming Main Event. I had enclosed the letter in a card with delicate white crocuses on the front and inside the words, "In the wet and cold meadow a timid flower is born."

Stranded in Chicago - My Negative New Harmony

The story I never wrote to my sister was the account of what had happened to me in Chicago several months later. It was a fateful summer weekend trip from Notre Dame to visit a nun friend from Minnesota. We had become good friends while on a government grant to study French at Kansas State Teachers' College several summers prior.

I rode up to Chicago with a group of priest friends from Notre Dame who planned to drop me at the Museum of Modern Art on Friday afternoon and pick me up there again on Sunday afternoon. In between I spent a pleasant afternoon with my friend from another order. She was wearing regular clothes as I was and even smoking cigarettes, a questionable habit I had never cared to imitate.

When I returned to the museum Sunday afternoon, I waited and waited. Without any way to get in touch with them, I continued to wait. And I waited some more. But the men never showed up and I never did find out what happened to them. But everything seemed to go awry from the moment I realized I was stranded in Chicago.

I was sure my nun friend had already left the college where she had been staying so I couldn't reach her. To make matters worse, I only had about five dollars left of the weekend money. As sundown approached, I knew I had to do something. Waiting any longer was not an option. I tried to reach several of my friend's friends in the dorms at Notre Dame, but it was dinner time and no one answered.

Then I remembered that my friend Earl asked me to call his brother who lived in Chicago while I was there. When I called and explained my situation to him, without a second thought he said he'd pick me up, give me bus fare and drop me at the Greyhound station. How relieved I was to hear his answer to my prayers.

After he dropped me off at the bus depot, I thought, "Whew, I'm home free." That is, until I walked up to the counter to buy my ticket and the agent announced, "Lady, the 8 o'clock bus just pulled out and there won't be another one till 1 in the morning." I didn't want to believe my ears. Another waiting game had begun. In the meantime I kept trying to reach my friend Joellen at the university, but my attempts continued to be futile.

Then another problem reared its ugly head. I needed coins for the phone, but everyone I asked took one glance at my wrinkled green dress and my frightened ashen face and refused to even check their pockets or purses to see if they could help. Eventually, my frustration led me to start to cry which only made me a more pitiful mess of a down and out woman. I was an expert at keeping my emotions pent up inside, closed away and ignored, as we nuns had been instructed to do. But this evening I simply couldn't care who saw me sobbing. What did it matter? Exhausted, I sank down in a one armed chair in the grungy and shabby waiting room. How amazed I was at the absurdity of my situation when, lo and behold, sitting beside was a one armed man! If I hadn't been so distraught, I would have laughed out loud for everyone to hear but instead streams of warm tears ran down my face.

Around 11 p.m. I finally reached my friend. I could hardly believe it when I heard her familiar voice come through the receiver. After several more calls, which meant I now only had a dollar or so in change left in my purse, I felt relieved because everything was finally arranged. As soon as they could, Joellen and a mutual priest friend who had a car on campus, would make the two hour drive from South Bend to downtown Chicago to pick my sad self up.

When at last I saw them coming down the escalator about to release me from the prison of the smelly Greyhound bus waiting room, I nearly collapsed in relief. The next morning for the first time in my entire school career, I skipped my classes and slept in.

The Communication Workshop and Revelations

During '69 I had been seriously debating whether or not I should stay in the convent. Trying to face all the pros and cons directly. Through an Ecumenical Bible Group I was part of in my late twenties, I became a good friend of a woman who used to tell me because my face was broken out, "What you need is an affair." Considering my Vow of Chastity, I laughed at the absurdity of the suggestion.

This same friend urged me to attend a Communication Workshop in St. Louis at the end of that summer. It would be especially hard for me because my priest friend would not be returning to Notre Dame. I decided I'd go to the workshop despite some initial problems getting the money for it. Understanding my situation and need, one of the assistant priests in my current parish paid for the workshop fees and my airfare. Before I left, I sent notes to each of my close friends at the time to pray for me that weekend because I "knew" it was going to be an important one thanks to my strong intuition.

A Communication Workshop, not a Sensitivity Workshop, it was attended by mostly priests and nuns. Furthermore, the facilitators were several priests and a nun, some who would later leave their orders or the priesthood.

The overall group was divided into clusters of eight with a mix of male and female in each. One of the men in mine was Basil Pennington, Trappist monk and writer, who became known for a resurgence of Centering Prayer and later Abbot in Conyers, Georgia. This method of prayer is quite different from the meditations in the convent based on Franciscan St. Ignatius' writings. Instead Basil wrote about a renewal of contemplative prayer with an emphasis on interior silence.

In the beginning this Communication Workshop did seem like a kind of Sensitivity Workshop. We threw pillows around to get our emotions out. Also, for the first few days I could do nothing except make insightful comments about everyone else's lives and problems. Never my own. Though it began Wednesday evening, it wasn't until Sunday morning that something profound transpired.

A Resounding Breakthrough in Tears

The whole group was assembled for the first time to listen to a tape by Carl Rogers, a writer/psychologist in the field of human development. As I listened to his own personal admissions of insecurity and low self-esteem, I increasingly felt he was sharing with me the same negatives I felt about myself. As that awareness intensified, tears started to flow from my eyes, slowly at first and then like a dam opening, they gushed out.

We had always been told to hold back any signs of emotion in the convent or in public. It was virtually a sin to show any feelings, even joy. For example, if one of us young nuns laughed too heartedly, the older nuns wondered what she was laughing at, presuming it had to be something wrong, possibly replete with sexual overtones. As a result I was a poker face most of the time, forcibly bottling up all my feelings.

For once, though, on this momentous day, none of those previous rules kicked in. I cried and cried. I didn't care who saw me. My tears were ones of relief and release and made me feel so good I couldn't wait to share my breakthrough with my group. As it turned out, the priest facilitator of that particular session, a handsome, engaging man, came in fifteen minutes after I had bared my soul about the implications of my experience listening to the Carl Rogers lecture. So when he finally did come in at the tail end of my story, he seemed determined to agitate me to share more because he sarcastically announced, "Well, that was a colossal waste of time!" At that comment I vehemently emphasized how crucial this breakthrough was to me.

At that he asked, "Are you going to stay or leave the convent?" I insisted that wasn't the point I was making. Rather, it was an issue of "leaving or staying me." Of accepting or rejecting me. After that he asked, "Why have you always felt so negative about yourself? What do you think I see when I look at you?"

I answered with the words, "A funny looking person." After that admission he explored all the things I had never liked about myself: my odd shape, my thin hair, my teeth. Along with the group he began helping me to get beyond this obsessive negativity about my appearance. By the end of the workshop, I was on an emotional high of self-acceptance and confidence, one that I couldn't have gotten with any doctor prescribed medicine.

From St. Louis to Indiana

When I literally and figuratively flew out of St. Louis, I was not wearing my habit. I had brought regular clothes with me because I had planned in advance to make a side trip to visit my dear priest friend from Notre Dame. No one back home except my closest women friends knew anything about this extension of my workshop weekend. When Earl picked me up at the airport, he couldn't help but proclaim, "You are flying so high, you didn't need that plane or this car!"

Again it was my "baby" sister to whom I had written all the details of these magnificent experiences. I specifically selected the two inches longer and two inches wider than standard sheets of light green paper. It symbolized new life. It was fitting for the story which I wrote exactly a week after it happened. Here is an excerpt from the letter.

That night Earl and I walked down by the Ohio River together. His secretary had lent me a pair of dangling earrings to accent my regular clothes.

For most of the evening into the early hours of the morning, we had the most serious open talk, a real extension of the workshop sessions - direct hard confrontational feelings and insights. It was all so good and necessary.

When he dropped me off at his secretary's place where I was staying, he asked, "Would you like to visit a nearby historic town tomorrow?"

> As Earl waited for my answer, I stood in the crisp night air. Carefree insects flew around the car's headlights and crickets sang their evening songs. How could I have even imagined what my "Yes" would ultimately mean....
>
> The next morning when he picked me up, I was aware of a different attitude toward him. He noticed this as we were on our way to visit that town about an hour out of the city. I said it was because I had been affected by a passage from Eric Fromm's <u>Art of Loving</u> I read that morning. The idea of the quote was that one cannot love unless and until he is at one with his central being, in touch with himself and only to the degree to which he is can he love. I explained I felt this was my main problem.

Here is the full quote from Eric Fromm that affected me so deeply. I couldn't write the whole thing in the letter...

"Love is possible only if two persons communicate with each other from the center of their existence, hence if each one of them experiences himself from the center of his existence. Only in this 'central experience' is human reality, only here is aliveness; only here is the basis of love. Love, experienced thus, is a constant challenge; it is not a resting place, but a moving, growing. working together; even whether there is harmony or conflict, joy or sadness, is secondary to the fundamental fact that two people experience themselves from the essence of their existence, that they are one with each other by being one with themselves, rather than by fleeing from themselves. There is only one proof for the presence of love; the depth of the relationship and the aliveness and strength in each person concerned; this is the fruit by which love is recognized."

The Day of a New Harmony and Spiritual Birth

The Momentous Day was born with a profound beauty. A day that would change my life forever. A stunningly gorgeous Indian summer day September 1, 1969. The sun bright. The temperature in the high 70's. The sky azure. The air pristine.

September 8, 1969

Dear "Baby Sister,"

Sit down - get ready - be patient. I have so much to tell you I don't know if I'll manage it to tell it all. I find it hard to write about. It would take a book if I went into total detail.

After arriving in the historic town Earl suggested, we first visited a famous place called the Roofless Church. All across the front of the large area were closely growing crab apple trees in full bloom - red and glorious - covering the entrance walk. This place was surrounded by eight to ten foot red brick walls, a large rectangular area - an open courtyard like place inside which to the far left is a fantastic unique fluted umbrella-like high structure.

I know exactly where I was standing in the middle of the open area of the church - with the sun shining on my face - when I had a sense. A sense that if I let come what I somehow "knew" was about to happen, I was going to cry. Did I even have any tears left after all the ones I had cried out in

Chicago and St. Louis? At this point I consciously chose Life.

"Whatever you want, Dear God, whatever you have in store for me, I'm ready." This I prayed as I walked across to the narrow balcony overlooking a newly plowed field on the loveliest of Indian summer days. While I stood there at noon gazing out over that expanse of green, I felt a sparkling sensation in my fingertips then an awareness of Being Born. What Euphoria!

I was born to me, great and good and wonderful. Finally able to accept that I was worthy of the real sense of mission I consciously felt as a new nun in '58 during a May Day evening ceremony and at high noon in '65 as I stood in the middle of St. Peter's Square in Rome.

All this I cried out to my friend, the first adult man who cared about me as an adult woman. I admitted openly how I've been questioning my vocation holding my arm to the plow looking back - wanting everything but not accepting me as worthy of a mission.

I can't communicate in words all this meant. What a decisive beginning of my life this experience was. I wanted to burst the bounds of my being, feel breeze and sky and warm - fly, sing, cry, laugh, be all to all the world. How does one communicate ecstasy?

Needless to say, my friend was his fine understanding self. He sat quietly while I was somewhere else beyond him. When it seemed like I had come back to the earth, Earl asked if I was ready to go to lunch. After eating I would have to change from my black and white sheath back into my habit then hurry to the airport for my 3:20 p.m. flight. My mundane life teaching at Greensburg Central was waiting for me.

On the way back it began to rain - a lovely, growing, soothing rain. I put my head and arms out the car window to feel rain-ness, to be rain and water and breeze. "Almost Baptismal," I gloried in it coming in the back window of the old station wagon. Then since it was coming in too much, my friend pulled off the road to close the window. I leapt out in my stocking feet to pick two of the loveliest bright yellow daisies - one for him and one for me - growing by the side of the road and ran my hand through the warm muddy puddle there.

When we were off again, out of nowhere as if from a dream, I asked my friend what he had said the name of the town we had just visited was called. And he said "New Harmony!" I couldn't believe it! I was overwhelmed again. His first reaction was to laugh but when he realized the true uncanny significance of the whole thing, he, too, was moved.

Then the sun came out again luscious and warm. And I was happiness! New Harmony. New Harmony. What peace! What joy! What a feeling of being right with the whole world!

Though I think I'm beyond the high, high, emotional peak of last week, I am more than ever convinced of all I've learned. Why I even see my Chicago nightmare now a true and vital preparation for all of this. It seems I've finally been unshackled of all my self-consciousness and self-pity so much so that I feel I could stand up to anyone.

I want to go on and on, but words are so surface to all I want to communicate. Talk about mysterious adventures into the Green Unknown: New Harmony!

Love,
Ree

For the first time in the thirty years of my life, I glowingly accepted myself as Great and Good and Wonderful. I embraced My Birth and changed from an overwhelming personal negativity to a loving acceptance of all I was and could and would be from that day on. Earl told me later he shared my story about New Harmony in a homily at one of his Masses.

**THE DRESS I WORE AT
NEW HARMONY**

THE ROOFLESS CHURCH IN
NEW HARMONY, IN

Here is an excerpt from an old flyer published by Historic New Harmony, Inc. detailing the early history of this wonderful town.

"From 1814 to 1824, Father Rapp's Harmony Society carved a uniquely civilized and prosperous town out of the wilderness of the Indiana Territory, a town acclaimed as 'that Wonder of the West.' The Harmony Society moved east in 1825, selling its property to the Welsh-born social reformer and industrialist, Robert Owen. Owen made New Harmony the site of an ambitious utopian experiment, which brought together a group of eminent naturalists and educators. These men and women made New Harmony an American center for scientific and intellectual inquiry."

Flying in Style

When we returned to where I was staying, it was clear I wasn't ready yet for re-entry. I had trouble getting the parts of my habit together right. My trembling fingers wouldn't cooperate with my intentions. As a result we arrived at the airport late and found out that my seat had been given to someone else. But that wasn't a problem. I had planned an extra day of wiggle room if I needed it. Yes, I would have been more than happy to stay longer but curiously remained resigned to whatever was going to happen.

To my dismay a few minutes later, I was told I had been given a seat, albeit in First Class. I said my sad goodbye to my friend, not knowing when I'd see him again, and was escorted to the plane in the pouring rain by a steward holding an umbrella over my head. Most likely I "disedified" the other passengers, a convent expression meaning to upset someone without understanding. They probably shook their heads as they wondered to their seat mates, "How did that nun have the money for a seat in First Class?"

Back to Normal?

At my parent's house for a welcome home celebration later that evening, it took a lot of effort for me to hold in the story of that afternoon. It was not the right time to share my wondrous experience. But when my sister was driving me to the new convent in the country where I was to teach that school year, I told her and her husband the whole story. I'll never forget her reaction after hearing the intense chronicle of events, "I don't know who's driving this car but it isn't me!"

When we arrived at the new convent, it was 11 p.m. and, as usual, the building was locked up like a tomb. I managed to get in because my friend Sister Christina Marie was awake waiting for me. Since I didn't know her well enough at that time to share my fantastic experiences, I just talked to her a few minutes and said goodnight.

Then all of the emotion and the pure joy of the day led me to run out of the house in my habit at midnight and dance barefoot in the wet grass. If any of the nuns in the house had glanced out her window, she probably would have thought the dancer on the lawn was drunk. In a way I was that night - high and drunk on my New Life. My New Harmony Life.

And so I had been born both privately and publicly to a higher degree thirty years after the biological fact but in a way at the same moment. In retrospect I realized that the St. Louis workshop was a vital onset of the labor of my birth at New Harmony. Furthermore, my traumatic experience in Chicago several months before that workshop was also an important preliminary event. I would thereafter refer to these as my "Negative New Harmonys." Truly, my experience of Birth at New Harmony made the rest of my life possible.

After my impromptu dance on the wet grass at midnight to honor the "Out of Body" experience of my birth at New Harmony, I felt genuinely happy at the beginning of the '69-'70 school year. My teaching job was in a new high school next to a new convent in the country. My woman friend who had originally told me about the St. Louis workshop kept warning me, "Be ready when you come down. You've got to be prepared for what happens when you get back to normal and the real world gets to you again."

The Other Side of Light

"God of my numbered hairs, I speak as one
redeemed but still at odds with blood and bone.
            Pittsburgh Poet Sam Hazo "Epitaph en Route"

The Roofless Church
New Harmony, Indiana
September 1, 1969
Noon.

I stood moved, shaken,
Oddly knowing yet oblivious.
A magnificence
A spectaculance
Before me!
If I let feel whatever is coming,
I'll cry I knew and said.

Then from inside the words,
"I will. I will. I will
let happen the inevitable
whatever it is or becomes."

I walked slowly out
beyond to where sky and field
lay summer beautiful.
I breathed,
I sighed.

Ah, Glory!

A tingling,
a sparkling
in my fingertips
Life came as though
I were fully conscious
of light and surge and
my exit from the womb.
As though finally born
only thirty years
After.

Life! What Joy!
Resolution! What Relief!
Insight clear and crystal
Happiness only tears could express!

And now...
Now the other side of light.

Now the pinching, piercing, probing,
gnawing questions,
the whys of the night.

"At odds with blood and bone."
Where is the Light, "Oh God of my numbered hairs,"
And why is the Dark so impenetrable?

(Published in <u>Burning Light</u> - 1993)

Part Four

**"This is the world,
what do you expect?"**

> **Awakening and Transforming**

'69-'70

Coming full circle,

My time was up.

Greensburg and The Green Lives On

T he school year of '69-'70 began rather well. I had been moved to a new school, predictably not questioning the reassignment. The notably named Greensburg Central High School was thirty-five miles outside Pittsburgh in the countryside. The convent building had four wings, one for each different Community.

Although it sounds unbelievable, I actually performed a yoga demonstration for all the nuns in the convent. After introducing myself I presented the curious audience with a series of yoga poses and explanations. We served drinks at the end of my "show." Screwdrivers to our friends and straight-up orange juice to the others.

Notably, in my cell that year I had a few potted plants, a first for anyone in the house. Some nuns would visit my cell to see these wonderfully green and growing plants.

CFL WINNERS—First place winners in diocese-wide Catholic Forensic League competition, who will compete in the National CFL tourney in Chicago May 30-June 1, were given trophies last Saturday at Greensburg Central. Winners in various categories, left to right: Douglas Heinrichs, St. Vincent Prep, Latrobe boys' extemp; Harry Giglio, St. Vincent Prep, original oration; Marilyn Hoili, St. John, Uniontown, girls' extemp; Mercy Sister Mary Raymond, diocese CFL director, who presented trophies; Barbara Molinaro, Geibel High, Connellsville,

The Meeting of the Year

At the end of September '69, the Community was to have an important "all hands on deck" meeting back at the Motherhouse. This was a potentially crucial event considering the letter about wearing regular clothes I had written and been so rebuked for just the year before.

So it was the big meeting of the year, one which would have ripple effects on all of our lives. Its topic was unrelated to education or to our service to the poor or even to anything spiritual. At the end of that month of September, less than a year after our request about wearing regular clothes just in the convent after hours and its condemning response from the Mother General, this meeting of the whole Community concerned full Optional Habit. In effect, our infamous letter helped to get the ball of change in motion.

When the day finally came, three fellow Sisters from my Community and I who lived at the Greensburg convent, got in the car for the hour trip into the city to the Motherhouse. We were in such high spirits of anticipation that the nun who was driving got pulled over for speeding.

"Oh, Officer," she purred, "we're dressed in our best habits on the way to an important meeting of our Community in Pittsburgh and we're all so excited."

Charmed by her story, he let us off with a warning.

Standing Up to Be Counted

In eighth grade Sister Mary Thomas
repeatedly advised us,
"Don't be like the other jelly fish
going down the stream."
in other words, "Stand up and be counted
for what you believe."

Sixteen years later I traveled
from our convent in the country
into the city of Pittsburgh
with three other nuns of my order
to attend the first meeting
of our entire religious community
during the twelve years
I had been one of them.

It was to discuss a topic
considered quite controversial
particularly by the old nuns:
Optional Habit.
Weeks before I had told my closest friends
that I "knew" this meeting would be a decisive one.
What I didn't and couldn't say out loud, though,
was that I also "knew" then
I would be a significant part
of whatever occurred that day.

These friends understood my past upsets
when confronted with issues I felt strongly about.
They knew how I seethed inside during these times,
yet had no voice to speak my peace publicly.
So it was no surprise to them that morning
that I found a seat in my usual safe place
at the beginning of the first session
in the middle of the back of the auditorium.

The young nun,
whom I had taken under my wing
as her "Angel" when she entered,
got up to explain that she
and several others
were NOT shouting obscenities at the police.
They had been arrested
in the Hill district,
a black area of town,
where they worked.
The press had reported hearsay about them.

Some "holy" old nuns called out,
"If you had been wearing your habit,
this wouldn't have happened!"
A cheap attack on the issue of
wearing an Optional Habit.

The whole time I seethed at their hypocrisy
since on my lap lay the program for the day
filled with beautiful "Love Your Brothers and Sisters" quotes
particularly from St. Paul in the New Testament.

Later during the coffee break,
I felt my organs shift inside my body
and knew I couldn't remain quiet any longer!
So when I returned to the auditorium,
I took a seat on the aisle of the third row
to be near the microphone
to be ready when My Time came.

The second half of the session started
like the first with recriminations and denials
and further recriminations and more denials.
My spirit mourned this lack of charity
as I sobbed with all my soul and body,
refusing to leave the auditorium when a nun
sitting behind me, who's still in the Community today,
pointed out the nearby exit to me.

As soon as I regained my composure,
I stood up feeling beautiful and powerful,
walked across the front of the auditorium,
picked up the microphone
and for the next few minutes
spoke my deepest feelings in glory and grace
beginning with an acknowledgment
of how hard it was for me to do so.

I admitted my past torment
yet inability to speak out.
I even told them
I loved a priest from graduate school
who had helped me to reach this point
of acceptance of myself.

I particularly described
the wrenching pain
as I witnessed
the lack of charity
that they had just shown their own Sisters.

Finally, I spoke my main point
with increasing vehemence in my voice:

**"If I were convinced that what I had just witnessed,
was indicative of the Community as a whole,
or of the Catholic Church as a whole,
or of Organized Religion as a whole,
I Would Leave All Three!"**

At that announcement
my high school math teacher,
sitting right in front of me,
called out this challenge,
"Well, why don't you?"
Later I was told others
had joined in her dare as well.

And I knew at that point
I had the Community's future
in the palm of my hand.
For if I had chosen to walk out,
I believed fifty would have followed me.
Some said even a hundred.
Which would have been the largest rift
the Community had ever faced.

"But you missed the point I'm trying to make."
My voice rang out loud and clear across the room.
I told them I desperately wanted to make them realize
the contradictions in the way they were acting
and in what they were saying.
In particular their blatant uncharitableness
toward each another.

For the rest of the day
after My Time had passed,
an openness grew among the nuns,
both young and old,
that I in my twelve years in the Community
had never seen or heard in any meeting.
Some even cried on stage.
Others laughed.

All shared their deep personal
but particularly negative feelings.
The elderly ones admitting their vanity.
No wanting to uncover their thin grey or white hair.
Not wanting to expose the wrinkles on their necks
or the varicose veins on their legs.
Not wanting to give up the natural face lift
our tight head piece afforded them.

Nevertheless, the debate about Optional Habit
and all it meant was a decision
that would bring everyone together,

not drag them apart.
For by the end of that momentous day,
the Community agreed to the change.

I realized
that many didn't know the world
or the vanity of women,
whether they be dressed
in long black flowing habits
or street length shortened ones
or in colored suits
or dresses or slacks.

Which they would eventually wear
if they chose
instead of the habit
only a short time after the morning
I stood up in their midst to bare my soul.

Over the years I've come to believe
that if the main or only reason
I was to remain in the convent
for more than a decade
was to stand up and be counted
on that One Magnificent Morning,
it was more than worth it.

So our Superiors decided to permit optional habits
realizing their decision was in keeping with the spirit of
Vatican II. That day they began to hear each other's openly
feminine human needs whether expressed by someone young
or old.

As Fate would have it, those events of September in
'69 set the stage for the drama of the rest of my life.

Eleven Years '57-'68

"Have patience with everything unresolved in your heart and try to love the questions themselves as if they were locked rooms or books written in a foreign language. Don't search for the answers, which could not be given to you now, because you would not be able to live them. And the point is to live everything. Love the questions now. Perhaps then, someday far in the future, you will gradually, without even noticing it, live your way into the answer."

> From Letters to a Young Poet, written by Rainer Maria Rilke to Franz Xavier Kappus

Eleven years
Eleven.
Am I who I was?
Would I know me now?
Who can say?

Eighteen then -
Twenty-nine now -
Am I still me
Or someone else?

Eleven years as me?
No... no... no!
One of Sister Rose Marie.
Nearly ten of Sister Mary Raymond.
Two summers of Soeur Marie Raymond.
One of Mary,
Rose,
Rosemary,
Rosie,
Rosemarie.
Now three months
as Sister Rose Marie once more.

Will the circle close itself
Rounded off now
Through an eleven year cycle?

Or is there one opening left?
To drop the "Sister"
To drop the eleven years?

To be me
The old me again
The Rose Marie Engle Me
A unique somebody who everyone calls
Me
Rose Marie
Me
"Ree"
Me
Rosie
Me
Rose
Me
Rose Marie
Me just Me
Whoever I am.

Is the circle complete?
Has it all come full circle?
How can I,
Dare I,
Will I,
Find the answer?

On the Paths to Myself

Despite all the hats I've worn
on the Paths to Myself,
I'm still "here or there or elsewhere
in my beginning," as T. S. Eliot wrote.

And to paraphrase Emily Dickinson,
Myself behind
Myself concealed.

My thoughts today echo Mary Oliver's,
    "When it's over, I want to say:
    All my life I was a bride
    married to amazement.
    I was the bridegroom
    taking the world in his arms"
as I continue down the Paths to Myself.

The Search at Mercy Internationale

As I think about all the names that I've had in my life, I recall Sister Mary Kay, the nun who took me on the tour of Mercy Internationale in Dublin. She was trying to locate my name in the register of the 55,000 women who took vows, beginning in Mother McAuley's day. For some reason the hard copy of the computer program had been lost. As she calmly worked at her desk searching through the names, I looked out the window and asked Mother McAuley for help. Minutes later, Sister found my entry as well as Sister Regis' in the register. Coaina

V. Grace from Dennison, Ohio became Sister Regis and was 90 when she died on July 14, 1979, the night before the first reunion of the ex nuns of the Community. Her ID number is 406; mine 303.

THE ENTRANCE TO MERCY INTERNATIONALE

Getting to Know My Brother
For the First Time

Early in that school year of '69-'70, I had a chance to visit my parents and siblings. It was the first time I started to get to know my "Baby Brother" who was only nine when I left home. Now he was nineteen and we spent the forty minute drive back to my convent in the country getting to know each other. Then we sat in his car in the convent parking lot continuing our discussion. Some nun had to notice us there and presume he was a man I was "seeing" on the sly. But no one ever asked me about who he was. It was as though they knew I was guilty of whatever they imagined. No judge. No real evidence. No jury. No simple question to me about who that man was.

If I could go back I would make a poster for the bulletin board with the tall words, "He was My Baby Brother!"

The "Crime" of Using The Convent Phone

The real "stuff hit the fan" that next month in October of '69. I invited two girls who were sisters in my senior Speech class, to come and work on a school project in my order's Community Room one night. They needed to use a tape recorder for this assignment and had borrowed one from a guy in the class. After eight that night was the only time they could use the machine.

They worked until 10 o'clock that night at the end of which they needed to call their Father to come and pick them up. But there was no place nearby where they could go at that hour to call home. The school was locked up and there weren't any stores or payphones within walking distance. There was only one place for them to make a call and that was in the convent. I let them walk down the hall past nuns' cells to the telephone.

Somehow the word of my "wicked" deed - the permission I had given those two girls to walk through the hall of the convent - got out. Could some "holy" nun have been up watching for anything to gossip about? Was someone spying on us the whole time, curious and suspicious?

As a result and without ever being spoken to directly, I became the brunt of multiple scathing notes of condemnation posted on the convent bulletin board. The Superior of the house had written the notes after somehow apprised her of my "transgression." I might as well have paraded a male lover down the convent halls for all the hassle I was subjected to.

Unfortunately, this kind of abusive behind-the-back treatment wasn't new. I had been condemned like this in front of students or other nuns at other local houses or schools. Sometimes it was for not being with all the other nuns as they watched television from right after school into the night. According to their hasty judgments, I was a "smart young thing running around town," undoubtedly up to no good. I'm reminded of a relevant Tibetan proverb:

> "The best of men speak only when necessary.
> The mediocre speak only when questioned.
> The worst speak behind your back."

However, the nuns never seemed to acknowledge the fact that in addition to teaching five classes of English to Juniors and Seniors in the high school, I was a Speech and Debate Coach. I practiced with my students after school and on weekends accompanied them to meets across the state as well as to National Competitions in Florida and Illinois.

Sister Christina Marie, my friend in the Community from the "20's Crowd," was also perturbed by this chain of events related to the absurdity of letting two girls use the convent phone. Every time another derogatory note appeared on the board, she seethed as well. These notes kept turning up throughout the next few weeks on a regular cycle without any noticeable rhyme or reason.

The Final Note That Sent Me Out the Door

T hen on November 19, 1969, when I naïvely thought the irksome bulletin board notes were things of the past, another one appeared. It was the last draw. Walking into our Community Room at 7 p.m. that night, I announced calmly to Sister Amadeus, one of the other nuns in my Community, "I think I've been fooling myself for a long time." Inherent in that line was the belated awareness that my overworking self in service to God had kept me from facing a clear reality - I was not meant for this life. At that point my thought the night I entered, "Oh my God, it's Saturday night and look where I am!" came back to me with a stunning clarity.

I left the building and started to walk around the track of the school. Like the hours after New Harmony, it was drizzling. I sat down on the wet bleachers overlooking the town of Greensburg, the county seat. It was another emotional watershed event. It followed my exquisite private moments at the Roofless Church in New Harmony. Also my glorious public event "Standing Up to Be Counted" at the Motherhouse.

Then I announced to myself calmly and emphatically, "This is it. I've fought the good fight. It's over."

From that awareness that evening, I have never turned back. No regrets. My decision was definite and final. I even repeated what my high school boyfriend had tried to convince me of thirteen years before, "You can save your soul in the world." A Life Changing Epiphany.

Caught in the turmoil of those last days and nights, I recall staying up unusually late. In those last few months I would secretly pray stretched out on the floor in front of the altar in the convent chapel - a kind of timeless parallel to the prostration of my Final Profession ceremony seven years before. Innumerable thoughts wafted through my mind during those nights.

In many ways I was a workaholic during my second six years in the convent and this easily kept me from questioning my future. Every day while on my teaching break I'd talk to Father Joe, the counselor of the school. We were close friends and we shared our observations on life and living. He became the first person I told of my momentous decision.

"I am going to leave the convent," I declared to him as he sat at his desk, noticeably taken aback by the announcement.

To which he responded, "How can you do that? You're my Mainstay."

The Principal Who Wouldn't Understand

When the time came, I made that same announcement to my Principal, a Catholic man of about fifty. He was one of the first men to head a high school with all nun teachers. With overflowing machismo, he steadfastly refused to accept I had deep personal reasons for making the decision to rejoin the world. In his mind I was leaving for a man.

Perhaps some of the nuns at the school presumed Father Joe and I were an "item" because I frequently spent my "prep time" talking to him in his office. He ultimately left the priesthood years later but not for me. I was also a professional friend with Jim, the Speech and Debate Coach at St. Vincent's, a nearby school. But we'd just see each other at competitions and only as colleagues. So there was no man I was leaving for; I was leaving for one person. A woman. My Own True Self.

Becoming the Path Ahead: A Dream

After making my decision to leave,
I'm outside walking down a wide path
with green bushes in full splendor on both sides.
Ahead I see the path stretch into the distance.
I have the sense of being or becoming the path,
the ground, the bushes and especially the Green.
The day and the horizon ahead.

What a fine sequel this was
to my wondrous Waking Dream
of being born at the Roofless Church
when I wanted to be the sun,
the clouds and all the glory of the day.

I never deviated from my decision that night sitting on a bleacher overlooking Greensburg. I was meant to leave the convent three months before turning thirty just as I was meant to enter three weeks after turning eighteen.

Decision. Finality. Relief.

November 19, 1969 Evening
While sitting on a Lone Bleacher
at the Football Field
at Greensburg Central High School

Decision. Finality. Relief.

It's over.
I've given all I have to give.
I can't be true to who I am and stay.

Can I see the path
into the distance
or the place
beyond and into?

A long time coming.
Thirteen years.
I had given Him
all I had to give
in that hallowed world.
My years as a nun are over.

Decision. Finality. Relief.

Choices and Consequences

A young nun dancing barefoot in the wet grass at midnight.
What did it mean?
Did any of the other nuns see her?
And what if they did?

A young nun standing up for what she believed.
What did it mean?
Why did she dare?
Some called out, "Why don't you leave?"

A young nun letting two girls use the convent phone at night.
What did it mean?
Even if it was an infraction...
Why was it such a big deal to the others?

A nun realizing she'd been fooling herself for a long time.
What did it mean?
How could she stay now that she understood?
Did she even have a choice once she knew?

A young nun leaving the religious life.
What did it mean?
There was only one answer.
On the other side of the door.

A Young Woman being true to herself.
That's what it meant.

During those months I was completing my Master's thesis in English at Notre Dame University. "Man's Search for Meaning in Absurdity" was my study of a key play of the Theater of the Absurd, Samuel Beckett's "Waiting for Godot."

Life imitated art as I rode a Greyhound bus from Pittsburgh to South Bend, Indiana to meet and confer with my professor advisor at Notre Dame. On this trip I had the following farcical experience.

The Confession

Thrusting himself into the seat beside me, the burly man appeared to have singled out this place from all the other vacant seats on the bus. I didn't want to be trapped into talking with him during the three hour ride. "Why this seat? Why here?" I complained to myself.

After all, I had just spent the past hour and a half in a discussion about Vietnam with Anthony, another seat mate recently out of an Army stockade for having been involved in a My Lai type massacre. At the first rest stop I avoided going for coffee with him by staying in the ladies' room, emerging only when the bus was preparing to move out.

Anthony now ambled back on to the bus. As he passed his already occupied seat, I tried to communicate a silent, "I couldn't help it," but he still shook his head in disapproval as he pushed past me to find another place.

In an annoying way the new man now beside me squirmed in his seat. His restless movements seemed to keep repeating, "Talk to me. Talk to me."

Ignoring him, I instead buried myself in the novel I had vowed to read on this trip. It was not a casual read because it was related to my graduate studies. Duly apprehensive about the pending conference with my thesis advisor, I wanted to make a good first impression by being well-prepared. I didn't have time to waste with another talkative guy in pants.

After several chapters a squealing and screeching brought me back to the bus from the intrigues of Isabel in Portrait of a Lady. The aggravating man next to me was now playing a game of some sort with the two little kids across the aisle. "Only another ploy to get my attention," I thought. "Why can't he get the message that I'm not interested? Men can be so dense," I grumbled to myself as I continued reading.

About ten minutes later the man beside me announced, "Get ready. I'm going to take off my coat now." I reluctantly glanced over. He was smiling at me in that certain ingratiating way more like an outright smirk, an unwelcome facial expression. The kind that turned me off.

"So what's your problem? A hang-up about talking to new men?"

I remained silent.

"For the love of God, Lady, do me one little honor and answer me."

Without wanting to, I resigned myself to the inescapable situation and responded, "I just want to read. Do you mind?"

"Damn right I mind. A guy gets on a bus, sees an empty seat next to a good-looking dame and decides that's the best place for him. Got some gripe against that?"

"It's just that..."

"Oh stuff it, either you and me talk like two civilized people sitting beside each other on a bus or we don't. But don't get me wrong, I'm not trying to beg you to talk. Still we're both stuck here together for another couple of hours. Hell, why don't we make the best of it? Who knows, you might find out I have something to say. Or maybe you do."

At this point the man's head shot back and a hearty laugh roared out of his mouth. In spite of my previous resolve, I heard myself say, "My name's Rose. What's yours?"

"So you want to know my name, do you? I'd say that's a little forward for such a quiet..."

"More like shy."

"Sure, sure, my Mother always told me to watch out for you shy ones. Yes, sir, you are the kind to be careful of. You bet I'm right, Babe. See I've been around. Met lots of different kinds of broads. Known lots, too, if you get my drift."

"OK, so what's your name?" I was trying to change the subject.

"Mr. Buck Carlin is the name." As he said it, he acted like he was "somebody." Not that he wasn't, but I just didn't care.

"So what kind of work do you do?"

"Government in Panama. I'm just back in the states for a bit of a rest. What about you?"

"I'm a teacher... high school English."

"What'd you say? English teacher? I don't believe it. I never was any good at all that reading, grammar and compositions you gals always forced on us. Lucky I even passed. Hmm, and I notice you're not married neither. Always make a point of checking. Yup, avoid a lot of bad scenes that way. So you've got all the makings of an old maid except for the looks. Shoot, I don't get it! What is your thing? How come no guy's hitched up with you yet? And don't go giving me that too shy excuse. It's all worn out if you ask me."

"It's not that. Just haven't met the right man." I bit my tongue as this trite lie flowed so easily out of my mouth. I was astonished at myself.

"Still I don't get it, you being such a good looker and all. Say, you should come to Panama. The teachers I know there are something else. They sure swing! Lots of us men for them all, too. By the way, mind if I hit you with another personal question?"

"All right," I replied reluctantly.

"Honestly now, weren't you glad when I got on the bus and sat down here beside you?"

Without skipping a beat, I threw a "No" at him.

"That does it. Hell, you are something else! I thought so when I first spied you and now I'm damn convinced. But what's the use of arguing? Back to Panama. Like I was saying, the women I know there are all real winners. But there's this one chick in particular. Man, she's some kind of a broad and a half and then some. Wants me to marry her and all that but I just can't see it. Piece of ass now and then is good enough for me. And what a good piece she is. Met her at a swinging cocktail party. Lots and lots of long blond hair and great legs too. To boot it all, she's a 42 D. Overall, a real piece of work if you know what I mean."

My stomach churned. What did I care about this guy and his sensational woman? The whole story was disgusting. How I hated being trapped next to him. Liquor had loosened his tongue beyond my endurance. "Well, he'll be sorry," I vowed to myself with a secret smile.

Still he rambled on, words jumping out of his mouth as if gasping hungrily for air. "There ain't no broads like that one around here. That's for damn sure. Sonya can turn me on big time. But none of them old wedding bells for this guy. I like to eat my cake and have it too. Get that play on words, Teach?"

The obnoxious man roared another embarrassingly loud belly laugh and audibly farted as he did. I grimaced quite unabashedly.

Oblivious to my reaction, the man did, however, soften his voice to a more restrained bellow as he continued, "Say, I bet I could give you some real good pointers on how to land a guy since you're still out there on the prowl. First off, get yourself an overseas job. Lots more men and fun for you single gals over there. Then remember them eyes. Sounds funny, eh? But they're the main things - eyes. Man always knows what kind of woman he's talking to by her eyes. Let 'em talk and tell him you want him. Say you'd like him to light your fire and turn you on and keep him begging for more. No doubt about it. You know some broads can show the hots they have for you just by the way they look at you. Can give a guy a hard-on right on the spot!"

At this point I could only mumble a weak, "Oh." Repulsion was now surging so wildly within me that I knew I couldn't take this man's abuse for much longer. But If I told him about my identity, he was going to be provoked and it could get even worse, God forbid.

"Eyes. Yes, sir, the eyes," he kept repeating. "Sock it to 'em, Baby. Sock it to... Hey, wait a minute. Hold on one freaking minute, Lady! You're staying too damn quiet. By now after all this time, you should have let me have it straight and admitted you'd like to get it on with me sometime. But you just keep on playing it cool. I know your kind. Want the guy to lay all his stuff out on the table and butter you up real good. Well, Babe, that's not going to happen, you hear. No, sir, Buck don't bow down to no broad. They give him the come on first or else I just bug off, see?"

"Then bug off," I thought, but I bit my lip and remained silent. My Confession would take care of everything. Yes, it was the only way to squelch this man. It will settle him down and maybe even shut him up. Smiling to myself, I waited for the perfect moment to lay it on him.

The man refused to give up. "Hey, Babe, I bet you could be something else to get to know. I mean become intimate and all that with. So what do you say? Maybe we could get it on some time. You could sign up for Panama. They always need lots of teachers there. We'd have one hell of a time - you and me. One hell of a swinging time, I guarantee you. Good whiskey. Wine. Beer. Lots of laughs. Fun and games!" Again he laughed so loud I felt the seat beside me vibrate.

"Just wait for the knockout punch...." I said to myself and inadvertently laughed out loud.

"There you go, Doll. Now that's better. Go ahead, relax and enjoy, Honey. You're too uptight for your own good. Just take it easy and go on laughing. Me and you are going to go places together. We'll have one hell of a good time maybe even before I leave the states again."

The man beside me was on the edge of shouting now. My face reddened even more as new waves of embarrassment surged unmercifully throughout my body. There was no way the other passengers couldn't overhear his obnoxious comments and obscene laughs. Probably the soldier whose seat he took was having a good laugh at my expense too.

"So, come on, Baby Doll, what's the good word, eh?"

No response.

"Ah, shoot! You are without a doubt one hell of a damn stubborn broad. Now just what is your problem? Jesus Christ, you must be some kind of weirdo!"

Now the man's sneering bellows echoed even louder up and down the aisles of the bus. Again I winced. What a disgusting show he was putting on.

Blaring out even louder, the man swore again, "God damn it! How's a guy supposed to enjoy a bus ride with a weird broad like you sitting beside him?"

Pursing my lips, I angrily jerked toward the man and looked directly into his glassy brown eyes for the first time. Then as casually as I could, I asked him, "How securely are you seated in your seat, Buck?"

His usual blustery laugh preceded his nonchalant reply. "Fine. Just fine. No question about me. You're the one with the God damn problem."

I shook my head as I announced, "No, but I have something to tell you... something you should know." I swallowed hard and continued resolutely as I looked directly at him...

"I'm a nun."

Speechless at last, the man could now only stare at the girl? woman? nun? beside him. It was as though I had delivered a powerful punch below his belt which knocked all the gusto out of him.

Still uneasy, I regretted that I'd told him. If only I had just ignored him and let him ramble on and on. Surely, I could have managed somehow to be more civil with the drunken man and his macho display of bravado. But he deserved to be knocked down. It was his fault anyway; I didn't ask him to sit next to me. I didn't encourage him to tell me how to get friendly with men. How to be such a grand sexual success. He was the epitome of an obnoxious misogynist loser.

A barely subdued yet angry voice from the man interrupted my thoughts. "Damn you! You think you're smart, don't you! You... you... smart-ass English teacher, waiting until I get into things so deep that I bury myself. A good joke but it won't work. Why I ought to...." His voice trailed off as though someone had just levied another swift blow to his groin.

Then he stopped short and snorted, "Wait ... wait just one God damn minute, Little Lady! Tell me just one thing. Are you or are you not putting me on? You a holy nun? Living in a nunnery with no men to get it on with? How do you expect me to believe that? Your hair's showing and your legs, too. And what about that fancy coat you're wearing? You've got to be shitting me! Oops, pardon my French."

Shaking my head, I softly replied, "Some of us wear regular clothes now."

"So I'm supposed to believe you're a nun just because you say so? Sure, you caught me off guard, but get this straight, no one puts ol' Buck Carlin down. Least of all an odd broad like you whatever you say you are." He glared a threat at me, pounding his hairy fist angrily on the armrest between us.

At this I squirmed even more uncomfortably in my seat. What time was it? Shouldn't we be close to the next stop by now? Wouldn't I ever get rid of this loudmouth "Lizard man" beside me? Wasn't there any way to shut him up? He refused to let himself believe me. Maybe he would have believed something else.

When the bus finally jerked to a stop, I watched this disgruntled man push into the surging line headed toward the door. No, he had not believed me. How could I have convinced him? Would he have accepted "lesbian?"

As I waited to retrieve my luggage, he walked beside me and asked in a restrained but gruff voice, "Why couldn't you have been just some ordinary woman I met on a bus?"

("The Confession" was published in my book of short stories Unsettled Lives.)

The whole salacious tale was a prime example of the absurdities we all face in this imperfect existence. As the subtitle of my thesis eventually indicated, this was part of everyone's ongoing search "to find meaning in absurdity."

Absurdity in Action:
The Thesis Advisor and His Faux Pas

Arriving on campus at Notre Dame, I went straight to my thesis advisor's office in an imposing brick building. Goosebumps covered my body indicating my nervousness to meet him. All of our interaction thus far had been through the mail. In his letters to me, he was very direct, which was fine but I felt the need to prove myself in person. Walking into his office, he smiled, stood up to greet me and shake my hand. Without registering a reaction, I noted the zipper of his pants was down. From this point on, I felt relaxed and at ease. It affected me like the old public speech method of imagining the people in the audience in their underwear.

Here is the title page of my thesis.

WAITING FOR GODOT:
MODERN MAN AND HIS SEARCH FOR
MEANING IN ABSURDITY

A Thesis

Submitted to the Graduate School
of the University of Notre Dame
in Partial Fulfillment of the
Requirements for the Degree of

Master of English
by
Rose Marie Engle, B.A.

My thesis involved Samuel Beckett's quintessential play "Waiting For Godot." I delved deep into the examination of the search for meaning in absurdity and its relationship with schizophrenia.

In an essay by William Oliver entitled "Between Absurdity and the Playwright," he indicates that "A confrontation with the absurdity of one's condition is the escapable prerequisite if one hopes to live sanely, this is reasonably." So when Beckett's two homeless men in "Waiting For Godot" repeat the following exchange,

"Let's go.
We can't.
Why not?
We're waiting for Godot."

They're describing in a nutshell what I in particular am continuing to do - keep on keeping on - waiting for God.

As I also wrote in my thesis,

"Beckett manages to give the bold, beautiful truth to Camus' salient comment on existence, 'Living is keeping the absurd alive.' As long as the two clowns continue their waiting game with life, the absurd lives on also. Beckett gives no outright indication that things will change, that Godot will one day really appear. Hardly. For in the last analysis he seems to say that there is simply no way to escape the essential fact of human existence - the hard truth that man must face the absurdity of life."

As my thesis progressed, my advisor wrote in a critique that it was becoming "too psychological" because of my discussion of schizophrenia. Yet I continued writing only adjusting it slightly. After the group of advisors at Notre Dame accepted it a few months after I left the convent, that same professor wrote, "I knew you could do it all along."

"Running Around Town"

At Greensburg Central, which would become the last convent of my life, I was experiencing a real honest-to-goodness chapter in my own story of absurdity. Repeatedly condemned behind my back because I tried to help all the people I could. Being chastised for being "out there" in the world all the time. A moral and spiritual contradiction: A Rule for a Rule for a Rule's sake, no matter the consequences, which over the years I realized didn't make sense. But the frustration of those days remained. I was being condemned for trying to help the people I was sacrificing my life for. The belief, never said to my face, was that I was "running around town." Which I was literally doing in service to others, but not in an untoward or selfish way as they imagined. I was living the absurdity attempting to find meaning in it.

One evening in '69, I made a hot crayon art banner on cloth. The quote I chose to transcribe was a prayer which has stood me in good stead over the years.

"May the Lord only preserve in me a burning love of the world and a great gentleness and may He help me persevere to the end in the fullness of Humanity."
          Teilhard de Chardin

Driving Episodes from 1956 to 1968

Praying for perseverance towards the end of my years in the convent leads me to remember 1956 when I got my driver's permit at sixteen. But I only could drive my boyfriend Brian's Dad's car at night while on a date. (My Dad wouldn't let anyone drive his one luxury, his Chrysler.) Because I never practiced parallel parking it was no surprise that I didn't pass the driving test.

In '67 we Sisters of Mercy were now permitted to drive. So I signed out the convent car to take the test again. When I didn't pass because of the parallel parking problem a second time, I vowed that was It. I Would Not Fail a Third Time. So I practiced and practiced then practiced some more. Occasionally, one of the gracious assistant pastors even lent me his car.

By the time I returned to take the test the third time, I had carefully memorized all the movements and turns for the process. After I successfully parallel parked, the insightful policemen advised me, "You can breathe now, Sister." (I was wearing our new grey shorter habit at that time.)

After that announcement the young policeman took advantage of my profession and proceeded to ask me some religious questions such as "How did you decide to become a nun?" and "Do you think priests will ever be allowed to get married?" My companion watching from the window of the waiting room couldn't imagine what I'd done wrong when I was still on the course for about fifteen minutes after the test.

So the Third Time was The Charm. Over ten years after getting my learner's permit, I finally passed and became a certified driver although I still don't like to parallel park and avoid doing it whenever feasible.

Prayer For Safe Travel

"God's Angels guard and keep you
All the way that you must travel
Till earth's days are past
When blossoms fade and
Time is fleeting fast
In times of purest joy
Or pain and fear
God's Angels guard
And keep you safe."

The Storm and The Guardian Angels

The first time I was told by my Superior to drive, it was only a week later. This turned out to be a more difficult test than the official one with the armed policeman. Five nuns over fifty, none of whom had been behind the wheel of a car, got into the convent's blue Chevy sedan with me behind the wheel. Our mission was to go to the Pittsburgh airport.

It was during a particularly threatening storm replete with stunning lightening flashes and deafening claps of thunder. It felt like I held my breath the whole trip. The rain was crashing down in heavy sheets. I was praying nonstop as we slowly drove the forty minutes across town. The traffic was slow going, the going arduous. No one talked; they sat and stared out the windows bewildered. Then, in addition to the challenge of my first real world time behind the wheel and furthermore in such horrendous weather, I had to then circle up five floors of the narrow indoor garage. Talk about a Test of Tests! The all too silent nuns in the car didn't realize what it took of me to keep us safe. Each woman seemed to be saying her Rosary with deep devotion. Since our Guardian Angels were working overtime, we all lived to enjoy another day.

Duck Dinners, Church and the Porcelain Altar

On a snowy Christmas break in '69, I traveled to Cleveland to visit my priest friend George from Notre Dame. We prepared a celebratory duck dinner then a friend who had been in the seminary with George arrived. We three enjoyed our meal along with a number of glasses of wine and plenty of laughter. The funniest thing was when the two of them had to help me pull on my tall winter boots. I was so inebriated I could barely do it myself. Then I tried not to stumble as we walked over to George's church where we attended an ecumenical Bible service. After the church event was over, I slipped into the convent next door where I was to stay for the night. Fortunately, I got to the bathroom just in nick of time before I promptly lost my dinner.

During my previous visit with George, I stayed at his home and in his bed. He slept in the attic. But before he said goodnight he instructed me to "not answer the phone." The rumor mill didn't need to know some young woman was sleeping at his place.

At Easter break I saw Jim again to enjoy a dinner and a dance together. Because in my heart I had already left the convent, it wasn't a big deal for me. Months later after I actually left, he helped me move into my first apartment.

Confronting the Mother General

After this trip to Cleveland during the Christmas break, big things were about to go down. Following my sister Pat's insistence, I lined up a visit with the Mother General to tell her I would be leaving. However, I "knew" she would say, "Well, if you're that sure, go at semester break."

Again I turned to my friend George for advice. He told me to "stand my ground and tell her like it is." Before I left I wanted to land a job so I chose to stay for the second semester. Wouldn't you know it, Mother said what I thought she would, "If you're that convinced, leave at semester break." Brushing aside her suggestion, I insisted I would remain at Greensburg Central until the end of that school year.

At the end of our talk, she asked me, "Why are so many of you leaving?" I had no answer. About ten woman were leaving each year, but I could only speak for myself.

Letter of Resignation

Here is the official letter I wrote to the Mother General indicating my intention to leave the Community.

January 5, 1970

Dear Sister Thomas Aquinas,

Early in November of last year I made a decision to leave the community. It was the result of many years of searching to find who I am. Since the year before my Final Profession through these past six years, I have experienced many new things, major of them the beginning of an understanding of me as I am. I have at last been able to face this unique person and finally accept the truth of what has been plaguing me with varying degrees of intensity these past seven years particularly.

In effect, then, I am stating what I sincerely believe to be my one course of action if I am going to be true to me at this point in time. I am convinced that my mission in life somehow is leading me beyond this life to some unknown one. I am leaving the community in order to follow whatever way of life I have become convinced God is leading me to through certain vital occurrences and their resultant insights, particularly through the summer and fall of this past year.

The following are my explicit reasons for making this decision:

1. I feel I entered under questionable pretexts, I looked into the life in the first place simply because I had the health, intelligence and normal (?) desire for dedication. I entered, then, thinking the life was for me basically because I was

accepted by the community. Then, too, in my mind was the unconscious reasoning that I'd be getting my education at the same time, something that would have been difficult otherwise.

2. I believed for a long time it was good to be unhappy, to suffer, not to have any or very few satisfactions and particularly that I was no good, had nothing or very little to offer and therefore I was extremely self conscious and self depreciating. I was never really settled inside about my life as it was in religion. For most of my professed years teaching, I was almost a pure activist, jumping into every activity, taking every chance to get out and, all in all, somehow managing to keep pushing out of my immediate vision the questions and the doubts about who I was, what I should be, what I was and whether or not I would be able to survive as such.

3. It has only been the last few months directly influenced by a communication workshop I attended at the end of August that I have begun to face who I want to be square in the eye. Having done that as honestly as I ever have as an adult, I am convinced I cannot be true to what I have learned if I remain in a way of life I don't believe is meant for me.

Even though I am convinced that I must leave, I do want to honor my current teaching commitment to the community at Greensburg Central until June. During the intervening months I hope through further serious prayer, discussion and increased self knowledge in and through my work and whatever hardship it involves to penetrate deeper into whatever God's specific plans are for me outside.

I am depending on your prayers.

Sincerely,
Sister Rose Marie Engle

One thing I left out of that letter was my real reason for remaining in the convent a while longer - I had to find a job before I left. In addition, there were a number of hurdles I had to jump through before leaving. One was to write to the Vatican requesting to be released from my vows. I was determined that even if Rome didn't respond, I was going anyway.

Another hurdle was to change from a five year non-thesis program for my Masters degree at Notre Dame to a four year thesis program. This was because I wouldn't have the money to pay for another summer semester once I left. Why not? Because my Vow of Poverty meant I had zero dollars of savings.

In the Spring of '70, I got one phone call from the Motherhouse from Sister Regis who asked me, "Are you still going to do this?" I answered, "Yes." Then I became one of the only nuns of the Community not required to take a psychological test before leaving. The head ladies knew my mind and probably wanted me out of there.

> "Ah, but I was so much older then.
> I'm younger than that now."
> Bob Dylan

Job Interviews in Maryland

S ince I had insisted with the Mother General that I would stay through the school year, that Spring I lined up a series of interviews for a teaching position in the Baltimore area. I also scheduled an interview in Montgomery County but I left it for last because I thought it was odd and intrusive to require fingerprinting.

As Fate would have it or by the Will of God, I never heard a word from any of the Baltimore schools. By the time I had my final job interview in Montgomery County, I was ready for some action. I even asked the interviewer, "When will I hear whether I have a position?"

To which he answered in his deep and authoritative voice, "Well, there are two hundred applicants for every opening." After his next breath, he surprisingly added, "But don't do anything until you hear from us."

That was the last week of April '70. For the next seven days I chaperoned several students at a National Speech and Debate Competition in Hollywood, Florida. I even took a side trip to Nassau with several who didn't place in the competition. To my overwhelming joy when upon returning, I found the Montgomery County Schools' teaching contract under my cell door.

Future Finances

Before I left in June, the Community gave me $300 for my eight years of teaching. They paid for my BA and MA so that was something. In addition, I agreed to accept a $1,000 loan from the Community that I would pay back "religiously" at the rate of $50 a month. With my five-figure teacher's salary in Montgomery County, Maryland starting the next year, I was going to live comfortably. I'd be in a whole different ball park financially than a woman who had left in '67 who wasn't given a single dime when she left her contemplative order.

Mother McAuley's Resting Place And My "Death" as a Nun

As I stand at Mother McAuley's grave site at the end of my visit to Mercy Internationale, I recall "my death" as a nun leaving one world for the next. Much like Catherine did for good on November 11, 1841 at only 63 years young.

Mother's grave is marked with a plain cross. Her wish was to be buried in the ground like the poor and not in a crypt. In 1869 a flat marble slab was put over this hallowed spot and an honorable inscription added forty years later. A memorial chapel is now built around and over the slab.

Interestingly, the tabernacle in the main Chapel nearby is decorated with jewels some of the early Sisters brought with them to the new Community.

I had come a long, long way from the days I was a new Sister to the day when I chose as a young adult woman to move out, move on and, in effect, die to that life.

The Song of My Last Year in the Convent

A variation on "If That's All There is, Let's Go on Dancing."
by Peggy Lee from her popular song in the late '50's

Dedicated to Chrissie, Barbara and Anna Mary,
"The Scarlet Women of the House" as Barbara dubbed us

One day we young nuns didn't say our required psalms
because we were sick in bed.
And nothing happened.

Another day we didn't say them
because we lost track of time and forgot.
And nothing happened.

Then another day we didn't say them
because we didn't feel like it.
And still nothing happened.

Finally, one particular day
we purposely didn't say them
And Still Nothing Happened Again.

On none of these occasions
did the Earth open up
and suck us into the depths

of fire and brimstone forever.

Mephistopheles wielding a mighty pitchfork and
dragging a long black tail behind him
didn't pounce on our bodies
and cart them back to Hell.

Peggy Lee's song became a metaphor
for all we as "good Sisters"
had accepted hook, line and sinker,
never realizing in the early years
that we had been so duped.

It was a form of control as one old nun put it,
to impress on the "fleshy tablets of our hearts,"
that serving God meant giving up everything,
even down to what makes us human:
our thinking feminine selves.

A decade down the line
when we finally saw through
the facade of "their" power over us,
we sang with a rollicking lilt in our voices,
"If that's all there is,
let's go on dancing!"

So I did right out the door.
I had come full circle.
I had "fought the good fight."
But now my time was up.
Exactly 12 years and 283 days.

The Day dawned beautifully
sunny and warm.
June 7, 1970.
The end of the cycle
that began on another bright day
September 7, 1957.

The night before two of my former students
had frosted my hair blond to highlight my brown.
For the first time I wore a sheer spring green
and sparkling pink flowered short dress
with matching green earrings and sandals.

What a way to go.
I'd come so far
from my late teens and twenties
when most of my face, neck and breast
were covered all the time.
With long black robes
hanging down to my "old lady" shoes.

I was on my way out now.
There was no turning back.
My life as a nun had run its course.

I was about to climb over the wall,
Mini dress and all.

My Return to the World
in a Green Dress

It's no surprise that Green was the color of the dress I bought for my Leaving Day. What a long road I've traveled from June 7, 1970, the day I left the convent. Have I kept the dress I bought for that momentous occasion? Yes, indeed.

My Return to the World Dress - a lovely one with a green and pink flowered design - belted and flared - with green earrings to set it off. My hair frosted the day before and curled and styled by two former students from Saint Xavier's. With green sandals to boot. All symbols - signs of where I was going - On and Out and Up with Green as my Ongoing Hope Sign.

Handing in My Ring and Habit

Sister Christina Marie drove me to the Motherhouse for the unceremonious visit. I had my Habit in a bag and my ring from Final Profession in my pocket. Both I dutifully handed in. Was the ring ever given to anyone else? But who would want "Maranatha" or "Come Lord Jesus" as a motto engraved inside it? If no one still wears it, I would like to have it back as a symbol of my coming full circle from all those long ago years.

After that final visit to the Motherhouse, Sister and I drove to the house of my friend who had told me about the Communication Workshop which officially began my exodus from the convent. There we celebrated with fine wine and cheese. Afterwards Sister dropped me off at my parents' home where I stayed that night. The next morning I drove to Notre Dame for my last summer there in the car my friend George lent me.

Through it all - the ebb and the flow, the destructive and the constructive, the somber and the joyful times - all the opposites inherent in living this life - I know my Green Has Never Died. In fact, it has blossomed and grown....

All the Difference
(A Dialogue with the Over Twelve Years I Was a Nun)

So, Convent Days, all these years since I left you,
how does it feel that I continue to be there with you,
in a way still connected with you,
though technically disconnected?
How does it feel
that I'm here talking to you?
You who brought so much pain
to my Mom and two sisters.
I never knew how my Dad
felt about my entering
but he essentially lost his daughter.
And my baby brother Chuck
was only nine,
did he even understand?
You who brought such despair
to my boyfriend when I left him for you.
And now I'm realizing
I never left you.

> How does it feel you ask?
> Strange but good.
> Good for you
> and your awarenesses of the present time.

You know your inherent contradictions
did lead me out officially from you.
I was repulsed by the have and have not world
I saw inside your walls.
I was sickened by the age prejudice,
the status prejudice,
the holiness prejudice I witnessed there.
I was hurt by the implications of the awareness
that all these prejudices lived within even your walls.
It was virtually a sin to be happy there.

I was disgusted by the denials of my womanhood,

my personhood, my sexuality
we learned from your heads.
I revolted against your rules that seemed heartless
and meaningless and worthless.
And yet in the overall analysis,
I know that those years in your world
were unique growing years for me.

Years I was meant to have by the series of choices
willingly made in the idealism of my youth.
I would not have gone to Notre Dame or met Earl
or had the out-of-this-world glory of New Harmony
had it not been that I was with you.
You made that possible.
You sheltered me
but pushed me
out on my own.

Most important of all,
by leaving the world for those years,
I found who I was
so I could grow from that awareness.

I found that seed of me deep inside.
I held it there and planted it
in the deepest fertile ground
inside the caves of my being
and it rooted and grew
leading me out to other people.
Most of all to me.
More and more my own person.

            And so, Rose, has it all been worth it?
            You don't regret giving up
            your youth to be with me?
            You don't regret giving up
            your femininity
            and your voice?

No, dear Convent Days.
I've never lost my youth.
I've never been getting older.
I've been getting better and better.
We do what we have to do when we do it.
And when the time is right,
we move on leaving some parts
of ourselves in one place
but always taking the core
of ourselves with us
with all we've learned
and been hurt by and grown with.

No, I've never really left you.
I've brought you out to the world with me.
You Have Made All the Difference in My Life.

Going Forth

"For ye shall go out with joy, and be led forth
with peace: the mountains and the hills shall break
forth before you into singing, and all the trees
of the field shall clap their hands."
          Isaiah 55:12

Always a Nun

It's an awareness
that first came to me
out of the proverbial blue
in recent years.

On some level I'll always be a nun.

I can go to the silence of my soul
at will without strain.
I can center in prayer
whenever and wherever I am.

On this level I'll always be a nun.

I can quote scripture
usually only to myself
but as necessary
to others as well.

On this level I'll always be a nun.

And of late I've realized
more and more that in some ways
I'm a Former Nun/Minister
all these years after the convent.

Life is Strange.

Today there are three men I know
who call me "Sister."
Even a Minister friend
who addresses me as "Sister Rose."

Another casual friend
who has told me he's shared more
with me about his life than anyone else,
initially dubbed me his "Mother Confessor.'

But after I reminded him
he's only three years younger than I am
so I can't be his "Mother Confessor,"
now he says I'm his "Sister Confessor."

My longtime priest friend recently told me,
"Listening is a Ministry."
Also my current friend
of the masculine persuasion
calls me a "Pseudo Nun."

Me a Minister: A Dream

I've become a kind of minister/priest. I'm in a Confessional and two women, a younger one and an older one come in to confess to me. I leave and it's the middle of the night but a table is being set by a guy. Is he a priest preparing the altar?

Later I note a whole entourage of young and old including little kids go into this room and come out formally dressed up. I know it's because they are pretending that they are the family of a person on his deathbed. They will fool him into thinking his family has come.

A Dream

Words that come to me....
A little child shall lead them.
How can this be done, Lord?
I will lead you. All in good time.
In the fullness of morning.
Sleep.

The Bishop and the Little Girl: A Dream

Sports cars driving, driving as I'm waiting. I see people across the way cooking a great meal and having fun.

I'm with several people and realize I'm not going to get back in time to teach my noon class. Kathy asks several of us to come to a party or some kind of special dinner stressing how good it will be.

Then "The Event" happens before everyone is ready. There's a stirring outside the place, the vestibule of a church. A Bishop comes in. A small girl kneels or actually stumbles down to kiss his ring. He passes the other few people by and goes to a side place with thin curtains facing the congregation and raises his hands to bless them.

I'm nonplused over the Bishop's arrival. Readiness is all. The little girl is blessed individually but the others are passed by in the vestibule or at the door. Then the Bishop blesses people to the right behind or on the other side of the curtain as a group. There are two sides on either side of the altar except the curtain opens across and so a person can sort of see out from behind. Also I'm reminded of a contemplative situation. I'm behind the curtain with a small group of men and women and children on the Bishop's side while the general group or population is on the other side.

I have fun and am relaxed before "The Event" while waiting and feel a kind of awe when the Bishop comes. I feel togetherness with strangers and non-strangers.

Thoughts on the Bishop Dream

Beach? School? Mix of convent/seminary. A mixed group waiting.

Married clergy together sharing? A Cross-sex community? The wave of the future?

Oh God, coed contemplatives - married couples or individuals married not to each other working and planning and waiting sharing, cooking, doing the mundane things of life like a dinner party.

I'm a child again.

Curtain - see through but there ("We see now through a mirror darkly but then face to face.")

I wait out on my limb, Oh God, passionately. I wait listening, recalling, writing "messages" of dreams. I'm at peace waiting. I marvel at what you're sending from my deepest self when at first I thought there was nothing in this dream except four cars in a row driving, driving.

Thank you, God, for these awarenesses although I don't quite grasp them yet. Thank you, too, that I'm remembering them so I can study and re-experience them.

I have to find someone. A holy woman? Should it be a man? My flowing is toward such a different way. Would I be able to even get through to him or her with all the media hoopla and the fact of a Vatican censor. Would it be worth trying? Why not? I also must write and sound out Rosemary Radford

Reuther about her article and her Harper and Row book - Women and Church.

If as George said years ago and Jung or Perls concur, you are in a way everyone in your dreams then I'm both the Bishop and the little child.

At a healing Mass I remember thinking how I would begin a sermon with "Brothers and Sisters in Christ." I recall noting that there were no women in the service doing reading on altar except one giving out Communion. Are they representative of the Church as a whole now? I felt the need to pee throughout most of the time - coldness of air conditioner - little warmth from service, little real music, fun or joy. Woman singing off key, powerful, sitting next to me is me.

I'm going to start a group - a community situated by beach, significant water. I will be in as regular member with men and women and also hold the dual role of Bishop and Little child with humility despite honor and position. I recall other people who got ideas in dreams for scientific inventions, creative ideas and religious insights.

How can this be, Lord?
When the time is right, you'll know. You'll meet the right people. You'll find that spiritual leader or director. It will all

come to pass in the fullness of time. As the morning dawns. As light follows night.

Help me, Lord. Help me, a foolish vessel, a broken vessel. Image - I'm on the edge of a cliff. I swoop and fly. Flying free.

Last night laughing smiling much more than usual. Talking about flowing in dance. Singing but not caring whether or not on key or in step. Now I sing a lot more.

I never gave myself full love and acceptance for all I could do, for my potential, always concerned about what others would say, how they would react to me. Simply hung up on that. For all to happen as I'm being led, I need to have even more love for myself and belief in my mission to stand strong against tide of the traditional, to flow against backward waves, to be rooted in myself, to trust in my deepest self.

So I continue to be led down multiple paths on my Search for Continued Fulfillment. On the way I have been blessed beyond belief as I continue my journey. It's as though in my next poem my Best Self is talking to me, reassuring me, urging me on, being there for me during my ongoing exploration....

Continuing My Search

Search is who you are.
You will find
but you will still
Search.

The Search is You.
Embrace it. Be it.
The Search is You.
You are The Search.

The Search you know is ongoing.
The Search you know is uniquely You.
Rose, you've got to believe.
Give your pearls.
So what if there are swine
who take them.
They can turn to men
and be like Circe in the Odyssey.
What more
did you know as a teenager?

Go for that gold.
The Gold is your Search.
The Gold is You.
The Infinite Loop.

It is all there, Lovely Lady.
You've got to believe
even when the Search
seems more than the Find.

You will find
But you've got to know
the Find will always lead
to another Search.
Inner places are vast
like the reaches of intergalactic space.

Believe it.
You are The Search.
The Search is You.
You are The Gold.

Synchronicity of the song,
"Dream When You're Feeling Blue."

A recollection of a Dream...

Going down stairs
to find the leader of a workshop,
a man in the kitchen
"working on his books."
Scene of living room being flooded
with the water of new life.

Thoughts:
The living room of myself
is being flooded
with the water
of my new future
as my male side -
my animus -
continues to write.

"You have found us
worthy to stand in your presence
and serve you."

I know I'm being primed
for more,
led to more.
I am the Search.

With Hopkins, I need to
"Glow, glory in thunder
and bless when I understand."

Could I have ever dreamed it
in those dark cold lonely nights
curled up in my stark white single bed
desperate to be held and cherished?

A Nightmare I had to deal with:

I'm seeing millions of insects,
thin furry legs, rattlesnake tongues,
Rottweiler teeth, eel skin and bat wings.

I wake in a panic wet and disoriented
in the middle of the night
cuddling up close to myself.

How I would have preferred and loved instead
to be sitting across from a handsome man.
He looking at me lovingly and long.

Could I have ever even imagined then
that I would be able to connect
to any person, place or generation
when I put myself down so ruthlessly,
not without encouragement
from well meaning Retreat Masters?

I've wondered
what my dreams might have been
as I tried to adjust to the classroom
full time as a young nun?

What must my dreams have been
at Saint Xavier's
when certain older nuns
were out to get me
any way they could
and would cut me to shreds
in front of my students.

What a challenge.
What must my dreams have been
during those nights afterwards?

And what about the surprising "Waking Dream"
the day those older nuns as a group
were all changed to other schools
on the Community's annual List?

Probably most of my dreams at the time
had to be frustration nightmares
but somehow I learned from them
as they became frustration dreams.
And I made it.

And there must have been some
powerful compensatory dreams
with wondrous events.

Nevertheless, they helped me to go back
and face it day by day
surviving and coming out on top.

Understanding what my insights let me.
Again I bless when I understand.
And I bless understanding.

I see now how vital
those junior high days were.
They pushed me out
making my anima,
my feminine side,
as well as my animus,
my masculine side,
stretch and reach and Rise.

The Good, the Bad, The Worse
made all the difference
during my convent dreams.

Memory's Natural High

RememberingRemembering...

the wondrous closeness
of my Dad to me
as we knelt together
at the foot of my bed
and said the Our Father
in the nights when I was three
before my sister was born.
1942

RememberingRemembering...

my excited fascination
as I watched in awe
the sparkling multicolored lights
on the houses we passed on the way
to Grandma and Granddad's house
each Christmas night
for dinner and presents.
1944-1950

RememberingRemembering...

the warm hug of understanding
and shared grief as I embraced
my Mom after her Mother died suddenly,
my first real experience of feeling
sadness at another's loss.
1953

RememberingRemembering...

my only slow dance
to Elvis' "Love Me Tender"
with my high school flame,
I announced to my Mom, "he's the only guy

I'd stay home from the convent for"
if he said he cared about me
which he never did.
1957

RememberingRemembering...

the delectable sweetness
of holiday chocolate treats
and Sister Alma's fresh grape juice
at "Collation" after Midnight Mass
as a nun in my teens.
1957-1960

RememberingRemembering...

the solemn stillness
of midnight every year
as I knelt at Holy Hour
on New Year's Eve
in the Novitiate Chapel
and prayed for the world.
1957-1960

RememberingRemembering...

the fun of riding a motorcycle
down the street and back
at someone's picnic...
while in my long habit.
1963

RememberingRemembering...

the angelic quality
of the Mont St. Michel monk
shrouded in white muslin
ringing the massive Angelus bell.
1965

RememberingRemembering...

the visit home my sister and I,
as young women in the convent,
were given permission to enjoy
for the celebration of our parents'
25th Wedding Anniversary.
On the back porch
watching my Dad swing my Mom
around in an impromptu dance.
1967

RememberingRemembering...

the delicious delicacy
of the daily quart of strawberries
I picked each June from the patch
outside the St. Xavier's refectory
to eat for lunch.
1964-68

RememberingRemembering...

the exquisite feel
of Earl's strong hand in mine
as we two graduate students,
a nun and a priest,
walked together in the dark
on a summer evening across the campus
of Notre Dame University.
1966

RememberingRemembering...

George leading a group of us
Notre Dame nuns and priests
across the front of a theater
to find a better seat

as if announcing to everyone,
"Yes, here we are to see
one of the first nude scenes
in a mainstream movie."
Knowing I could've been "called in"
by my Superiors for seeing "Hair."
1968

RememberingRemembering...

being escorted down the aisle
at my sister's Wedding
by my only brother
but not permitted
to attend the Reception,
not minding that Rule
since I was leaving for Notre Dame.
1968

RememberingRemembering...

THE Ecstasy of My Out-of-Body
Experience of Birth
at New Harmony, Indiana!
1969

RememberingRemembering...

The Joy of walking
out and on and to
the Rest of My One Life.
1970

RememberingRemembering...

Even in the winters of my being,
the Rose of Myself blooms
with a delicate sweetness and light
as well as an abiding joy in life.

Not Shedding a Goodbye Tear

As I left home and said "goodbye" to my Mom and Dad my resolve was firm and my eyes were dry. Not even one tear was shed. Years later when I confronted this fact, I sobbed and sobbed for all the years I missed with them. For all the experiences I never had with them. For all it meant for me to give up my life and leave them to become a nun.

Regrets about becoming a nun, I have none. I learned a number of crucial life lessons while I was purportedly cut off from "the World, the Flesh and the Devil."

Becoming a Better Person

The Positive Things I Learned in the Convent
That Have Stood Me in Good Stead
Decades Later in the Other World

Prayer.
Meditation.
The Joy of Silence.

Multitasking before I knew it was a word.
Having to be occupied sewing
or doing something else
at recreation in the convent.
Not just talking.

True friendship through all its

ups and downs.
Patience and perseverance.

Responsibility.
Being the youngest in the community
to chaperone eight girls in France
for six weeks one summer.
In addition to teaching for eight years
and coaching Speech and Debate.

Discernment.
Determining finally with certainty
that I couldn't remain true
to the person I had become
and remain in that way of life.

Being dedicated to a cause.
Staying on task despite distractions.
Studying well even with limited time.

How to deal with authority.
How to stand my own ground.
How to stand up and be counted.
How to be my own person.
How to find my Center.

How to sew.
Becoming proficient
using a treadle machine.

How to learn and to teach.
How to flow and be flow.
In fact, I flow more now
than I did when I flowed.

How to appreciate the finer things in life
like chant, classical music and drama.
How to be a better person/woman/human being
glorying in my inherent good qualities.

How to share with others.
How to listen and fully hear.
How to start to be all I could be.

How to be a tree
opening my arms
with solace for all.

A flower bringing sweetness and joy to others.
A sponge soaking up all that is good in the world.
A clean sheet of paper willing to be written on.
A gift offering my encouragement to empower others.

The Negatives I Learned in the Convent

To nitpick for my shortcomings
To lock up inside any criticism
of the way I am or things are.
To be afraid to speak out
against the system or "The Rule."
To sublimate my femininity.
To deny my sexuality.
To put on a facade of happiness.
To accept whatever kind of indoctrination.
To negate who I was to such a degree
that I refused to believe I could have
anything of worth to offer the world.

Still Answers Elude
and Questions Abound

A challenging malaise
continues to assail me
plaguing me with questions.
Their answers elusive at best.
Nonexistent at worst.

It's as though I'm back in eighth grade
in Sister Mary Thomas' class
on the top floor
the room by the stairs.
Being able to see her coming
in the reflections
on the glass front
of the bookcase in the hall.

After which she would always ask,
"Who here talked while I was out?"
Listening to Sister's admonition
across decades and hundreds of miles,
"Don't be like all the other jellyfish
going down the stream together.
Dare to Be Different."

The same year watching my friend
walking down the aisle
in Church on Mary Crowning Day
with an oversized safety pin
pulling the top of her gown together.

Feeling all oozy and excited inside
any time I heard my "Secret Love" that year
talk with his deep, sexy drawl.

Memories wash over me
like warm bath water.

I smile and am refreshed
reliving my naïve lost innocence.
And so I come back to now
to the same recurring question of my life,
"What do I want?"

And I hear
a resounding reply...

To be honored
sought after
well recompensed for my art
adored and listened to
patted on the back
honored
cherished.

To be able
to sit back
and
ponder
create
cogitate
plan
contemplate
publish
become known
accepted
and sought out.

"But wait," my Self responds,
"You don't do these things
even for yourself.
How can you expect others
to uphold and cherish you
and applaud you?"

How to hold on?
How to love and honor me?

How to be my own best friend?
How to do all these things?

In little ways each day
preferably not with food
or new clothes
or travel
or anything
that costs money.

How then?

By removing the self pitying,
self depreciating,
and self denigrating
audiotape inside my head.

Playing instead an upbeat one,
that applauds all my gifts
and accomplishments:
my stories and poems
and especially
the wondrous work
of the Art of Myself.

Believing without a doubt
that I am by and with God
as I realized so powerfully
in the Roofless Church.

Even if no one else thinks so
or tells me so or even hints.

I have to do all of this
first for just me.
Otherwise I can't expect
or yearn for it from others.

But how to take the first giant step

that genuinely counts?
How then to keep on
taking that step
over and over
and finally move on
somewhere, somewhere
over the proverbial rainbow?

How to exorcize "Neggie,"
my negative self
once and for all?
Is it conceivable to remove him?
When all is said and done,
he's my 90% gold shadow part.
Must find a way or make one
to use him to my advantage.

Dialogue with my Negative Stuff

Tell me, "Neggie,"
What do you want from me?

        Dig deep into yourself. You know what I want.
        I want you to be that skinny girl
        nicknamed "Sour Puss."
        I want your insides eaten away again
        with the acidic bile of my cutting you down.
        I want you defeated by me.

No, I refuse to let you.

        You invariably vacillate
        day after day
        right back into my arms.
        Only hanging on
        by your cuticles.
        No matter how far you think you've come
        beyond me or in spite of me.

Well, you're right but....

> No buts.
> You'll see.
> You're nearly mine.
> No matter what you think.

Forget that. I refuse to believe you.
Or let you burn me away inside.
I have too many gifts to offer.

> You can keep deluding yourself.
> But what are you going to do about me?

Just stay out of my way.
I'm going to flow
with the tides of my life
in and out
in sickness and in health
from sunrise to sunset
despite you.

> Good Luck.
> You'll need it.

I exorcize you from my life!

> See ya.

My Old Habits

Thinking about it....
How am I trapped by old habits,
old ways of doing things
personally
professionally
socially
spiritually?

What is it about the various ways
I continue to act
that perpetuate my old habits,
some being bad habits?

My actual "Old Habit:"
the protective garb of my religious habit:
the floor-length flowing pleated black serge gown
and sheer long black veil surrounding
heavily starched face and bodice coverings.

All of it
Restraining.
Enveloping.
Masking.
Distorting.

Old habits.
The Ways of the Past.
Conforming religiously.
Following unquestioningly.
Accepting wholeheartedly.

And yet in my deepest self
always the spark
the thread
the touch
the flicker

of the New and Different.
Flowing Dancing Swimming
Flying Flowing Free.

Old Habits.
New Habits.
The True into the Untried.
The Protected into the Open.

What cost the new?
What worth the old?

How separate.
integrate and
assimilate
the best of both?

How wed old and new
with the best of both?

How develop and embrace
the union and the bliss of both
flowing together as one?

Change only in spurts through decades.
A lifetime needed to resolve.

Wearing a habit.
Being a habit.
Becoming a habit.

Are we our habits?
Do they command us?
Or do we use them only for growth
for our daily comings of age to ourselves?

Old and New Habits
of my two lives,
speak to me with all that is

Good and Positive and Gold about you.

Stand me in good stead
when I need you to fall back upon.
But fly away from me
when I need to grow
beyond you.

Old Habits,
I will not
be trapped.

The Right Day

"There are only two days in the year that nothing can be done.
One is called yesterday and the other is called tomorrow, so
today is the right day to love, believe, do and mostly live."

The Dalai Lama

Looking for Sister Patrick
But Needing a Habit: A Dream

I'm in Pittsburgh and asked by Sister Patrick to be in a holy procession. I go to the Mount to talk to her or maybe to the Mother General, Sister Thomas Aquinas, or Marietta. I don't have a habit to wear which is not good. I start walking upstairs to the Novitiate. On the second floor there's a class in session including young kids and teenager guys. I move on up to the third floor. Another group is there in a wide open area. It is where Sister Patrick's cell used to be but now the bed and dresses are out in the open. I'm wearing a free-flowing black small flowered short robe-like dress. A few people here know me. I see Marietta and she tells me I don't need a habit.

Questions about a Life Long Past

Will I think of the past years of my life
as seconds, as dots, as instants,
as virtually no time?

Am I wishing my life away?
Would I want to go back?
No, I wouldn't want to return to the convent,
but sometime I do miss
the quiet, the meditation, the peace.
Yes, there was the Quiet of the Grand Silence.
My meditations in the throes of sleep
every morning.
The peace of not knowing any better
or different.
Believing I was meant to be there.
That it was My Grand Vocation
God had willed for me for all eternity.

How I had accepted it all
without question or guile.
The negativity. The self abasement.
The "offering up" of my pains,
physical or emotional, believing
"my reward will be great in Heaven."
How I followed the Rule exactly
even feeling guilty for those who didn't.

What did I know?
Whom did I know?
Not myself.
Or what I was meant to be.
Or being primed all along to become.

Insights and glimpses
of what could have become of me
from where I was being led
to wherever I was to go.

Lifetimes away.
Lifetimes between.
My life to be given up and gained.
To be lost and found.

Across hundreds of physical miles
and though millions of psychological ones.
Of acceptance and understanding
of me as I am and others as they are.

I have so many things I still have to find out.
Like being a teenager and "knowing" everything
then walking into a multiple level college library
and realizing how little I know.

Where is the line drawn between
how much self love is needed before
being able to love another person?
Where is the line drawn
between audacious pride
and serene acceptance
of all the gifts
I've been blessed with?

Recalling Rilke's words
to a young poet years ago,
will I vow to continue
"to live along into the answer(s)?"

Reiteration

I do not regret
what I decided to do
with my life at eighteen.

I did what I did
and left when I knew
I had to at thirty.

What was was.
I am now because
of what I lived then.

In the World
but not of it.

In the Flesh
but not yet experiencing
the fun of it.

Believing in my "Holy Days"
that the Devil was constantly trying
to win me over.

But I held out and on
so that My Green inside
Never Died.

In fact, it bloomed and blossomed
and made me the Flower of My Name.

Where Have All the New Nuns Gone

Every Day We Really Live and Love is a Mysterious Adventure into the Green Unknown. I also believe Saint Paul's assurance, "To those who love God, all things work together unto good."

In a variation of a classic 60's song, I wonder about the Community I was in, whose average age is now eighty-one...

> "Where have all the new nuns gone
> long time passing?
> Where have all the new nuns gone
> long time ago?"

And I hear Bob Dylan in '63 reply, "The answer is blowing in the wind." Pete Seeger's song, popularized by The Byrds in '65 and based on Chapter 3 of the Book of Ecclesiastes, sums it all up with...

Turn! Turn! Turn!
by Pete Seeger

"To everything
Turn Turn Turn
there is a season
Turn Turn Turn
And a time for every purpose
under Heaven.
Λ time to gain, a time to lose.
A time to rend, a time to sew.
A time for love, a time for hate.
A time for peace.
I swear it's not too late."

Moving on to Find Answers

"A time for every purpose under Heaven."

How those words in particular
resonate with me
as I continue to relive
my chosen life.
There was a season for me then
and a reason for me to be a nun at that time.
"A time for every purpose under Heaven."

I am not remorseful about my decisions.
It was a time for me to live and a time to die.
A time to laugh and a time to cry.
A time to suffer and a time to glory.
But once it was over.
It was Over.
And I moved on to find answers
still "blowing in the wind."

Life. Love. Joy. Peace.

What is Life
But the living of it?
A Way of Awakening.
A Dawn.
We wander far from ourselves.
Only to find it there
In us all along.

What is Love
But the accepting of it?
A Way of Cherishing.
A Caress.
We search for it far and wide.
Only to realize finally
We must give it to ourselves
So that we can share it.

What is Joy
But the glorying in it?
A Way of Flying.
A Bird.
We search for it but
It so often eludes us.
It's just around the corner
On our back step all the while.

What is Peace
But the relishing of it?
A Way of Thankfulness.
A Warmth.
We wander searching the world for it.
Only to find it hidden deep
Within us all our days.

What is Heaven
But the glorying in it?
A Wave of Happiness.
An Orgasm.
We expect it in the Other World.
Only to find it fleetingly
Within our hearts and souls here.

So through the years
I held out and on
so that my Green Inside Never Died.
Instead it bloomed and blossomed
making me the woman I now am.

(Published in my book of poetry Stairs to the Attic)

Rose, Rose, I Love You

Delving into
my Deepest Self
for the deepest meaning
of my name
Rose.

Images of Rose.
A Flower Always Blossoming.

Red:
powerful, angry, emotional.

Pink:
feminine, soft, loving, motherly.

Yellow:
sexy, fun, creative, flowing.

White:
calm, introspective, spiritual.

Me as a Rose
unfolding to all the colors
of my unique self.

Me as a Rose
growing,
blooming,
becoming.
As inner layers
like petals
flow off.

Truly I am a Rose of a Rose
and my own "Lova" of Rose.

I have to believe that the Past
is truly only Prologue.
The Present is a present - a gift
for the Future waiting in the wings
to fly me on the stage
of my own true life.
My one true happy,
fulfilled, fun life
which is to come not only later
but sooner as well.

I have to believe.
I have to trust.
Be at peace
and wait on the Lord.

As Progoff, a Dialogue Workshop leader, repeatedly said,
"When the time is right, it'll all happen."
When the time is right.

I knew all those years ago
it was the Right Time
to fly away to the rest of my life
happier, more fulfilled,
renewed and rejuvenated
filled with joy and friendship.

I have to believe
in myself
and all my gifts.
And that He will always be there for me.

It's just that His time
is not my time.
His time is outside
and beyond my time.
Beyond time itself.
His time will bring me
all I want and need.

All I yearn for.
All my heart pleads for.
All my soul aches for.

What's waiting for me on the other side
of the Green Door of the old song?
My search in '57 led me
to new knowledge,
to new experiences
and ultimately to a new life.

Green Door:
Door of hope.
Door of the unknown.
Door to the future
to a new life
to new opportunities
to newness of all kinds.

I hear myself insist now,
"Look, Rose,
you hang on and in.
Show everyone
what you got."

And so this is the time
to ready myself
to open myself
to avail myself
of all I can be.

A jar waiting to be filled.
A cave to be explored.
A well to be savoring the rain
All to prepare for the rest of my life
here in this vale of tears.

To serve Him as I wait.
To be a willing open vessel

ready to follow Him
wherever He leads me.
To fly and flow
free and frolicking.

Perspectives on What Is

I n '69, the year I made THE decision for my future life, my spiritual and emotional questions did not subside. Joni Mitchell sang a song that continues to speak to me on many levels.

> "I've looked at life from both sides now
> From up and down and still somehow
> It's life's illusions I recall
> I really don't know life at all."

One thing I do know is that there are numerous other experiences I could write about my years supposedly away from "the World, the Flesh and the Devil." Additional layers upon layers upon layers of memories of my life during those dramatic days connected with friends who have chosen to remain in the convent and those "out" like me. As a friend of mine puts it, "What was was" then and "What is is" now. I am who I am because of who I was.

The Eternal Spirit

During the same trip to Ireland to tour Mercy Internationale, I visited the grave of John O'Donohue, Irish poet and former priest and writer. He was the favorite poet of Father Michael Fish, our pilgrimage's spiritual leader. I was struck by O'Donohue's profound words, especially several lines from the poem "For a Time of Necessary Decisions."

> "We drift through this gray, increasing nowhere
> Until we stand before a threshold we know
> We have to cross to come alive once more."

A variation on Goethe's lines...

> "Transformation and again transformation,
> the eternal entertainment of the eternal spirit."

And so I end this memoir with a short poem. Encapsulating my life and journey, the lines speak to me about appreciation and forgiveness.

Transition to Transformation

This morning the sky is
a mix of dark smooth clouds
over a blanket of light silver gray.

The sun is shining
in and out
streaming in on my hand
as I write out these words.

A metaphor for where I am
in the cycles of my Life?

While I savor the warmth
and the sparkle
of the elusive sun,
they reassure me
that waiting and wondering
will lead to ongoing revelations.

Waiting is for Ever
but once Ever has passed,
Fulfillment is for Eternity
for Love alone will last.

While all the while,
My Green Has Never Died.
Amen. Hallelujah!

EPILOGUE

The year after leaving the convent during the summer of '71, I went on a vacation trip to Mexico with a group of singles. There are many stories I could recount from this wild time but one takes the cake for its poetic justice. On the unforgettable last night I met a local man who would inadvertently give me some fine advice for the rest of my life.

The Two Hundred Peso Man

Acapulco: the last leg of my long-awaited two week Mexican vacation. How anxious I was for a three day respite from the singles tour group which included thirty women and only one man. The guide gave him the choice to join another group but he declined. We had traveled together from Mexico City to this town after stopping at notable spots along the way.

On the last day of the trip, determined just to relax poolside lapping up fresh pineapple tropical drinks, I passed on the prepaid boat tour. I rejected even the thought of spending one more afternoon bussed around Girl Scout style with a group of giddy women with voracious appetites for worthless trinkets and trivial conversation.

Since my roommate didn't feel the same way, she left early in the morning for the excursion with the others. Now for once in the whole trip, I was free to do whatever I wanted without any deadlines for meals or the need to dress up and be sociable. Slipping into my new azure bathing suit, I threw a few things into my beach bag: a romance novel, a fresh tube of sunscreen and a colorful towel with dolphins on it. Then I skipped to the elevator, singing, "Sun and cool water, here I come!"

When I first stretched out at the edge of the pool, I noted there were only a few people around. Only a handful of young Mothers stretched out on lounge chairs keeping tabs on their children splashing in the water. They reminded me of some of the women on the tour - flabby, over made up, bored and boring. How ecstatic I was to be away from all of them. Sighing a swoon of relief, I closed my eyes and breathed in and out deeply. The yoga exercises I'd been recently practicing helped me to ease my tensed muscles at will.

After dozing for several moments or maybe a half hour, I opened my eyes and felt exquisitely renewed. Since there wasn't anyone around worth getting interested in, I decided it was time to enjoy a fresh Piña Colada. Luxury of luxuries, I simply had to motion to one of the roving waiters and give him my order.

As I sat slowly sipping my luscious tropical delight, I spied a tall dark haired man walking toward me. "If I have to be disturbed by anyone, he would be worth it," I fantasized. Picking up my casual beach read again, I momentarily enjoyed a romantic dinner in the South of France with a handsome man named Jean-Paul. Before I could enjoy dessert with him, I was transported back to the pool where surprisingly I saw a real quite tall young man coming straight toward me. "The rest of the group can go on their boat tour; I'll enjoy a fine diversion right here at the hotel," I mused to myself.

After the man introduced himself as "José," we kibitzed about the hotel, the drinks and the ocean. I noted that not only was he good looking, he also had a remarkably cool and casual yet warm sense of humor. His brown eyes seemed to sparkle when he laughed or smiled. That was what really boiled me over from the moment we met. He smiled so easily and laughed so freely. Such a delightful change from the all too feminine world I had felt trapped in for the whole trip.

As we continued our friendly conversation, cliché or not, it did seem like I had known José for longer than an hour when, in his pleasing accent, he asked me, "Could you do me a favor?"

I didn't respond at first so he continued. "I can't get into my room right now. Could I take a shower in yours?"

I hesitated a few moments thinking, "Celeste is on the group tour. What harm would there be to let this guy use our shower?" so I said, "Yes."

In my naïveté I was unprepared for his increasingly demanding advances as soon as we got in the room. He wanted to kiss me, to hold me, to become entwined with me. But it was too much too fast. Barely out of the convent, I was not a swinger or into casual relations. I was a lady.

"No! Stop! Please!" I declared. Pulling away firmly from him with all my strength, he finally gave up and announced, "I'll take my shower now."

Relieved, I sat down on the bed anxiously waiting for him to finish and be gone. To add insult to injury, he let the water gush out of the shower enclosure and cover the bathroom floor to such a degree that it flowed out into the bedroom. What a freaking mess.

The next thing I knew he was standing towel-shrouded right in front of me. Since he was still apparently interested in more than the shower, I backed away, glaring my best Evil Eye at him. As I stood at the window ready to scream for help if need be, he got dressed.

Then suddenly, he walked over, grabbed my arm and roughly demanded, "That will be two hundred pesos!"

"What do you mean? Two hundred pesos for what?" I demanded, the incredulous words sticking to the sides of my mouth.

His nonchalant reply took my breath away and I nearly fell to the floor. His sultry macho Mexican accent made his words feel cinematic and scripted. "Yes, two hundred pesos. This is the world, Baby, what do you expect? Everyone knows me around here." His voice then changed as he became serious. "You give me two hundred pesos or there could be real trouble."

I caught a glimpse of myself in the dresser mirror at this bizarre request. My face looked like a freight train was barreling down the tracks at it. Who was this guy? As soon as he asked to use my shower in my room, I should have realized there was more he had in mind.

As soon as this "Lizard Man" got dressed, I managed to push him out the door without forking over a single measly peso, let alone two hundred. His final statement as he left, "This is the world, Baby, what do you expect?" still rang in my ears.

Thoroughly upset, I telephoned Sandra, one of my new friends from Canada who had also decided not to go on the boat tour. She listened to my disturbing story and then advised, "When the tour guide returns, he'll know what to do."

I hurried down to the lobby then to wait for Mr. Alvarez with outlandish visions of becoming involved in an international scandal. Would I be hassled by the hotel administration or an embassy employee for not paying up?

While waiting on edge in the lobby, I saw the loser José on the far side of the lounge laughing with a group of his friends. Surely I was the brunt of their guffaws.

Finally, the tour guide strolled into the hotel. I stopped him before he reached the elevator and cried out, "Oh, Senor Alvarez, tengo un gran problema!" I wanted to avoid sounding like a spoiled American by speaking some Spanish.

"What's the matter, Rosie?" he asked, looking at me with concern and curiosity.

"It's all so crazy. I didn't go on the tour today because I just wanted to lounge at the pool. A guy asked if he could take a shower in my room. Then...."

"Stop right there. You let him in and he wanted something more, right?"

"Oh, I'm such a fool. After I pushed him away, he actually took a shower and then said I had to pay him two hundred pesos! He told me that everyone in the hotel knows what he is and I better pay up or else." My voice broke at this point, but I forced myself to hold back the tears hanging on the fringes of my eyelids like drops of rain left on the leaves of a plant.

"Now settle down, Rose. This man's whole deal was a scam. There's nothing he can do to you now."

I was so relieved as Mr. Alvarez's reassuring words penetrated my agitated mind that I nearly hugged and kissed him. He smiled and left me sitting in the lobby with happy tears of relief in my eyes.

That evening I enjoyed another super fine Piña Colada while hanging out with my friend Sandra. We sat in the hotel lounge right on the edge of the dance floor. José came over and knelt down by my chair. "Did you find a key in your room?" he asked in his seductive Mexican accent.

I assured him I hadn't and told him, "Go away."

Hours later when I returned to the "scene of the crime," I did see an odd key lying alone on the edge of the dresser. The last thing I was going to do was attempt to look for José to return it. Instead I attached it to my key ring which still reminds me today not to be so naïve.

Life Expectations and The World

So it was that the "Two Hundred Peso Man" unwittingly gave good advice for my future. "This is the world, Baby, what do you expect?" Assuredly, this *is* the world and I have to live it as it comes along with the unpleasant, the joyful and the bothersome. José's words about expectations rang true as well. "What do you expect?" neatly encapsulated all of my youthful and misguided expectations living as a Sister of Mercy.

When I could no longer reconcile my vocation to a Higher Calling with the reality of the pettiness of the convent, I had to leave to find myself elsewhere. As Teilhard de Chardin wrote, "We are not human beings having a spiritual experience. We are spiritual beings having a human experience."

Words I've Lived By

As Sister Regis would say,
"Live it to the hilt and love it."

To which my Mom would
have surely added,
"Yes, you've got to like it
whether you like it or not."

And I would insist further,
"Indeed. Live Life every moment."

As my dream self urged me,
"Reach for the stars
and they will come down
and bless you."

Having now looked back and relived my past life as a
nun with all its ebb and flow in this memoir, I declare once
more that my Green Has Never Died.

Despite inner winters of psychological snow and ice
from covert denunciations and religious contradictions, I
survived and thrived as my Green wondrously continued to
live inside.

NOTRE DAME FRIENDS LIVING LIFE

JOELLEN, ROSE, GEORGE, JANE, DICK

Rose Gordy's stories, poems and essays have appeared in the following publications:

Association for the Study of Dreams Newsletter
Burning Light
Dream Network Journal
Futuremics
Ginseng
Grab Your Tiger: How 110 Women Made the First Move
   to Capture the Men of Their Dreams
Ideas Plus of The English Journal
Jungian Literary Criticism
Mad Alley
Networker of the Women Business Owners
   of Montgomery County, Maryland
New Women - New Church
Nothing But The Truth So Help Me God: 73 Women on
   Life's Transitions
Pablo Lennis
Pittsburgh Mercy
The Critic
The Dana California Literary Society
The Journal of the National Association of Poetry Therapy
The Journal of the National Council of Teachers of English
The Maryland English Journal
The Merton Seasonal

New Book "Nothing But The Truth So Help Me God: 73 Women on Life's Transitions" Released

Anthology contains an essay, "The World, the Flesh, and the Devil," by former nun Rose Gordy concerning her transformative experience in the convent of the 1960's.

(Press Release) - *May, 2014* - *Nothing But The Truth So Help Me God: 73 Women on Life's Transitions* is the highly anticipated follow up to *Nothing But The Truth So Help Me God: 51 Women Reveal the Power of Positive Female Connection.* From becoming a mother to dealing with religion, recovery from disease and addiction to starting a business, this new anthology of essays and art sheds light on all the times along our evolution when changes shake us up and make us who we are.

73 Women on Life's Transitions features work from NY Times best-selling authors Kelly Corrigan and Gabrielle Bernstein, notable trailblazers like Belva Davis and Rita Henley Jensen, poets such as Rose Gordy, esteemed businesswomen like Janet Hanson and social entrepreneurs like Megan Calhoun, as well as many new women, eager to share how transitions in their lives brought them unexpected gifts, lessons, and growth.

Nothing But The Truth So Help Me God: 73 Women on Life's Transitions is the handbook for all women to know they are not alone as they navigate through the many transitions we go through in life. The book is available on Rosewords.com and at http://tinyurl.com/p3vnv3m as well as Books Inc.

ISBN-10: 098837546X
ISBN-13: 978-0988375468

310 Pages

NOTHING BUT
THE TRUTH
SO HELP ME GOD

73 Women On Life's Transitions

a book compiled by A Band of Women

CONTRIBUTORS: Christine Beirne, Kim Bender, Cristhal Bennett, Kelly Parichy Bennett, Judy Johnson Berna, Gabrielle Bernstein, Jessica Braun, Mary Susan Buhner, Jennifer Bush, Megan Calhoun, Nancy Calef, Katie Clarke, Dolores Coleman, Ashley Collins, Christie Coombs, Kelly Corrigan, Belva Davis, Aubree Deimler, Kerri Devine, Abby Ellin, Nora Feeley, Kim Festa, Jane Ganahl, Sierra Godfrey, Rose Gordy, Ginny Graves, Janice L. Green, Shelly Guillory, Janet Hanson, Terry Sue Harms, Camille Hayes, Kelley Hayes, Claire Hennessy, Laurel Hilton, Stephanie Hosford, Vanessa Hua, Kat Hurley, A.C. Hyde, Rita Henley Jensen, Nancy Davis Kho, Mihee Kim-Kort, Christine A. Krahling, Heather Kristin, Leslie Lagerstrom, Vicki Larson, Shannon Lell, Christi Levannier, Barbara Libby-Steinmann, Karen Lynch, Katherine Mariaca-Sullivan, Abby Maslin, Eileen McIntyre, Jenny C. Mosley, Siobhan Neilland, Shasta Nelson, Silvia Poloto, Gina Raith, Eva Schlesinger, Susan Schneider, Marcia Sherman, Jan Shively, Valerie Singer, Tonja Steel, Tanya Strauss, Lisen Stromberg, Christie Tate, Sierra Trees, Johanna Uribes, Dawn Elyse Warden-Reeder, Shannon Weisleder, Katrina Anne Willis, Karen Young, Lauretta Zucchetti

ADRIFT IN WAKING DREAMS

A Novel by
Rose Gordy

Waking Dream: A notable experience which a person has while
awake that has qualities of a sleeping dream. The dreamer may
realize that what happened is of consequence and potentially
instructive in his or her search for meaning in life.

"Adrift in Waking Dreams"

Rose Gordy's absorbing book about intertwining dreams

(Press Release) Rosewords Books is pleased to announce a new novel by Rose Gordy. Titled "Adrift in Waking Dreams," this tome is now available for purchase on the Rosewords Books website, **Rosewords.com**.

"Adrift in Waking Dreams" involves a woman who, although attractive, was an insecure victim of angst. Still this woman, Laura, determined it was imperative to delve into her dreams. She had to find out why her night visions were so compelling, bothersome and somehow invigorating. But then Ryan, a man of the road, was waylaid in town after an earthquake and her life got switched on. Their animal magnetism was palpable yet painfully unspoken. With her sex life ultimately activated, Laura's dreams only intensified, including her newly discovered "waking dreams."

(**Waking Dream**: A notable experience which a person has while awake that has qualities of a sleeping dream. The dreamer may realize that what happened is of consequence & potentially instructive in his or her search for meaning in life.)

Until a thrilling "waking nightmare" tragedy reared its head and brought them hand in hand, the lovebirds almost shattered each other's hearts. But will her "hush-hush" past hinder their budding intimacy? Furthermore, will the ominous other men in Laura's life sit idly by without voicing their melodramatic desires? Unlikely. And who was that strange girl in her dreams? The one who she always tries to save from the wrath of the waves. Could it be the daughter she tragically left behind? The dreams that make her cry are the most beautiful.

"Adrift in Waking Dreams" is now available in paperback and eBook format and can be ordered through the publisher's website: **Rosewords.com**,

ISBN: 1499236352   264 Pages

Rosewords
YouTube Channel

Featuring HD Book Trailers
and Special Interviews with Rose

http://youtube.com/RosewordsBooks

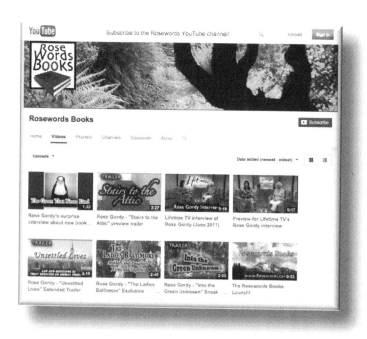

Lifetime Television Welcomed Author Rose Gordy to Interview About Her New Book

Rose interviewed about her dramatic life and her book "Unsettled Lives - A Collection of Short Stories"

(Press Release) After the economy crashed in 2008, many people lost their homes and nest eggs, but worst of all they were left with unsettled lives and uncertainty. With the economic crisis ongoing, people are searching for solace, resolution and a new acceptable normal. On June 24th, 2011, Rose Gordy was interviewed on Lifetime TV about how she has weathered the storm and her new book "Unsettled Lives."

Author and dream counselor Rose Gordy spent thirteen years of her early life as a nun effectively cut off from the "the world of the flesh and the devil." Through her experiences in the convent as well as decades of teaching in the classroom, she has woven a compelling story honoring the lives lost and changed forever by triumph and adversity.

"Unsettled Lives - A Collection of Short Stories" presents numerous tales of people caught in the second-guessing, soul-searching, and uncertain decision-making periods of their lives. In dealing with their lives of quiet and not so quiet desperation, the book's characters may rise above the pain and face new tomorrows with hope and joy. Or perhaps some of them may find their fate in hapless distress and melancholy. What threads of life's twists and turns will determine the direction and destiny that awaits them?

"Having Rose Gordy on 'The Balancing Act' has brought yet another inspiring story of perseverance to women, one that will have a real impact, and help them balance their lives. This is the essence of solutions-based programming, and we're proud that we can bring this to a wide audience."

To view the interview, please visit Rosewords.com

What will be found...?

Stairs to the Attic

A Collection of Poems

Expanded
Second Edition

by

Rose Gordy

"Stairs to the Attic - A Collection of Poems" - Available Now

A sweeping compilation of poems by Rose Gordy illustrating an unusual earthly life relevant to society's oxymorons.

(Press Release) – Rosewords Books is pleased to announce a new book by Rose Gordy. Titled "Stairs to the Attic - A Collection of Poems," this title is now available for purchase on the Rosewords Books website, Rosewords.com. This is the fourth book by Rose of Maryland, following "Into the Green Unknown," "The Ladies Baltimore," and "Unsettled Lives."

"Stairs to the Attic," a book which instinctually eschews the conventional, presents a collection of poetry down to earth yet otherworldly. Amidst the hundreds of adventures within these pages, readers will find themselves transported to places and feelings familiar and fantastic. One could watch TV but nothing captures an experience like the timeless rhythmical synergy of song & speech which civilization calls Poetry.

The poem which gives this book its title, Stairs to the Attic, paints a picture of youth restrained but always one step away from the truth. Will a group of ex-nuns find out the secret their convent held from them? What could happen when these liberated women return decades later full of latent curiosity?

Other poems delve into the dreamscape, the synchronistic, the blood bonds, the shadow memories, the earthiness, the maternal instincts, the harkening forward and the eyeful. Filled with 42 original photographs and over 150 poems this unusual book will break the proverbial mold.

"Stairs to the Attic" is available in paperback and can be ordered through the publisher's website: Rosewords.com.

ISBN: 1466226269

Unsettled Lives
A Collection of Short Stories

Rose Gordy

"Unsettled Lives" - A Collection of Short Stories

A wide-ranging collection of short stories delving into the unstrung lives and rattled experiences of modern society.

(Press Release) Rosewords Books is pleased to announce a new book by Rose Gordy and a completely redesigned Rosewords website. Rose's latest book is duly titled "Unsettled Lives - A Collection of Short Stories" and is now available for purchase on the Rosewords Books website, Rosewords.com. This is the third book by Rose of Maryland, following "Into The Green Unknown" and "The Ladies Baltimore."

"Unsettled Lives - A Collection of Short Stories" presents numerous tales of people caught in the second-guessing, soul-searching, and uncertain decision-making periods of their lives. Will the myriad characters opt for the "right" path seemingly laid out for them? Yes, they may eventually find their way... but they may otherwise stumble into unexpected and unique journeys we call the "Human Experience."

Throughout 21 short stories, numerous situations of emotional and social consequence will be offered to the reader. In "Lila, The Love of His Lonely Life," will Charles ever come to grips with his ephemeral obsession? What is Sister Alberta in "Masquerades" aiming to discover by ingenious cloak-and-dagger operations? Furthermore, what could the doctor in "Joy's Esperanza" tell open-minded Joy that would send her into serious self-doubt?

So please join us for psychological jaunts into the various lives within "Unsettled Lives" ... and don't forget to choose the right door in your own.

"Unsettled Lives" can be ordered through Rosewords.com.

ISBN: 1456420097

THE LADIES BALTIMORE

Mothers and Daughters
ALONE and Together

Rose Gordy

The Ladies Baltimore: Mothers and Daughters Alone and Together

A riveting and sweeping account of several seemingly divergent women in Baltimore, MD.

(Press Release) Author and dream counselor Rose Gordy spent thirteen years of her early life as a nun effectively cut off from the world. In spite of the conditions within the church, she managed to leave and make a life for herself including getting married and having three sons. Through her experiences in the convent as well as decades of teaching in the classroom, she has woven a compelling story honoring the lives lost and changed forever by adversity.

In "The Ladies Baltimore: Mothers and Daughters Alone and Together," an aged nun, a depressed waitress, and a lively teenage girl cross paths on a luncheon cruise in the Baltimore Harbor. Each woman will have a succession of unexpected and unique experiences related to mothers and daughters and to the various men in their lives. Spanning eight decades, the story organically unwinds in non-linear fashion as does life.

But will emotional resistance to the unknown lead them to destroy their vital links to the past? Or will they, through a cascading series of apparently chance encounters and fateful incidences around Baltimore, finally realize how they are profoundly connected? Perhaps time will tell if their lives are sublime results of synchronicity or merely chance encounters.

Also don't forget to visit the Rosewords.com website, where you can find the latest on Rose Gordy's books and other projects. Thank you for your curiosity.

"The Ladies Baltimore" is available now in paperback and can be ordered through Rosewords.com.

ISBN: 978-0-557-418718

Into the Green Unknown

Green Unknown

Second Edition

and other Science Fiction Stories

Rose Gordy

"Into the Green Unknown" and Other Science Fiction Stories - Now Available in Paperback

Attention Earth People... Special Announcement about an Interstellar Book by Rose of Maryland

(Press Release) Earth heralds the release of Rose Gordy's book, "Into the Green Unknown," a collection of 21 science fiction stories and 6 poems, available now at Rosewords.com.

Years in the making, these astounding adventures range from everyday events turned bizarre, to fantastic realms under Earth's oceans, to incredible worlds beyond human perception. Stories such as "The Announcement," "Living Waters at Lucia," and "The Man From Somewhere Else" take readers to strange places they can't possibly journey. Or can they...?

In "Subterfuge," will Madame President be able to protect L.A. from takeover by mind-controlling visitors? In "Lost Tides," can two nervous parents protect their children from a celestial disaster and its ramifications? In "The Genetic Casino," will the abducted Ronatta want to discover how she was chosen or remain ignorant and blissful? At the frenetic pace modern science is progressing these tales may be science fact by the time you cast an eye over them. That is, if they have not already transpired....

So join us for a jaunt on the Earth, in the Earth, in the Clouds, and among the Stars.

"Into the Green Unknown" is available now in paperback and can be ordered at Rosewords.com. At Rosewords.com you can learn more about Rose Gordy's books and other projects.

Bon Voyage!

ISBN: 1456528904

Author Rose Gordy's e-books are now available on Apple's iBookstore and Amazon's Kindle

Rosewords Books has released Rose's published tomes for the iPad, iPhone, and Kindle e-Readers

(Press Release) Rosewords Books is pleased to announce the publication of Rose Gordy's five books in electronic book format. With e-book sales now surpassing print book sales on Amazon, the state of the book business is transitioning to a new and exciting era. Accordingly, Rosewords Books now has e-books for sale on Apple's iBookstore, where over 100 million e-books have been sold, and Amazon's Kindle Store, the industry leader in e-book sales.

Before the advent of electronic books, author and dream counselor Rose Gordy spent thirteen years of her early life as a nun effectively cut off from the world. In spite of the conditions within the church, she managed to leave and make a life for herself including getting married and having three sons. Through her experiences in the convent as well as decades of teaching in the classroom, she has written books which honor the lives lost and changed forever by triumph and adversity.

Her six books are titled "The Green That Never Died," "Adrift in Waking Dreams," "Stairs to the Attic," "Unsettled Lives," "The Ladies Baltimore: Mothers and Daughters Alone and Together" and "Into the Green Unknown." All are available at Rosewords.com.

Stop by for a visit

Rosewords.com

The Dream That Got Away

An excerpt from
"Stairs to the Attic: A Collection of Poems"
by Rose Gordy

Was it one whose message
I wasn't ready to face?

Or one too good to be true?
Or too strange
disconcerting
disturbing
to be remembered?

Or was it one that the Angel of my Dreams
kept from my waking self to protect me
to soothe me on a deeper
than conscious recollection level?

Was it one I'll "recall" someday
in a "déjà vu" experience?

Or one that will come back to me
as I live along into it in the future à la Rilke?

So, dear Dream That Got Away,
more power to you.
You're only another dream away.
I sleep for you again tonight.

Published in Dream Network Journal 1995

Rosewords.com

60166100R00239

Made in the USA
Charleston, SC
23 August 2016